T0327128

DISCONTINUITY

TO

CONTINUITY

DISCONTINUITY

TO

CONTINUITY

A Survey of Dispensational & Covenantal Theologies

Benjamin L. Merkle

LEXHAM PRESS

Discontinuity to Continuity: A Survey of Dispensational & Covenantal Theologies

Copyright 2020 Benjamin L. Merkle

Lexham Press, 1313 Commercial St., Bellingham, WA 98225
LexhamPress.com

Print ISBN: 9781683593874
Digital ISBN: 9781683593881
Library of Congress Control Number: 2019957131

Lexham Editorial: Thom Blair, Elliot Ritzema, David Bomar
Cover Design: Kristen Cork
Typesetting: Sarah Vaughan

23 24 25 26 27 28 29 / US / 12 11 10 9 8 7 6 5 4 3 2

CONTENTS

ABBREVIATIONS

BDAG   Bauer, W., F. W. Danker, W. F. Arndt, and F. W. Gingrich,
       *A Greek English Lexicon of the New Testament and Other
       Early Christian Literature*. 3rd edition. Chicago, 2000.
BSAC   *Bibliotheca Sacra*
CTR   *Criswell Theological Review*
EBC   *Expositor's Bible Commentary*
JETS   *Journal of the Evangelical Theological Society*
TRINJ *Trinity Journal*
MSJ   *The Master's Seminary Journal*
WTJ   *Westminster Theological Journal*

ACKNOWLEDGMENTS

It is a great privilege and joy to be able to write books that are for both the church and the academy. This undertaking is never done in isolation. Even if I had written this book while on a personal retreat in a cabin in the mountains, I would have had as conversation partners all the saints whose works are referenced in this book. They all have taught and challenged me along the way, and I am grateful for those who have diligently studied Scripture and have sought to present a biblical and coherent theological and hermeneutical system.

Although I have my preference of theological system, I have tried to silence my own opinion. Instead, this book is descriptive in nature. My goal is mainly to inform rather than persuade. It is often only when we are adequately informed that the viability of our own position is challenged. The reality is that no one has a perfect system, and so we need to humbly learn from others. Not only is life a journey, but our understanding of how the Bible fits together is also a journey. I am thankful that God is patient with us along this journey.

I am also grateful for all my students over the years who have taken my Advanced Hermeneutics course (also known as Ninja Hermeneutics). The idea for this book came directly from teaching that course and sensing the need for students to be able to analyze and assess views other than their own. They have helped modify the structure and questions that are central to this book. Special thanks to Michael Guyer, who helped me draft the introductory chapter, and Alysha Clark, who double-checked every reference in the footnotes and proofread the manuscript. I am incredibly grateful for the six scholars who offered valuable feedback for those chapters that represent (or nearly represent) their views. In particular, I'm appreciative of Tommy Ice (classic dispensationalism), Michael Vlach (revised dispensationalism), Craig Blaising (progressive dispensationalism), Steve Wellum (progressive covenantalism), Richard Lints (covenant theology), and Kenneth Gentry (Christian reconstructionism). The feedback I received from them has helped fine-tune the explanations of their views. Any deficiencies are my own and do not reflect their input.

Finally, I am grateful for the word of God, which reveals Jesus as the fulfillment of God's promises to his people. All the promises of God are "yes" and "amen" in him (2 Cor 1:20).

PRELUDE
FOUR (INTENDED) RESULTS
OF READING THIS BOOK

Before you delve into the heart of this book, allow me to share four practical ways in which I believe every person reading this book should seek to benefit from it. Although they may not be your main purposes in picking up this book, I think it would be helpful for every reader to seriously consider them.

KNOW WHAT YOU BELIEVE

Sometimes we don't know how much we don't know about a topic until we begin to learn how much there is to know. As you read this book, you may not be confident in precisely how you would answer some of the questions that are addressed. Or, perhaps you will realize that your view is a smorgasbord of various systems with no noticeable consistency. Many of us have places in our theological "system" where the right hand does not know what the left is doing—in other words, we are guilty of affirming an inconsistent theological system. I am not necessarily referring to those places where we acknowledge that we don't have a suitable answer for our beliefs but places where our theological positions are incompatible, so that if our right hand did know what our left hand was doing, our right hand would vehemently object.

By studying various theological systems, we are able to test the consistency of our own. Maybe we affirm a particular position but aren't sure why we do so. Hopefully, this study will cause you to think deeply about what you believe and why you believe it. And if you find some glaring inconsistencies, you can humbly search God's word for answers. In the end, we want to know what we believe—not only to know the *word of God* better, but to know the *God of the word* better. We want to rightly handle the word of truth (2 Tim 2:15) so that we won't be ashamed or bring shame to Christ. We know that "we who teach will be judged with greater strictness" (Jas 3:1), and therefore should make serious effort to "teach what accords with sound doctrine" (Titus 2:1).

APPRECIATE THE VIEWS OF OTHERS

When we don't understand others' theological systems, it is easy to *dismiss* their views or, worse, *demonize* them. It is far too easy to attach some impure motives to those who disagree with us and question their spirituality. For example, if someone disagrees with your view of baptism, it is easy to think that they (1) don't know the Bible well, (2) have hidden sin in their life that keeps them from knowing the truth, or (3) have been deceived by some false teaching. From our perspective, their view makes no sense and seems utterly ridiculous.

But once we understand someone's theological framework and hermeneutical commitments, and not just their interpretation of a particular text, their view begins to at least make sense. It might be true that their view seems unlikely according to our theological perspective, but once we put on their theological spectacles, their view begins to seem possible and even plausible. Now, this does not mean that truth is relative or that all options are equally viable. But it does mean that there is probably a good reason why a view has been affirmed and held by many faithful Christians throughout the history of the church. By learning the systems of others, we are able to understand and even value that which we don't necessarily affirm.

RECOGNIZE THAT YOUR THEOLOGICAL
SYSTEM IS NOT PERFECT

I sometimes tell my students that they should not agree with *all* my doctrinal beliefs since I am certain that I am wrong in some areas. The only problem is that I don't know where I am wrong. And if I did know where I was wrong, I would change my beliefs. But since

I think that I am right, I am stuck where I am. Yes, my system is not perfect, but it's where I am until I am convinced otherwise.

I fear, however, that some people really think that their theological system is nearly perfect. Oh, they would probably admit they are wrong somewhere, but they assume that they are probably hovering in the upper 90s on the accuracy scale. Of course, regarding some of the basic doctrines, Christians have a high percentage of consistency. But if we honestly consider all the minor or more peripheral doctrines and all the various passages that have debated interpretations, suddenly our percentage of accuracy is greatly diminished. For example, I'm fairly convinced that my view of the millennium is correct. But I also realize that (1) it is not a central doctrine, (2) it only occurs explicitly in one passage in the Bible (Rev 20:1–10), and (3) solid theologians whom I respect hold to differing views. It is perfectly fine for me to think that my view is correct (and I do believe I'm correct). But I also believe there is a good possibility that I might be mistaken. This is a difficult (but sometimes necessary) place to be and requires both conviction and humility.

STRIVE TO BE A PERSON OF THE BOOK

Finally, we must all be continual students of Scripture. But it is not just a matter of seeking to master the content and doctrine of the Bible. We don't want to be guilty of knowing *about* God without knowing God. The fact that we don't have all the answers and will never have all the answers should always keep us close to the source of truth—God's revealed word. We must strive not only to know God but, more importantly, "be known by God" (Gal 4:9). Like Paul, we must be willing to admit that we have not already arrived but continue to press on (Phil 3:12). We should strive to work hard for the kingdom, excelling in all that we do. But at the end of the day, we must confess that "it was not I, but the grace of God that is with me" (1 Cor 15:10).

God's word is our source of truth. But his word is also our source of life (Phil 2:16; 1 John 1:1). As Christians, we need to meditate on God's word day and night (Ps 1:2–3), not only to formulate our doctrine but also to grow in the likeness of Jesus Christ. Jesus not only demonstrated knowledge of and trust in God's word but he demonstrated humility. In fact, he was the word of God made flesh (John 1:14). So, a person of the book is not merely someone who knows the Bible well but someone who has the mind of Christ (1 Cor 2:16); that is, someone who is humble and willing to consider others better than self (Phil 2:3–5). May God continue to work in us to conform us to the image of his Son through his word and the power of the Holy Spirit.

CHAPTER 1
AN INTRODUCTION TO THEOLOGICAL SYSTEMS OF DISCONTINUITY AND CONTINUITY

Theological systems are constructed in an attempt to understand the overall message of the Bible. Ideally, they result from a faithful interpretation of the Bible. Once formed, however, they also influence how we interpret the Bible. This makes understanding theological systems a hermeneutical endeavor. Such theological systems are often discussed in light of two broad positions: dispensationalism and covenant theology. Nevertheless, presenting the options as a mere dichotomy is an oversimplification. John Feinberg rightly notes, "Evangelical positions can be placed on a continuum running from belief in the absolute continuity of Scripture to belief in the absolute discontinuity of Scripture."[1] On the side of discontinuity is dispensationalism and on the side of continuity is covenant theology. Feinberg also notes, "While there are varieties of both kinds, it is unlikely that any actual systems are exactly at either end of the continuum."[2] To understand these theological systems, we must identify the various positions on this continuum and explore the hermeneutical framework of each.

Moving along the continuum from discontinuity to continuity, this book will address six different theological systems. Three of these positions will be related to dispensationalism and three will be related

---

1. John S. Feinberg, "Systems of Discontinuity," in *Continuity and Discontinuity: Perspectives on the Relationship Between the Old and New Testaments* (Wheaton: Crossway, 1987), 64.

2. Ibid.

to covenant theology. Recent developments within dispensationalism have highlighted three different positions on the side of discontinuity: classic dispensationalism, revised dispensationalism, and progressive dispensationalism.[3] On the side of continuity, the traditional position has been covenant theology. However, two other positions also stress continuity. First, the recently coined "progressive covenantalism" position is meant to be a middle position between dispensationalism and covenant theology.[4] Second, Christian reconstruction represents the extreme position on the side of continuity. Chart 1.1 provides a visual of these positions placed on this continuum.

Taxonomy of Theological Systems

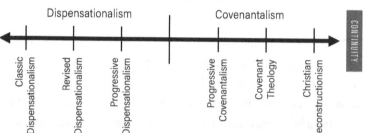

This spectrum of theological systems helps advance the discussion beyond the dichotomy of dispensationalism and covenant theology. Oftentimes, when people discuss or debate specific texts, they speak past each other because they are approaching the texts from different starting points. But knowing various theological systems allows a person to understand the foundational issues when discussing a text and also to evaluate the consistency of his or her own position. As a result, this book will not only help readers better understand their own views, it will also enable them to understand and appreciate the views of others. In the end, understanding these theological systems will be beneficial for interpreting the Bible. In order to explain and assess these systems, this book will examine the hermeneutical framework of each system by answering four key questions.

---

3. See Craig A. Blaising and Darrell L. Bock, *Progressive Dispensationalism* (Grand Rapids: Baker, 1993), 21–56.

4. See Peter J. Gentry and Stephen J. Wellum, *Kingdom Through Covenant: A Biblical-Theological Understanding of the Covenants*, 2nd ed. (Wheaton: Crossway, 2018), 34.

FOUR KEY QUESTIONS

Each position poses different answers to four hermeneutical questions. These questions are hermeneutical in nature because each of these theological systems seeks to interpret the Bible as a whole. The discussion of each position will start with the most general question and proceed to more specific questions. While these questions will be addressed separately, they are in many ways interrelated. Furthermore, the answers to the earlier questions will impact how the latter questions are answered. First, we will seek to identify the basic hermeneutic for each position. Second, we will look at how each position understands the relationship between the covenants. Third, we will address each position's stance on the relationship between Israel and the church. Fourth, we will consider each position's understanding of the kingdom of God. Below I will briefly explore each question in order to provide a guide to the discussion that will unfold in the following chapters.

1. WHAT IS THE BASIC HERMENEUTIC?

Literal or Symbolic?

The first and broadest question relates to the basic approach to Scripture employed by each system. The divide between dispensationalists and covenantalists has typically been construed as an issue of a literal versus non-literal, or spiritual, interpretation. Vern Poythress suggests that nearly all the problems between these two systems relate to the question of a literal interpretation.[5] John Feinberg, however, argues, "Both sides claim to interpret literally, and yet they derive different theological systems. This suggests that the difference is not literalism v. non-literalism, but different understandings of what constitutes literal hermeneutics."[6] Traditionally, dispensationalists have viewed a literal interpretation as the

---

5. Vern S. Poythress, *Understanding Dispensationalism*, 2nd ed. (Phillipsburg, NJ: P&R, 1994), 78.

6. Feinberg, "Systems of Discontinuity," 74.

historical-grammatical interpretation. In other words, a literal interpretation aims to understand the author's intended meaning by interpreting the text in light of its historical and literary context. In fact, dispensationalists have traditionally set themselves apart by noting their consistent use of a literal interpretation.[7]

Covenantalists, however, also often claim to interpret the Bible literally. By this they mean that they interpret the Bible non-allegorically and in accordance with the intended meaning of the author (which allows for figurative or symbolic language). In addition, covenantalists also employ the Reformation principle of the analogy of faith, namely, "Scripture interprets Scripture." This is not opposed to the historical-grammatical interpretation, but rather emphasizes the importance of the whole-Bible context for interpretation. Thus, the parts of Scripture must be understood in light of the whole and the whole in light of the parts. This dynamic opens up the possibility of a non-literal or spiritual interpretation, especially in regard to Old Testament prophetic texts.

If both types of systems affirm a historical-grammatical interpretation, what accounts for the differences between them? The answer, in part, is the priority given to either the Old Testament or New Testament. Herbert Bateman explains, "Testament priority is a presuppositional preference of one testament over the other that determines a person's literal historical-grammatical hermeneutical starting point."[8] Feinberg concurs with this assessment when he states that one of the foundational issues of the debate is "the relation of the progress of revelation to the priority of one Testament over the other."[9]

While dispensationalists and covenantalists agree that the New Testament fulfills the Old Testament, the latter tend to emphasize that the New Testament has priority for understanding the Old Testament, and the former start with the Old Testament and move to the New Testament but caution against reinterpreting the Old

---

7. See Charles C. Ryrie, *Dispensationalism*, rev. and exp. ed. (Chicago: Moody, 2007), 91–97.

8. Herbert W. Bateman IV, "Dispensationalism Yesterday and Today," in *Three Central Issues in Contemporary Dispensationalism*, ed. Herbert W. Bateman IV (Grand Rapids: Kregel, 1999), 38.

9. Feinberg, "Systems of Discontinuity," 74.

Testament in light of the New Testament.[10] This becomes the distinguishing issue as it relates to a literal or symbolic interpretation of various Old Testament passages, especially prophecies of the restoration of Israel. Since covenantalists tend to emphasize the priority of the New Testament, they allow later revelation to shape their understanding of the Old Testament. While covenantalists may employ the same basic hermeneutic as dispensationalists (historical-grammatical interpretation), they understand a particular passage in light of the more complete revelation of Jesus Christ contained within the New Testament. Thus, the New Testament clarifies the proper understanding of the Old Testament, and the Old Testament must be understood in relation to its fulfillment in Jesus Christ. Dispensationalists agree with this view of the New Testament as the completion of the Old Testament. They disagree, however, with the conclusions drawn from it. Dispensationalists believe one's basic hermeneutic must remain anchored in the Old Testament and that the New Testament fulfillment of the Old Testament does not do away with the promises or meaning of the Old Testament texts in their contexts.

Systems on both sides of the spectrum try to determine the relationship between the Testaments. If the New Testament has a certain priority over the Old Testament, what happens to the meaning of an Old Testament text when used by a New Testament author? Is a historical-grammatical interpretation sufficient for understanding the New Testament use of the Old Testament? Furthermore, if Jesus is the fulfillment of all the covenant promises, do the New Testament authors see a future fulfillment for national Israel? Jonathan Lunde argues that the central question regarding the New Testament use of the Old Testament is, "When NT authors appeal to OT texts in order to support or validate their arguments, the relationship between their meanings and that which was originally intended by their OT forbears is the central question."[11] In order to distinguish between the various

---

10. Feinberg argues, "Generally, the more one emphasizes continuity, the more one places priority on the NT as normative for the understanding of the OT. And generally the more one stresses discontinuity, the more he takes each Testament on its own and the less he tends to see one Testament's understanding as normative for the other" (ibid., 79).

11. See Jonathan Lunde, ed., *Three Views on the New Testament Use of the Old Testament*

systems, I will address (1) the proper role of typology and (2) Old Testament restoration prophecies to Israel.

The Proper Role of Typology

Typology is a key factor in determining the differences between various systems on the spectrum of discontinuity to continuity. Mark Karlberg argues, "Resolution of lingering differences of interpretation among evangelicals depends, to a large extent, on a proper assessment of the nature and function of OT typology."[12] Poythress even suggests that further discussion of this topic may have the ability to bring dispensationalists and covenantalists closer together.[13]

For the most part, dispensationalists tend to dismiss or minimize the role of typology in biblical hermeneutics. The problem they see with typology is the possibility of changing or doing away with the meaning of the type in its Old Testament context after its fulfillment in the New Testament antitype. Such an approach would compromise the priority of the Old Testament and would violate the emphasis on using a consistently literal or historical-grammatical hermeneutic.[14] For some, this means denying any role of typology in their interpretation, while for others it means a very controlled understanding of typology limited to the ways in which the New Testament authors identify Old Testament types.[15] Behind this position also lies the con-

---

(Grand Rapids: Zondervan, 2008), 10–11. Lunde identifies five orbiting questions that help distinguish the three positions covered in the work. The questions: (1) Is *sensus plenior* an appropriate way of explaining the NT use of the OT? (2) How is typology best understood? (3) Do the NT writers take into account the context of the passage they cite? (4) Do the NT writers' use of Jewish exegetical methods explain the NT use of the OT? (5) Are we able to replicate the exegetical and hermeneutical approaches to the OT that we find in the writings of the NT? The three positions are: (1) single meaning, unified referents argued by Walter Kaiser, (2) single meaning, multiple contexts and referents argued by Darrell Bock, and (3) fuller meaning, single goal argued by Peter Enns.

12. Mark W. Karlberg, "Legitimate Discontinuities Between the Testaments," *JETS* 28.1 (1985): 19.

13. Poythress, *Understanding Dispensationalists*, 117.

14. Poythress argues, "The major weakness of classic dispensationalist interpretive theory, at this point, has been the neglecting of the integration of typological interpretation with grammatical-historical interpretation" (*Understanding Dispensationalists*, 115).

15. Zuck argues, "A type may be defined as an Old Testament person, event, or thing having historical reality and designed by God to prefigure (foreshadow) in a preparatory way a real person, event, or thing so designated in the New Testament that corresponds to and fulfills

viction that Israel is not a type of the church and that the church does not fulfill or experience the covenant blessings promised to Israel in the Old Testament. For example, many classic and revised dispensationalists see the new covenant blessings that the church enjoys as resulting from a separate covenant than the new covenant made with Israel in Jeremiah 31:31–34 and Ezekiel 36:24–28.

Some dispensationalists and the majority of covenantalists, however, see a greater role for typology in understanding how the New Testament uses the Old Testament. David Baker defines typology as "the study of types and the historical and theological correspondences between them."[16] He further defines a type as "a biblical event, person, or institution which serves as an example or pattern for other events, persons, or institutions."[17] Baker sees two principles as undergirding typology: (1) it is historical, and (2) it implies a real correspondence. Edward Glenny identifies four criteria necessary to establish such typological-prophetic connections between the Old Testament and New Testament: (1) the type must be linked to an historical fact (persons, actions, events, institutions); (2) the link to the antitype must be identifiable within Scripture; (3) a pattern must exist between the type and the antitype; and (4) there must be an escalation or progression from the type to the antitype.[18]

Progressive dispensationalists view typology as an aspect of a historical-literary interpretation since it "refers to patterns of resemblance between persons and events in earlier history to persons and events in later history."[19] Darrell Bock argues for a complementary hermeneutic, which means that previous revelation can have an added or expanded meaning if it is complementary to the original meaning. The New Testament meaning can develop or complement the

---

(heightens) the type" (Roy B. Zuck, *Basic Bible Interpretation: A Practical Guide to Discovering Biblical Truth* [Wheaton: Victor, 1991], 176).

16. David L. Baker, "Typology and the Christian Use of the Old Testament," in *The Right Doctrine from the Wrong Texts? Essays on the Use of the Old Testament in the New Testament*, ed. G. K. Beale (Grand Rapids: Baker Academic, 1994), 328.

17. Ibid., 327.

18. W. Edward Glenny, "The Israelite Imagery of 1 Peter 2," in *Dispensationalism, Israel, and the Church*, ed. Craig A. Blaising and Darrell L. Bock (Grand Rapids: Zondervan, 1992), 157–58.

19. Blaising and Bock, *Progressive Dispensationalism*, 52.

meaning of the Old Testament, but not in a way that would deny what the Old Testament author originally meant.[20] In other words, the New Testament antitype does not contradict the meaning of the Old Testament type in its context, but develops or expands it in light of progressive revelation. Consequently, this hermeneutic includes both a "historical-exegetical" reading and a "theological-canonical" reading of any given text. The former is concerned with understanding the original author's message to his immediate audience in their particular historical context. The latter is concerned with understanding a text in light of later revelation.

While progressive dispensationalists allow for a partial fulfillment of some Old Testament covenant promises within Christ and the church, they do not believe such connections exhaust or completely fulfill those Old Testament covenant promises. Feinberg argues, "If the NT antitype cancels the meaning of the OT type, the NT must tell us so. NT reinterpretations of OT passages are neither explicit nor implicit cancellations of the meaning of the OT. Likewise, NT antitypes neither explicitly nor implicitly cancel the meaning of OT types. Thinking they do misunderstands typology."[21]

Covenantalists allow later revelation to provide greater clarity to earlier revelation. This opens the possibility for a developed or expanded meaning beyond what the original author would have perceived. Progressive covenantalists Gentry and Wellum therefore advocate reading Scripture in light of three contexts: textual (immediate context), epochal (preceding context), and canonical (entire canon).[22] Covenantalists also understand the Old Testament types as shadows that divinely point forward to typological realities culminating in Jesus Christ and the new covenant.[23] Thus, Old Testament types give

---

20. Darrell L. Bock, "Single Meaning, Multiple Contexts and Referents," in *Three Views on the New Testament Use of the Old Testament*, ed. Kenneth Berding and Jonathan Lunde (Grand Rapids: Zondervan, 2008), 116.

21. Feinberg, "Systems of Discontinuity," 79.

22. Gentry and Wellum, *Kingdom through Covenant*, 118–29.

23. Glenny accurately summarizes this position, "Thus the whole OT economy and Israel's experiences *in toto* are symbolic, temporary, preparatory and typical. They are taken as a type of the true spiritual reality found in Christ and the Church" (W. Edward Glenny, "Typology: A Summary of the Present Evangelical Discussion," *JETS* 40.4 [1997]: 631).

way to the New Testament antitype. The different understandings of typology across these systems can perhaps best be seen in how they interpret Old Testament restoration prophecies to Israel.

Old Testament Restoration Prophecies to Israel

A key issue impacted by one's understanding of typology is how each system interprets the Old Testament restoration prophecies to Israel. Perhaps the most well-known, or at least, most discussed, Old Testament restoration prophecy text is Amos 9:11–15 and its subsequent usage in Acts 15:14–18. Saucy notes, "James' citation of the prophecy of Amos to support the Gentiles in the church (Acts 15:13–18) is another crucial text in discussion between traditional dispensationalists and non-dispensationalists."[24] In Amos 9:11–15 God promises a future restoration of the people of Israel in very concrete and geographical terms (e.g., land, walls, crops, defeat of enemies, etc.). In Acts 15:14–18 the Jerusalem church was faced with the question of how to incorporate believing gentiles into the church. The apostle James sees the salvation of the gentiles and their incorporation into the people of God as agreeing with or fulfilling what was promised in Amos 9:11–12.

Traditional (classic and revised) dispensationalists believe that Acts 15:16–17 confirms the Old Testament restoration prophecy to the people of Israel. *The New Scofield Study Bible* states, "James declares that Amos 9:12 shows that, at the return of Christ, there will not only be believing Jews ... but also believing Gentiles 'who are called by my name.'"[25] The logic here is that since there will be gentiles alongside believing Jews when Christ returns, the church should not make gentile believers become Jewish proselytes by circumcision. In other words, James' reference to Amos 9:11–12 in Acts 15:16–17 is confirming the future reality of the inclusion of the gentiles during the millennial kingdom but does not specifically address the present situation, other

---

24. Robert L. Saucy, *The Case for Progressive Dispensationalism: The Interface Between Dispensational and Non-Dispensational Theology* (Grand Rapids: Zondervan, 1993), 76.

25. C. I. Scofield, Frank E. Gaebelein, et al., eds., *New Scofield Study Bible* (New York: Oxford University Press, 1967; repr. 1988 with New American Standard translation), 1554 (Acts 15:16).

than by affirming that God is now calling out a gentile people to himself. Since Amos 9:11–12 is given to national Israel, it cannot find its fulfillment in the church. Furthermore, the use of a historical-grammatical hermeneutic emphasizes allowing both the Old Testament and New Testament context to maintain their own meaning without later revelation changing or cancelling out earlier revelation.

Progressive dispensationalists believe that Acts 15:16–17 introduces an already/not yet fulfillment of the Old Testament restoration prophecy. Kenneth Barker states, "What happened in Acts 15 constitutes a stage in the progressive fulfillment of the entire prophecy in Amos 9 (cf. Acts 15:12–15). It is an instance of direct fulfillment, but not the final and complete fulfillment, as the following verses in Amos (9:13–15) plainly indicate."[26] Progressive dispensationalism affirms that Amos 9:11–12 has been partially fulfilled through the inclusion of the gentiles into the church. Nevertheless, this does not negate its future, fuller fulfillment for national Israel in the millennial kingdom. Like traditional dispensationalists, progressive dispensationalists hold to a clear distinction between Israel and the church. Since Amos records specific promises to national Israel, progressive dispensationalists do not see any reason to dismiss these promises for national Israel.[27] Yet, their complementary hermeneutic allows for a partial fulfillment of Amos 9:11–12 regarding the inclusion of the gentiles into the church because of the inaugurated reign of Jesus (cf. Acts 2:29–36). Bock maintains that this type of hermeneutic "argues that we should continue to read the Old Testament as still telling us something about Israel in God's plan, while being sensitive to how the New Testament complements that hope by expressing fulfillment today in Christ."[28]

Covenantalists argue that Acts 15:16–17 should be taken as the fulfillment of Amos 9:11–12. Lehrer argues, "The restoration of national

---

26. Kenneth Barker, "The Scope and Center of Old and New Testament Theology and Hope," in *Dispensationalism, Israel, and the Church*, 327.

27. For promises to national Israel, see Amos 9:11: "I will raise up the booth of David … repair its breaches … raise up its ruins … rebuild it."

28. Darrell Bock, "Hermeneutics of Progressive Dispensationalism," in *Three Central Issues in Contemporary Dispensationalism*, 92–93.

Israel in Amos 9 is interpreted by God in Acts 15 to refer to the gathering of God's elect, both Jews and Gentiles, to be saved and brought together into the church."[29] Covenantalists argue that the throne of David has been restored in the resurrection of Jesus and his ascension to the right hand of the Father (cf. Ps 110:1; Acts 2:29–36) and that the kingdom of God has now been inaugurated in Jesus Christ. On this basis, covenantalists see the restoration promise to Israel in Amos 9:11–12 as being fulfilled in Jesus Christ through the inclusion of both Jews and gentiles into the church. While there is variety among covenantalists in how they arrive at this conclusion, the most influential reasons they do so are (1) their hermeneutic gives priority to the New Testament, (2) the nature of the prophetic genre, and (3) their understanding of the fulfillment of Israel's covenant promises in Christ and the church.

2. WHAT IS THE RELATIONSHIP BETWEEN THE COVENANTS?

The second question essential to each theological system's hermeneutical framework is the relationship between the covenants. Traditionally, dispensationalists have focused more on distinct dispensations within Scripture.[30] While these dispensations encompass many of the biblical covenants (i.e., Noahic, Abrahamic, Mosaic, Davidic, and new), the dispensations have served to provide a more holistic picture of how the Bible fits together. On the other hand, covenant theology emphasizes three theological covenants, which are derived from the biblical covenants. There is a covenant of works/creation and a covenant of grace, which both flow out of the eternal covenant of redemption. Covenant theology understands all the biblical covenants as different expressions of the one covenant of grace.[31] Newer positions like

---

29. Steve Lehrer, *New Covenant Theology: Questions Answered* (self-pub., 2006), 88.

30. A dispensation "refers to a distinctive way in which God manages or arranges the relationship of human beings to Himself" (Blaising and Bock, *Progressive Dispensationalism*, 11).

31. Poythress, *Understanding Dispensationalists*, 40.

progressive dispensationalism and progressive covenantalism have put greater emphasis on the biblical covenants themselves.

Conditional or Unconditional?

A major issue regarding the relationship between the covenants is whether certain covenants are conditional or unconditional. The biblical covenants include: the Noahic covenant (Gen 6–9), Abrahamic covenant (Gen 12, 15, 17), Mosaic covenant (Exod 19:3b–8, 20–24), Davidic covenant (2 Sam 7; Ps 89), and the new covenant (Jer 31–34; Ezek 33:29–39:29). Both dispensationalists and covenantalists have argued that most of the biblical covenants are unconditional, whereas the Mosaic covenant is conditional. When and how these covenants are fulfilled depends on whether a covenant is conditional or unconditional. Feinberg states, "I think the ultimate difference on the covenants between dispensational and non-dispensation systems is not just conditionality *v.* unconditionality, but which aspect(s) of the covenant promises one emphasizes."[32] Dispensationalists have tended to emphasize the land promises of the Old Testament, and covenantalists have tended to emphasize the genealogical aspects of the Old Testament (i.e., promises regarding children).

Furthermore, there is a growing movement that argues for an understanding of all the biblical covenants as both conditional and unconditional. Gentry and Wellum argue that the unconditional aspect of the covenants reveals the covenant-making and covenant-keeping nature of God. The conditional aspect of the covenants reveals the necessity of an obedient covenant partner. Wellum states, "In fact, it is precisely due to this blend that there is a deliberate *tension* within the covenants—a tension that is heightened as the Bible's storyline unfolds through the progression of the covenants and is only resolved in Christ."[33] So, the question becomes how each theological system understands the biblical covenants in light of Jesus Christ. Although dispensationalists tend to argue that the covenants point to their fulfillment in Jesus Christ, they maintain that many aspects

---

32. Feinberg, "Systems of Discontinuity," 80.

33. Gentry and Wellum, *Kingdom through Covenant*, 663–64 (emphasis original).

of the covenant have not been fulfilled in Christ and await a future fulfillment among the people of Israel. Covenantalists tend to argue that the covenants are fulfilled in Christ and the blessings promised to Israel in the Old Testament are now extended to the church.

Salvation for Old Testament Saints

Two issues closely tied to the relationship between the biblical covenants are the nature of salvation in the Old Testament and the role of Old Testament law in the life of the new covenant believer. First, the issue of salvation in the Old Testament revolves around whether God has saved people differently at different times in biblical history. Most dispensationalists and covenantalists would affirm that salvation is always by grace through faith. However, not all have held this position. Some critics point out that dispensationalism teaches two ways of salvation, "that during the era of law, obedience to it was a condition of salvation, whereas during the age of grace, salvation comes simply through faith in Christ."[34] For example, The Scofield Reference Bible states that in the dispensation of grace, "The point of testing is no longer legal obedience as the condition of salvation, but acceptance or rejection of Christ, with good works as a fruit of salvation."[35] Not surprisingly, the New Scofield Study Bible clarifies and even removes the confusing content in this note.[36] Instead, the object of faith becomes the decisive point. Covenantalists agree that salvation is by grace through faith across the Old Testament and New Testament. However, some covenantalists would emphasize the necessity of a consciousness of faith in the promised or anticipated messiah on behalf of Old Testament saints.

---

34. Daniel P. Fuller, "The Hermeneutics of Dispensationalism" (ThD diss., Northern Baptist Theological Seminary, 1957), 144–45.

35. C. I. Scofield, ed., The Scofield Reference Bible (New York: Oxford University Press, 1909, 1917; reprinted 1996 as The Scofield Study Bible), 1115 (John 1:17). All citations from The Scofield Reference Bible are taken from the 1996 edition, which uses Scofield's original notes without alteration.

36. Scofield, Gaebelein, et al., New Scofield Study Bible, 1477 (John 1:9). For the New Scofield Study Bible, first published in 1967, a revision committee led by Frank E. Gaebelein edited Scofield's original notes published in The Scofield Reference Bible (New York: Oxford University Press, 1909, 1917). All citations from the New Scofield Study Bible are taken from the New American Standard edition published in 1988 (see page 13, note 25).

Applying the Law Today

Second, the relationship of the law to the new covenant believer is intricately connected to the discussion of the biblical covenants. There are two primary ways for understanding how the law has been fulfilled and is thus determinative for the new covenant believer's relationship to the law. Either parts of the law have been fulfilled or the entirety of the law has been fulfilled. Traditionally, covenantalists view the law as comprising moral, civil, and ceremonial aspects. They argue that the civic and ceremonial aspects of the law have been fulfilled typologically in Christ while the moral aspect of the law remains intact for new covenant believers. Thus, new covenant believers are bound to the moral aspect of the law as were the Old Testament saints. Dispensationalists and some covenantalists, however, argue that the law should be understood as a unity. D. A. Carson argues, "Although this tripartite distinction is old, its use as a basis for explaining the relationship between the Testaments is not demonstrably derived from the New Testament and probably does not antedate Aquinas."[37] In such systems, the law has been completely fulfilled in the first coming of Jesus Christ (cf. Jer 31:31–34; Matt 5:17–20). New covenant believers are now "in Christ" and are no longer "under the law" (Gal 5:18) but are bound to the "law of Christ" (Gal 6:2). Still, there are other covenantalists (such as Christian reconstructionists) who believe that both the moral and civil law are binding on new covenant believers today.

---

37. D. A. Carson, "Matthew," in *EBC*, rev. ed., ed. Tremper Longman III and David E. Garland, vol. 9 (Grand Rapids: Zondervan, 2010), 174.

3. WHAT IS THE RELATIONSHIP BETWEEN ISRAEL AND THE CHURCH?

Does the Church Replace or Fulfill Israel, or Are the Two Distinct?

The relationship between Israel and the church is perhaps one of the most defining differences between dispensational and covenantal theologies. First, dispensational systems have traditionally emphasized discontinuity between Israel and the church. Thus, there is a distinction between Israel and the church with each having specific roles in God's redemptive plan. In classic dispensationalism, this distinction is in large part due to a dualistic understanding of God's redemptive purposes—one relating to earth concerning an earthly people (Israel) and another related to heaven concerning a heavenly people (the church). Because the church is a part of the heavenly people, God's purposes for the church will be fulfilled separately from his purposes for his earthly people (Israel). Thus, the church does not replace Israel but is something entirely separate and distinct from Israel.

Revised dispensationalism maintains this rigid distinction between Israel and the church. Charles Ryrie considers this distinction the *sine qua non* (i.e., the absolutely indispensable part) of dispensationalism.[38] He argues that the church is distinct in its character, in that it is made up of Jews and gentiles after the cross of Christ; distinct in its timing, in that it begins at Pentecost and is completed with the rapture; and distinct from Israel, in that Israel continues with her own promises and the church remains a separate work of God in this age.[39]

Progressive dispensationalism sees both discontinuity and continuity between Israel and the church. Bruce Ware explains, "Between the two extremes of a strict distinction between Israel and the church … and a strict identity of Israel and the church … there is a middle position that would suggest that Israel and the church share theologically rich and important elements of commonality while at the same time

---

38. Ryrie, *Dispensationalism*, 45–48. He writes, "The essence of dispensationalism, then, is the distinction between Israel and the church" (48).

39. Ibid., 144–50.

maintaining distinct identities."[40] A distinct future for national Israel during the millennium is maintained by progressive dispensationalists. Israel and the church, however, are viewed as the one people of God with the church presently experiencing the inaugurated blessings of the eschatological salvation that both Israel and the church will enjoy in the future.

Second, most non-dispensational systems have traditionally emphasized continuity between Israel and the church. Similar to progressive dispensationalism, progressive covenantalism argues for aspects of both continuity and discontinuity. Regarding discontinuity, Wellum points out, "The church is *new* in a redemptive-historical sense precisely because she is the community of the *new* covenant and thus *different* from Israel in her nature and structure."[41] Regarding continuity, the church is seen as the eschatological Israel by virtue of its union in Christ. Thus, White argues, "It is not that Israel equals the church, as Covenant Theology teaches, but that Jesus is the climax and fulfillment of Israel and the church is the end-time Israel *because it is united to Jesus Christ, her covenant head*."[42] In covenant theology, the overwhelming emphasis is on continuity between Israel and the church. This continuity is based upon an understanding of the covenant of grace that sees one people of God across the Old and New Testaments. In this view, the church is not the replacement of Israel, but its fruition, based on God's covenant of grace which is fulfilled in Jesus Christ.[43] Christian reconstructionism also sees continuity between Israel and the church. David Chilton argues, "From the beginning, God has always had His one covenant people. The New Testament church is simply the continuation of the true 'Israel of God' (Gal 6:16), after the false Israel had been cut off."[44] Many charge covenant theologians and Christian reconstructionists as holding

40. Bruce Ware, "The New Covenant and the People(s) of God," in *Dispensationalism, Israel, and the Church*, 92.

41. Gentry and Wellum, *Kingdom Through Covenant*, 801 (emphasis original).

42. A. Blake White, *What Is New Covenant Theology? An Introduction* (Frederick, MD: New Covenant Media, 2012), 45 (emphasis original).

43. Michael Horton, *Introducing Covenant Theology* (Grand Rapids: Baker, 2006), 131.

44. David Chilton, *Paradise Restored: A Biblical Theology of Dominion* (Tyler, TX: Dominion Press, 1985), 126.

"replacement theology."[45] However, representatives of both systems typically deny this charge.

How Are Romans 11:26 and Galatians 6:16 Interpreted?

To help further understand how each system views the relationship between Israel and the church, we will seek to show how each system handles some of the key texts relating to this issue, especially Romans 11:26 ("And in this way all Israel will be saved") and Galatians 6:16 ("And as for all who walk by this rule, peace and mercy be upon them, and upon the Israel of God").

4. WHAT IS THE KINGDOM OF GOD?

The Old Testament anticipates the coming of the kingdom of God. Jesus' message centered on the kingdom. The kingdom is central to apostolic teaching (Acts 19:8; 28:23, 31), and Revelation climactically concludes the Scriptures' teaching on the kingdom. Saucy states, "All this leads to the conclusion that the kingdom of God is one of the grand themes, if not *the* theme, of Scripture."[46] We will specifically look at how each system understands both the (1) *inauguration* and (2) *consummation* of the kingdom of God.

Dispensationalists tend to emphasize a future realization of the kingdom of God. First, both classic and revised dispensationalists envision the kingdom of God as entirely future. Jesus did not usher in the kingdom during his earthly ministry. He offered it to Israel, but when they rejected it, the offer was rescinded and the kingdom never came.[47] Some classic dispensationalists hold to a distinction between the "kingdom of God" and "kingdom of heaven." C. I. Scofield argued that the kingdom of God is universal, entered into

---

45. See Michael J. Vlach, *Has the Church Replaced Israel: A Theological Evaluation* (Nashville: B&H, 2010).

46. Saucy, *The Case for Progressive Dispensationalism*, 81.

47. For example, see Stanley D. Toussaint and Jay A. Quine, "No, Not Yet: The Contingency of God's Promised Kingdom," *BSac* 164 (2007): 131–47. They argue that "the kingdom is not present today, because when Israel rejected Jesus, the kingdom was postponed" (131).

only by new birth, and chiefly inward and spiritual. The kingdom of heaven, however, is "Messianic, mediatorial, and Davidic, and has for its object the establishment of the kingdom of God in the earth (Matt 3:2; 1 Cor 15:24, 25)."[48] Elsewhere, Scofield explains that the kingdom of heaven "signifies the Messianic earth[ly] rule of Jesus Christ, the Son of David."[49] It is primarily concerned with the fulfillment of Davidic promises (2 Sam 7:7–10) to national Israel through the Messiah. Thus, the "kingdom of heaven" began to appear in the ministry of Jesus, but upon being rejected by Israel it was postponed until the millennium. In the end, the kingdom of God and kingdom of heaven merge together in the eternal state. Ryrie, however, notes that the distinction that some make between the kingdom of heaven and the kingdom of God is relatively insignificant and not determinative of a dispensational view of the kingdom of God.[50]

Second, progressive dispensationalism sees the kingdom of God as primarily future but allows for some realization of the kingdom in the present.[51] It proposes a unified picture of the kingdom of God rather than separate kingdoms. This differs from classic and revised dispensationalism, which tends to see two separate kingdoms operating in conjunction with one another and ultimately merging together. Progressive dispensationalists understand God's universal rule over all creation as united and overlapping with his rule over Israel within the one eschatological kingdom of God. The relationship between God's rule over all creation and over Israel is developed throughout the progressive unfolding of Scripture. Special attention is given to the Davidic covenant and the reigns of David and Solomon, which serve as types of the coming eschatological kingdom.[52] The kingdom

---

48. Scofield, *Scofield Reference Bible*, 1003 (Matt 6:33).

49. Ibid., 996 (Matt 3:2).

50. Ryrie, *Dispensationalism*, 180–81. He comments, "Within the ranks of dispensationalists there are those who hold to the distinction and those who do not. It is not at all determinative" (180). He later adds that the distinction "is minor league and unimportant stuff" (181).

51. Feinberg notes, "The basic distinction here among dispensationalists is that older ones tended to see the kingdom relegated entirely to the future. More contemporary dispensationalists hold that the full realization of the kingdom for Israel and the world awaits the future, but certainly spiritual aspects of the kingdom are operative in the church" ("Systems of Discontinuity," 82).

52. Blaising and Bock, *Progressive Dispensationalism*, 229.

is inaugurated in this present age through the coming of Christ, the indwelling of the Holy Spirit, and the church's enjoyment of the spiritual blessings of God's rule in Christ.[53] While progressive dispensationalism allows for this type of present fulfillment, the kingdom of God is still primarily future and will be finally realized through the millennial reign of Christ on the earth and then the eternal state.[54]

Third, almost all non-dispensational systems hold to an already/not yet understanding of the kingdom of God.[55] George Ladd has provided perhaps the most notable definition of the kingdom:

> Our central thesis is that the Kingdom of God is the redemptive reign of God dynamically active to establish his rule among human beings, and that this Kingdom, which will appear as an apocalyptic act at the end of the age, has already come into human history in the person and mission of Jesus to overcome evil, to deliver people from its power, and to bring them into the blessings of God's reign. The Kingdom of God involves two great moments: fulfillment within history [already], and consummation at the end of history [not yet].[56]

Progressive covenantalism emphasizes the progressive unfolding of the biblical covenants and their fulfillment in Jesus Christ as central to defining the kingdom as a present reality and a future hope.[57] Covenantal theology views the already/not yet nature of the kingdom through its unifying theme of the covenant of grace. Christian reconstructionism views the kingdom of God as arriving in the ministry

---

53. Ibid., 255–62.

54. Darrell L. Bock, "The Reign of the Lord Christ," in *Dispensationalism, Israel, and the Church*, 57; see also Blaising and Bock, *Progressive Dispensationalism*, 268.

55. Michael J. Vlach, "New Covenant Theology Compared with Covenantalism," *MSJ* 18.1 (2007): 201–19. Vlach suggests, "The issue of the kingdom is one in which New Covenant theologians and Covenant theologians appear to be similar. Neither side claims that its system necessarily leads to any particular millennial view. It appears that, within both CT and NCT, one could be an amillennialist, postmillennialist, or historic premillennialist" (218).

56. George E. Ladd, *A Theology of the New Testament*, rev. ed. (Grand Rapids: Eerdmans, 1993), 89–90.

57. Gentry and Wellum, *Kingdom through Covenant*, 648–54, 718–46.

of Jesus and as being brought to completion through the church in this present age and culminating with the return of Christ.[58] While there is still a future realization of the kingdom for Christian reconstructionists, the major emphasis is put on its present reality. DeMar argues, "The Reconstructionist views the kingdom as a present reality that manifests itself as sinners embrace the gospel and live out their new lives in conformity to the Bible. There is no kingdom to bring in, since we are living in the kingdom."[59] Covenant obedience and the saving work of the Holy Spirit through the church in the world will characterize the present realization of the kingdom of God.

CONCLUSION

Trying to bring clarity to the difference between dispensational and non-dispensational (covenantal) systems is not new. Many others have done so in the past and most have helped advance the discussion.[60] Poythress rightly notes,

> In the dispute between dispensationalism and Covenant Theology, both sides cannot be right. It might be that one position is right and the other wrong. Or it might be that one position is mostly right but still has something to learn from the opposing position. So, it is important to seriously listen to more than one point of view to ensure that some significant truths have not been overlooked.[61]

This book seeks to have this conversation in an even more complete way by acknowledging the full scope of theological systems on a spectrum from discontinuity to continuity.

---

58. Gary DeMar argues, "This 'already-not yet' view of the kingdom is biblically sound and has been defended by numerous Bible-believing scholars from various millennial perspectives" (Gary North and Gary DeMar, *Christian Reconstructionism: What It Is and What It Isn't* [Tyler, TX: Institution of Christian Economics, 1991], 96).

59. Ibid., 99.

60. See, e.g., Feinberg, *Continuity and Discontinuity*; Bateman, *Three Central Issues in Contemporary Dispensationalism*; Poythress, *Understanding Dispensationalism*.

61. Poythress, *Understanding Dispensationalism*, 7.

By identifying the various theological systems and subjecting each of them to the same key questions, the reader will be able to more fully see what distinguishes these systems from one another. While the issues of Israel and the church and the kingdom of God often stand at the front of the discussion between the various systems, it is often the more nuanced issues regarding hermeneutics, understanding the biblical covenants, and the New Testament use of the Old Testament that provide the greater clarity between what distinguishes these systems. Since no position can be exhausted by any one author, this book will seek to interact with three key representatives of each system while recognizing there may be others who hold different views within each system. Classic dispensationalism will be represented by John N. Darby, C. I. Scofield, and Lewis S. Chafer. Revised dispensationalism will be represented by Charles Ryrie, John Walvoord, and Dwight Pentecost. Progressive dispensationalism will be represented by Craig Blaising, Darrell Bock, and Robert Saucy. Progressive covenantalism will be represented by Peter Gentry, Stephen Wellum, and key representatives of new covenant theology. Covenant theology will be represented by Michael Horton, O. Palmer Robertson, and Meredith Kline. Finally, Christian reconstructionism will be represented by R. J. Rushdoony, Greg Bahnsen, and Gary North.

CHAPTER 2
CLASSIC DISPENSATIONALISM

Taxonomy of Theological Systems

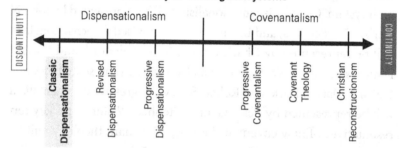

As explained in the introduction and illustrated in chart 2.1, classic dispensationalism represents the position of extreme discontinuity between the covenants and thus between Israel and the church.[1] After offering a brief history of the rise of classic dispensationalism, I will seek to answer our four key questions primarily through the voices of (1) John N. Darby, (2) C. I. Scofield, and (3) Lewis S. Chafer.

John Nelson Darby (1800–1882) is considered to be the father of modern dispensationalism.[2] Darby, a trained lawyer and Anglican

---

1. Of course, there are some positions that are more extreme that will not be covered in this survey. See Charles C. Ryrie, *Dispensationalism*, rev. and exp. (Chicago: Moody, 2007), 229–41 ("Ultradispensationalism").

2. Stephen R. Spencer, "Dispensationalism," in *The Encyclopedia of Christianity*, vol. 1: A–D, ed. Erwin Fahlbusch, et al., trans. Geoffrey W. Bromiley (Grand Rapids: Eerdmans, 1999), 854. The label "dispensationalism" is anachronistic because it was not applied during Darby's lifetime. Furthermore, to date the entire origin of dispensational thought with Darby is to ignore many indications of dispensational discussion throughout history. See especially Larry V. Crutchfield, "Rudiments of Dispensationalism in the Ante-Nicene Period Part 1 (of 2 parts): Israel and the Church in the Ante-Nicene Fathers," *BSac* 144 (1987): 254–76 and idem, "Rudiments of

priest, became disappointed at the lack of spiritual fervor in the church. He eventually came to believe that the established church was so corrupt that no true believer should remain.[3] But finding no comfort in other denominations, Darby sought something simpler and joined a group of individuals for Bible study and communion.[4] By 1840, this small meeting had grown to eight hundred people.[5] This was the birth of the separatist movement later known as the Plymouth Brethren. The appellation "Plymouth Brethren" was due to Darby's objection to denominational names. He preferred instead to use the New Testament term "brethren."[6]

Darby first published his dispensational views in a paper titled, "Apostasy of the Successive Dispensations."[7] A "futurist," Darby rejected the "historicist" approach in vogue in Britain in the early nineteenth century.[8] Darby added two novel elements to futurist theology. First, he saw a "gap" between the 69th and 70th week in Daniel 9:25–27.[9] This gap represented the church age. Second, he suggested that a "rapture" would end the church age,[10] thus inaugurating the 70th week, where the wrath of God will be poured out upon the unjust.[11]

Dispensationalism in the Ante-Nicene Period Part 2 (of 2 parts): Ages and Dispensations in the Ante-Nicene Fathers," *BSac* 144 (1987): 377–99. Also see Arnold D. Ehlert, *A Bibliographic History of Dispensationalism* (Grand Rapids: Baker, 1965), 12; Ryrie, *Dispensationalism*, 70–77.

3. Darby explains, "If it be alleged that the fallen and corrupt state of the church makes it now undesirable so to give it [i.e., the Scriptures], the answer is, God has graciously provided for us in this also. He has told us when the church was become utterly corrupt, as He declared it would do, we were to turn away from all this corruption and those who were in it, and turn to the scriptures which are 'able to make the man of God wise unto salvation'" (John Nelson Darby, *The Collected Writings*, ed. William Kelly [Oak Park, IL: Bible Truth Publishers, 1962], 20:240–41).

4. C. Norman Kraus, *Dispensationalism in America: Its Rise and Development* (Richmond: John Knox, 1958), 26–27.

5. Ryrie, *Dispensationalism*, 77.

6. Clarence B. Bass, *Backgrounds to Dispensationalism: Its Historical Genesis and Ecclesiastical Implications* (Grand Rapids: Eerdmans, 1960), 72.

7. Ehlert, *A Bibliographic History of Dispensationalism*, 49.

8. Spencer, "Dispensationalism," 854.

9. See Louis E. Knowles, "The Interpretation of the Seventy Weeks of Daniel in the Early Fathers," *WTJ* 7.2 (1945): 136–60.

10. A term derived from the Latin verb (*raptare*) "to seize"; cf. 1 Thessalonians 4:17 (ἁρπάζω).

11. Spencer, "Dispensationalism," 854.

In 1845, Darby returned from Switzerland to Plymouth, Britain. Controversy arose between Darby and B. W. Newton, another leader in the early Brethren. The first evidence of the controversy between Darby and Newton concerned the status of the church during the tribulation. Darby asserted that the church would be raptured prior to the tribulation. Additionally, Darby disagreed with Newton's view that the Old Testament saints were merely part of the church.[12] Bass comments, "Here is tangible evidence that the dichotomy between Israel and the church was forming in the thought of Darby, growing out of a rigidly applied principle of interpretation."[13] The conflict between Darby and Newton would snowball, ultimately resulting in Newton being forced out of Plymouth and the Brethren movement.[14] In the coming years, Darby and his followers would gain an attentive audience, particularly among American Presbyterians and Baptists.[15]

Several other individuals helped launch dispensationalism into a robust theological system. The first was Cyrus Ingerson Scofield (1843–1921). C. I. Scofield preached his first sermon in Dallas in 1882—the year Darby died.[16] In 1888, he published a booklet titled *Rightly Dividing the Word of Truth*, which has sold over a million copies and is still in print today. The pinnacle of Scofield's work and "the most important publication of this classic form of Dispensationalism was the *Scofield Reference Bible*, an edition of the King James Bible published in successive editions ... in 1909 and 1917."[17] The publication of the *Scofield Reference Bible* expanded the reach of dispensationalism. Scofield's contribution is so significant that "the label 'dispensationalism' was apparently used first in the 1920s to distinguish Scofield's dispensational theology from other approaches."[18] Indeed, while Darby's

---

12. Bass, *Backgrounds to Dispensationalism*, 74–76.

13. Ibid., 76.

14. Ibid., 87.

15. M. James Sawyer, "Dispensationalism," in *The Blackwell Encyclopedia of Modern Christian Thought*, ed. Alister E. McGrath (Oxford: Blackwell, 1993), 108. James Hall Brooks, a Presbyterian pastor in St. Louis, was among the first to follow Darby. He discipled Scofield after his conversion and is considered the American father of dispensationalism.

16. Ehlert, *A Bibliographic History of Dispensationalism*, 82–83.

17. Spencer, "Dispensationalism," 855.

18. Craig A. Blaising, "Dispensation, Dispensationalism," in *Evangelical Dictionary of*

work gave rise to much of systematic dispensationalism, Scofield's work was the catalyst for American dispensationalism.[19]

The second influential American who helped launch dispensationalism was Lewis Sperry Chafer (1871–1952). Chafer was the founder of Dallas Theological Seminary (DTS)—a school committed to the principles of dispensationalism. In addition to founding DTS, which would produce many notable dispensationalists throughout the twentieth century, two of Chafer's works have been particularly influential. The first was a sixty-page journal article for *Bibliotheca Sacra*, the journal of DTS of which Chafer served as the editor. This article presented a rigorous argument for classic dispensationalism. Second was Chafer's eight-volume systematic theology, "which became the standard theology of the 'Scofieldian' period of dispensationalism."[20]

1. WHAT IS THE BASIC HERMENEUTIC?

Is a Literal or Symbolic Hermeneutic Employed?

A foundational presupposition of dispensationalism is a consistent literal hermeneutic. For example, Chafer states that a "proper interpretation assumes that each word has its normal literal meaning unless there are good reasons for regarding it as a figure of speech."[21] But in addition to a literal hermeneutic, classic dispensationalism applied typology as a secondary theological observation. For Darby, the key was to apply a literal hermeneutic to texts related to Israel, whereas texts related to gentiles or the church could also have a secondary typological or symbolic meaning. Darby states, "First, in prophecy,

---

Theology, 2nd ed., ed. Walter A. Elwell (Grand Rapids: Baker Academic, 2001), 344.

19. It is important to note that Darby's brand of dispensationalism was founded upon an ecclesiology much different than that held by later "dispensationalists." Spencer comments, "Thus dispensationalism in America was and is an eschatological perspective built upon an ecclesiology quite different from the earlier British Brethren version" ("Dispensationalism," 854).

20. Sawyer, "Dispensationalism," 108.

21. Lewis Sperry Chafer, *Major Bible Themes: 52 Vital Doctrines of the Scripture Simplified and Explained*, rev. John F. Walvoord (Grand Rapids: Zondervan, 1974), 35. Elsewhere Chafer states, "The outstanding characteristic of the dispensationalist is the fact that he *believes* every statement of the Bible and gives to it the plain, natural meaning its words imply" (Lewis Sperry Chafer, "Dispensationalism," *BSac* 93 [1936]: 446).

when the Jewish church or nation ... is concerned, i.e., when the address is directed to the Jews, there we may look for a plain and direct testimony, because earthly things were the Jews' proper portion." He continues, "On the contrary, where the address is to the Gentiles, i.e., when the Gentiles are concerned in it, there we may look for symbol, because earthly things were not their portion, and the system of revelation must to them be symbolical."[22] Thus, when dealing with the Jews, a literal interpretation is demanded but not necessarily when the church is being addressed.

Scofield's hermeneutic was very similar to Darby's in that texts related to Israel needed to be interpreted literally, but those related to the church often included a spiritual or even allegorical interpretation. Thus, Scofield not only accepted that sometimes Scripture needed to be spiritualized, he also endorsed it. He writes, "It is then permitted—while holding firmly to the historical verity—reverently to *spiritualize* the historical Scriptures." He qualifies this statement by claiming, "Prophecies may never be spiritualized, but are always literal."[23] Thus, like Darby, Scofield did not hold exclusively to a literal interpretation of Scripture. When the passage of Scripture related to the church, a spiritual interpretation was sometimes permitted.[24] When a passage (especially a prophecy) applied to Israel, however, only a literal interpretation was accepted.

Additionally, if the New Testament appears to claim that the Old Testament prophecy regarding Israel is fulfilled in Christ and the church, then there are two separate fulfillments or the New Testament "fulfillment" is only an "application" or "partial fulfillment" of the Old Testament principle that will also be literally fulfilled in Israel.[25]

---

22. Darby, *Collected Writings*, 2:35.

23. C. I. Scofield, *The Scofield Bible Correspondence School*, vol. 1 (Chicago: Moody, 1907), 45, 46.

24. See the notes in the *Scofield Reference Bible* on Genesis 24:1; 41:45; Exodus 2:2; 15:25; John 12:24 as well as the section on typology (Scofield, *Scofield Reference Bible*).

25. See notes in the *Scofield Reference Bible* on Joel 2:28: "'Afterward' in Joel 2:28 means 'in the last days' ... and has a partial and continuous fulfilment during the 'last days' which began with the first advent of Christ (Heb. 1:2); but the greater fulfilment awaits the 'last days' as applied to Israel" (932; see also 1151 [Acts 2:17]).

According to Scofield, a text might have a spiritual fulfillment related to the church but must also have a literal fulfillment related to Israel.

In sum, early dispensationalists affirmed that the Bible should be interpreted literally, especially when related to Israel. But this hermeneutic was not rigidly applied to texts that were applied to the church. The uneven application of a literal hermeneutic demonstrates that the foundational commitment of dispensationalism is not a literal interpretation of the Bible but a commitment to maintain a firm distinction between Israel and the church.

What Is the Proper Role of Typology?

Are the New Testament authors employing typology? Do they allow for a spiritual or allegorical interpretation? Or is the Old Testament always fulfilled in a literal manner? For classic dispensationalists, the emphasis is usually on a literal fulfillment. Yet, as we will see, many classic dispensationalists also embrace the use of typology.

Scofield defines a type as "a divinely purposed illustration of some truth" (e.g., a person, event, thing, or institution).[26] He gives two rules for practicing typology. If the New Testament does not confirm the type, (1) it cannot be "dogmatically asserted" and (2) it can only be spiritually analogous.[27] He states, "Types occur most frequently in the Pentateuch, but are found, more sparingly, elsewhere. The antitype, or fulfilment of the type, is found, usually, in the New Testament."[28] Classic dispensationalism's understanding of typology is closer to a spiritual or even an allegorical interpretation when put into practice. For example, in Genesis 1:16, Scofield asserts that the "greater light" is a type of Christ (e.g., "sun of righteousness," Mal 4:2) and the "lesser

---

26. Scofield, *Scofield Reference Bible*, 4 (Gen 1:16). The 1967 revision drops all of Scofield's types.

27. Ibid., 100 (Exod 25:1). House summarizes: "In general, traditional dispensationalists would assert a single historical meaning for every biblical text that is a union of a divine and human meaning, though many traditional dispensationalists do accept a conservative form of *sensus plenior* or *reference plenior* in which the New Testament provides an extension of the Old Testament single meaning that is nonetheless controlled by the initial authorial meaning, thus different but not disparate" (H. Wayne House, "Traditional Dispensationalism and the Millennium," *CTR* 11.1 [Fall 2013]: 10 [emphasis original]).

28. Scofield, *Scofield Reference Bible*, 4 (Gen 1:16).

FROM DISCONTINUITY TO CONTINUITY

light" is a type of the church.[29] In addition, other types found in *The Scofield Reference Bible* in Genesis include the following:

- Eve is a "type of the Church as the bride of Christ" (8 [Gen 2:23]).
- Abel is a "type of the spiritual man" (10 [Gen 4:2]) and the sacrifice that he offered is a "type of Christ, the Lamb of God" (10 [Gen 4:4]).
- The ark is a "type of Christ as the refuge of His people from judgment" (13 [Gen 6:14]).
- Melchizedek is a "type of Christ the King-Priest" (23 [Gen 14:18]).
- Lot and Abraham are "types of the worldly and the spiritual believer," respectively (30 [Gen 19:36]).
- Sarah is a "type of grace" and Isaac is a type of (1) the church as composed of the spiritual children of Abraham, (2) Christ as the Son "obedient unto death," (3) Christ as the bridegroom of a called-out bride, and (4) the new nature of the believer as "born after the Spirit" (31 [Gen 21:3]).
- Abraham typifies God who "spared not His own son, but delivered Him up for us all" and the ram is a "type of substitution—Christ as a burnt-offering in our stead" (33 [Gen 22:9]).
- Both Joseph and Benjamin are types of Christ (53 [Gen 37:2], 62 [Gen 43:34]).

Scofield also saw all the elements of the tabernacle as typological, including the details:

- Comprehensively, the tabernacle represents (1) the church as a habitation of God through the Spirit;

---

29. Ibid. Regarding Genesis 1:5, Scofield states, "The use of 'evening' and 'morning' may be held to limit 'day' to the solar day; but the frequent parabolic use of natural phenomena may warrant the conclusion that each creative 'day' was a period of time marked off by a beginning and ending" (*Scofield Reference Bible*, 4).

(2) the believer; or (3) a figure of things in the heavens (101 [Exod 25:9]).

- The materials and colors of the tabernacle: gold represents divine glory; silver represents redemption; brass represents judgment; blue represents a heavenly nature or origin; and scarlet represents sacrifice (100 [Exod 25:1]).
- The material of the ark of the covenant: acacia-wood represents the humanity of Christ and gold represents the deity of Christ (101 [Exod 25:9]).
- The content of the ark of the covenant: the law points to God's law in Christ's heart, the manna represents his people, and Aaron's rod is a symbol of the resurrection (101 [Exod 25:9]).
- The use of the ark of the covenant: the mercy seat is a type of God's throne (101 [Exod 25:9]).
- The brazen altar is a type of the cross where atonement is made in the fire of judgment (101 [Exod 25:10]). It is also a type of Christ upon the cross who offered himself as a whole burnt offering (104 [Exod 27:1]).
- The elements in the temple: the showbread represents Christ, the bread of God (102 [Exod 25:30]); the candlestick represents Christ, our light (102 [Exod 25:31]); the inner veil represents Christ's human body (104 Exod 26:31]); oil is a symbol of the Holy Spirit (105 [Exod 27:10]); and the fine linen typifies personal righteousness (104 [Exod 27:9]).

Chafer likewise affirms the use of typology. He defines a type as "a divinely purposed anticipation which illustrates its antitype."[30] Although he laments the fact that many abuse typology, he in no way rejects it.[31] In fact, he readily acknowledges "there being upwards

---

30. Lewis Sperry Chafer, *Systematic Theology*, 8 vols. (Dallas: Dallas Seminary Press, 1947), 1:xxx.

31. Regarding typology, Chafer writes, "It is obvious that to neglect truth is a greater error than to overemphasize it or to misstate it" (ibid.).

of one hundred legitimate types," with a full one-half related to the Lord Jesus Christ.[32] When it comes to determining a type, Chafer even rejects the notion that a type must be clearly stated as such in the Bible. He argues, "There are many easily recognized types which are not directly sanctioned as such by any specific New Testament Scripture."[33]

It should be noted that most of the texts associated with typology are found in the Old Testament and not the New Testament. This apparent omission is caused by the belief that prophetic texts must be interpreted literally.[34] Many revised dispensationalists have moved away from this understanding of typology and focus more on a literal or historical-grammatical interpretation.[35] Consequently, the literal, plain reading always remains the rule, but early dispensationalists did employ typology. This typology, however, was not rigid or fundamental to a proper understanding of the Bible. Proper understanding is achieved by a consistent literal hermeneutic, especially in regard to prophetic texts.

How Are Old Testament Restoration Prophecies Fulfilled?

Regarding restoration prophecies, classic dispensationalists insist on literal fulfillment. For example, in Amos 9:11–15 Israel is promised a future restoration which involves a return to the land, rebuilt cities, bumper crops, and defeat of enemies. The heading at the beginning of this passage in *The Scofield Reference Bible* states, "Future kingdom blessing: (1) The LORD's return and the re-establishment of the Davidic monarchy" and "(2) Full kingdom blessing of restored Israel."[36] Since such prophecies have not come to fruition, we still await their fulfillment.[37] In Acts 15 this passage is quoted in relation to the gen-

---

32. Ibid.

33. Ibid., 1:xxxi.

34. According to Scofield, Matthew 2:15 (which quotes Hos 11:1 as being fulfilled) "illustrates the truth that prophetic utterances often have a latent and deeper meaning than at first appears" (*Scofield Reference Bible*, 995).

35. W. Edward Glenny, "Typology: A Summary of the Present Evangelical Discussion," *JETS* 40.4 (1997): 632.

36. Scofield, *Scofield Reference Bible*, 940.

37. See Darby, *Collected Writings*, 11:268.

tiles being accepted into the church. But instead of interpreting these verses as being fulfilled in the early church, Scofield insists, "These verses which follow in Amos describe the final regathering of Israel, which the other prophets invariably connect with the fulfilment of the Davidic Covenant (e.g. Isa 11:1, 10–12; Jer 23:5–8)."[38]

Chafer has a similar view. Regarding such prophecies, he writes, "The prophecies of the Bible are fulfilled in every instance by actual history. The Bible itself indicates that the acid test of all prophecy is its literal fulfillment."[39] The intended referent must always receive the fulfillment of the prophecy.[40] Classic dispensationalists reject any attempt to spiritualize or adapt prophecies. According to Chafer, James' use of Amos 9 in Acts 15 demonstrates the distinction between Israel and the church. In fact, apparently reading between the lines, he even suggests that this passage confirms "that a chiliastic belief that Christ returns before the thousand-year kingdom, was adopted by the church at its first council."[41]

Thus, classic dispensationalists tend to embrace the validity of typology but never at the expense of the literal fulfillment. The majority of the typology is found in the Pentateuch and relates to the person and work of Christ. When the New Testament writers quote the Old Testament, classic dispensationalists assume that the fulfillment is yet to come because the prophecy must be fulfilled by Israel and not the church. If the text states that a "fulfillment" has taken place, then the fulfillment is interpreted as either a partial fulfillment or as an application.

---

38. Scofield, *Scofield Reference Bible*, 1170 (Acts 15:13).

39. Chafer, *Systematic Theology*, 1:30.

40. Darby similarly states that in Amos 9:14–15 "we get what has clearly never yet been fulfilled, while it applies to temporal blessing in the land" (*Collected Writings*, 11:276).

41. Chafer, *Systematic Theology*, 4:269 (see also 5:329).

2. WHAT IS THE RELATIONSHIP BETWEEN
THE COVENANTS?

The word "dispensation" is essential to dispensationalism. The word
comes into English via the Latin translation (*dispensatio*) of the Greek
word *oikonomia*, the basic meaning of which is "management of a
household."[42] But the concept of dispensations is not unique to dispensationalism. A *dispensation* is often simply defined as "a period of
time." Scofield's definition for dispensation is "a period of time during
which man is tested in respect of obedience to some *specific* revelation of the will of God."[43] This definition not only involves time, but
also involves some concept of God's administration as well as man's
responsibility. Those three components—time, God's administration,
and responsibility—are the three crucial concepts for a dispensation.
Scofield lists seven distinct dispensations:[44]

1. Innocence (Gen 1:28–3:6) Creation → Fall
2. Conscience (Gen 4:1–8:14) Fall → Flood
3. Human Government (Gen 8:15–11:9) Flood → Babel
4. Promise (Gen 11:10–Exod 18:27) Abraham → Exodus
5. Law (Exod 18:28–Acts 1:26) Moses → John the Baptist
6. Grace (Acts 2:1–Rev 19:21) Pentecost → Rapture
7. Kingdom (Rev 20–21) Millennium → Great White Throne

Dispensationalists insist that God's progressive revelation and subsequent human failure necessitates various administrative periods
in history. The Bible is to be understood within this framework of
dispensations. Chafer writes, "The dispensational study of the Bible
consists in the identification of certain well-defined time-periods
which are divinely indicated, together with the revealed purpose of

---

42. BDAG, 697. See 1 Corinthians 9:17; Ephesians 1:10; 3:9; Colossians 1:25.

43. Scofield, *Scofield Reference Bible*, 5 (Gen 1:28). Chafer's definition is similar: "a dispensation is a specific, divine economy, a commitment from God to man of a responsibility to
discharge that which God has appointed him" (*Systematic Theology*, 7:122; see also 1:40). See
also Darby, *Collected Writings*, 1:124–25.

44. Scofield, *Scofield Reference Bible*, 5 (Gen 1:28). See also idem, *Rightly Dividing the Word
of Truth*, rev. ed. (Grand Rapids: Meridian, 1989), 21–26; Chafer, *Systematic Theology*, 1:40–41.

God relative to each. ... No accounting is possible as to the extent of error which is prevalent because of the careless reading into one dispensation or age of that which belongs to another."[45] Closely related to (but not identical with) the concept of dispensations are the biblical covenants since a new covenant often triggered a new dispensation.[46] Dispensations involve the historical outwork of God's plan whereas covenants involve the relationships between God and man. Like most theological systems, dispensationalism makes a major distinction between conditional and unconditional covenants.

Are the Covenants Conditional or Unconditional?

With regard to the Abrahamic, Davidic, and new covenants, classic dispensationalists see them as eternal and therefore unconditional.[47] The Abrahamic covenant guarantees everlasting blessings for Abraham, his offspring, and all people. As such, the Abrahamic covenant "is wholly gracious and unconditional."[48] Chafer claims this covenant "is unconditional in every part of it, being that alone which Jehovah declares He will do for and through Abraham. Being unconditional, it cannot be broken by man."[49]

Although Genesis 12:1 ("Go out from your land, your relatives, and your father's house to the land that I will show you"; CSB) includes a command (i.e., "Go"), this does not make the covenant conditional. When God declares his intention to act, that declaration becomes

---

45. Ibid., 1:xi.

46. Scofield clarifies, "The *dispensation* must be distinguished from the [Abrahamic] *covenant*. The former is a mode of testing; the latter is everlasting because unconditional" (*Scofield Reference Bible*, 20 [Gen 12:1]).

47. Dispensationalists also include the Palestinian covenant (Deut 28:1–30:32) as unconditional (see Scofield, *Scofield Reference Bible*, 250 [Deut 30:3]).

48. Scofield, *Scofield Reference Bible*, 20 (Gen 12:1). Chafer adds that the Abrahamic covenant is unconditional because "(1) No human element appears in any feature of the Abrahamic Covenant as it is announced by Jehovah, and (2) that both Abraham's position in Jehovah's covenant to him, and Abraham's imputed righteousness (Gen 15:6) are secured to him apart from meritorious works" ("Dispensationalism," 434). See also Darby, *Collected Writings*, 3:47–49; Chafer, *Systematic Theology*, 7:96–99.

49. Chafer, *Systematic Theology*, 4:313. Earlier he writes that the Abrahamic covenant is "without human condition" and that it "declares the unchanging purpose of Jehovah. It will be achieved in pure grace, apart from every human factor, and its accomplishments are eternal" (4:235). See also ibid., 5:317; Darby, *Collected Writings*, 3:48–49, 54.

binding. For classic dispensationalists, Genesis 15:5–21 further proves the unconditionality of the Abrahamic covenant. God himself ratifies the covenant while Abraham is placed into a deep sleep.[50]

The Davidic covenant is likewise unconditional, which assures three blessings to Israel: "The covenant made with David (2 Sam 7:11–16), like the covenant made with Abraham, is unconditional and everlasting in its duration. It guarantees (1) an unfailing house or line of David's sons—a king without cessation to sit on David's throne ... ; (2) a throne, the earthly throne of David to continue forever; and (3) a kingdom forever."[51] While the Lord can discipline the lineage of David, the covenant cannot be revoked (2 Sam 7:13–15).[52] The literal reading of the covenant ensures an earthly throne. To those who see a spiritual fulfillment, Chafer objects by stating, "There is no evidence that David foresaw an earthly throne merging into a spiritual reign. ... Nor is this kingdom and throne established in heaven."[53] When a consistent literal hermeneutic is employed, the unconditional language of the Davidic covenant could not be any more certain. The Davidic covenant will be fulfilled with Israel in a physical way, not in the church.

What about the new covenant? Because of the distinction between promises given to Israel and those given to the church, classic dispensationalists insist that Israel is the true and only recipient of the new covenant promised in the Old Testament (Jer 31:31–34; Heb 8:8, 13). This covenant is distinct from the new covenant that is now in force with the church. Unlike the covenant that was given through Moses, this covenant will be unconditional and will begin when Israel enters the millennial kingdom.[54]

There are, however, some differences as to how classic dispensationalists view the new covenant with the church in relation to the new

---

50. Chafer, "Dispensationalism," 432–33. For an extended treatise of unconditional and conditional covenants from a classic dispensationalist perspective, see especially 429–45.

51. Chafer, Systematic Theology, 4:314. Elsewhere he writes that this is "an everlasting throne, an everlasting kingdom, and an everlasting King to sit on David's throne" (1:43).

52. Scofield maintains that "disobedience in the Davidic family is to be visited with chastisement, but not to the abrogation of the covenant" since this covenant "is immutable" (Scofield Reference Bible, 362 [2 Sam 7:16]).

53. Chafer, "Dispensationalism," 435. Cf. Matthew 25:31–32; Luke 1:31–33; Acts 15:16–17.

54. Chafer, Systematic Theology, 4:315–16, 325.

covenant with Israel. Darby taught that the new covenant belonged solely to Israel in both the Old Testament and New Testament, though the church may participate in the benefits of Christ's sacrifice (Luke 22:20; 1 Cor 11:25; 2 Cor 3:6).[55] The church is related only to the blood of the new covenant and not the covenant itself. The good news of the gospel is not formally a "covenant" but instead is the revelation of God's salvation in Christ. Because the new covenant with Israel is still future, Jesus "has not [yet] accomplished the actual new covenant formally with Israel and Judah."[56] Scofield regarded the new covenant as applying to both Israel (in the millennium) and the church (the present age).[57] There is one new covenant that contains a twofold application: one related to Israel (future) and one related to the church (now). Thus, the church's relation to the new covenant is viewed as a partial fulfillment. Chafer affirmed a slightly different interpretation by maintaining that there are two new covenants: the new covenant mentioned in the Old Testament that will be fulfilled by Israel in the millennium and a different new covenant in the New Testament that will be fulfilled by the church in the present age.[58]

Despite these small differences, classic dispensationalists insist that the new covenant as revealed in the Old Testament was specifically related to Israel and would be fulfilled during the millennial kingdom. In addition, they affirm that the new covenant was unconditional. For example, Scofield maintains that the new covenant "is absolutely unconditional, and, since no responsibility is by it committed to man, it is final and irreversible."[59] Chafer explains that this new covenant, like the Abrahamic and Davidic covenants, rests on "the faithfulness of God and not at all on the unfaithfulness of men" and therefore is "unbreakable by men."[60] This covenant will not supersede the previous unconditional covenants but will supersede the law covenant that was broken because it was conditional.

---

55. See Darby, *Collected Writings*, 3:49–53.
56. Ibid., 3:52.
57. See Scofield, *Scofield Reference Bible*, 1297–98 (Heb 8:8).
58. See Chafer, *Systematic Theology*, 4:325; 7:98–99.
59. Scofield, *Scofield Reference Bible*, 1298 (Heb 8:8).
60. Chafer, *Systematic Theology*, 4:325.

Because classic dispensationalists see these three covenants as unconditional, there is nothing humanity can do to alter God's plan. As a result, the promises to finally restore Israel will certainly occur. Even though the church is now enjoying the benefits of the new covenant, in the future God will once again focus on Israel by making a new covenant with her.

How Were Old Testament Saints Saved?

The discussion of covenants is closely related to the issue regarding the means of salvation between the Testaments (covenants). Because dispensationalists maintain a strict distinction between Israel and the church, critics often accuse dispensationalists of suggesting multiple ways of salvation. For some classic dispensationalists, there is evidence that they taught that Old Testament saints and New Testament saints were saved differently. For example, Scofield writes, "As a dispensation, grace begins with the death and resurrection of Christ (Rom 3:24–26; 4:24, 25). The point of testing is no longer legal obedience as the condition of salvation, but acceptance or rejection of Christ, with good works as a fruit of salvation."[61] Because Scofield says salvation is "no longer" through legal obedience, the implication is that previously it was the condition of salvation. Likewise, Chafer comments, "A distinction must be observed here between just men of the Old Testament and those justified according to the New Testament. According to the Old Testament men were just because they were true and faithful in keeping the Mosaic Law. ... Men were therefore just because of their own works for God, whereas New Testament justification is God's work for man in answer to faith (Rom 5:1)."[62] Again, it is difficult to

---

61. Scofield, *Scofield Reference Bible*, 1115 (John 1:17). The 1967 edition has changed the language entirely: "Prior to the cross salvation was through faith (Gen 15:6; Rom. 4:3), being grounded on Christ's atoning sacrifice, viewed anticipatively by God" (Scofield, Gaebelein, et al., *New Scofield Study Bible*, 1477). Aldrich attempts to acquit Scofield of these charges by appealing to Scofield's note on Romans 1:16 (Roy L. Aldrich, "An Apologetic for Dispensationalism," *BSac* 12 [1955]: 49). In Romans, however, Scofield is clearly commenting on the salvation of NT believers. It is possible, if not likely, that when Scofield speaks of "grace," he is referring to the age or dispensation of grace, not grace itself.

62. Chafer, *Systematic Theology*, 7:219.

imagine that Chafer is not claiming that Old Testament saints were justified because of their good works.[63]

Typically, however, dispensationalists have rejected the charge that they promote two ways of salvation. The doctrinal statement that Chafer wrote for DTS states: "We believe that the dispensations are not ways of salvation. ... We believe that according to the 'eternal purpose' of God (Eph. 3:11) salvation in the divine reckoning is always 'by grace, through faith,' and rests upon the basis of the shed blood of Christ."[64]

How Is the Old Testament Law to Be Applied Today?

What relationship do New Testament believers have to the Old Testament law? Because the dispensations between the Old Testament and the New Testament are distinct, classic dispensationalists insist that the Old Testament law has no bearing on New Testament believers. Chafer argues, "There is no scholarly reason for applying the Scriptures which bear upon the past, the present, or the future of Israel to any other people than that nation of whom these Scriptures speak."[65] This also applies to some of the laws found in the Gospel accounts since the dispensation of grace was not inaugurated until the death and resurrection of Christ (Luke 22:20). For example, Scofield maintains that the law, including the Sermon on the Mount, does not relate to the Christian because Christians are saved by grace and not the law. Since the Sermon on the Mount is "legal ground,"[66] it is an ethic for Israel in the millennial kingdom and not for the church. It offers "the divine constitution for the righteous government of the earth" and as such is "pure law."[67] Consequently, the Lord's Prayer is not a prayer for Christians. Yet, there may be some "application" or principles found in the Sermon on the Mount that are appropriate for Christians today.

---

63. Some have suggested that Chafer was not advocating that works are the actual basis for salvation but that he is merely contrasting law versus grace.

64. Quoted in Aldrich, "An Apologetic for Dispensationalism," 50–51.

65. Chafer, "Dispensationalism," 406.

66. See Scofield, Scofield Reference Bible, 1002 (Matt 6:12).

67. Ibid., 1000 (Matt 5:2).

Chafer distinguished between *primary* and *secondary* applications. Since all Scripture is profitable for the Christian (2 Tim 3:16–17), it can, in some sense, be applied to Christians. It is, however, necessary for the New Testament believer to realize that "not all Scripture is *about* him."[68] Chafer writes, "The Scriptures are 'profitable' because they are pregnant with moral and spiritual values; this is true even when they exert only the influence of a secondary application."[69] Thus, Christians can appropriate the principles found in portions of Scripture outside the dispensation of grace. Nevertheless, they should not assume the words directly address them.[70] Like Scofield, Chafer associates the teachings of Jesus more closely with Moses than Paul. He comments, "The teachings of Moses and the teachings of the kingdom [i.e., Jesus' teachings] are purely legal, while the instructions to the believer of this dispensation are in conformity with pure grace."[71] For Chafer, the Sermon on the Mount is a "manifesto" in which "the King declares the essential character of the kingdom, the conduct which will be required in the kingdom, and the conditions of entrance into the kingdom. This kingdom rule of life is purely legal."[72] Indeed, Jesus' commands are more advanced than those given by Moses because they are "vastly more impossible," which intensifies the character of the sermon as being "strictly legal."[73]

The distinction between Israel and the church also affects the understanding of the covenants. Whereas covenant theology places various eras and economies underneath the umbrella of the covenant of grace, dispensationalism sees dispensations and covenants as separate categories. Thus, the covenants must be understood within the dispensation in which they were created.

---

68. Chafer, *Systematic Theology*, 1:116 (emphasis original).
69. Ibid.
70. See also Chafer, "Dispensationalism," 417–18.
71. Chafer, *Systematic Theology*, 4:225.
72. Ibid., 4:177.
73. Ibid.

3. WHAT IS THE RELATIONSHIP BETWEEN ISRAEL AND THE CHURCH?

Does the Church Replace or Fulfill Israel, or Are the Two Distinct?

Classic dispensationalists affirm a rigid distinction between Israel and the church. The two are different groups and should never be confused. Darby maintains that whereas Israel is earthly, the church is heavenly.[74] He further states, "Prophecy applies itself properly to the earth; its object is not heaven. It was about things that were to happen on the earth. … The church is something altogether apart—a kind of heavenly economy."[75] Similarly, Chafer comments, "The Dispensationalist believes that throughout the ages God is pursuing two distinct purposes: one related to the earth with earthly people and earthly objectives involved, while the other is related to heaven with heavenly people and heavenly objectives involved."[76]

At the most basic level, the difference between Israel and the church can be seen in how one becomes part of each group. Chafer writes, "Israelites become such by a natural birth while Christians become such by a spiritual birth."[77] The differences extend beyond origin to differences of responsibility, destiny, and promises. As a result, the promises for each group are distinctively different. Chafer contends that in spite of a few similarities between Israel and the church, the differences, which he observed to be more than twenty-four, far outweigh the similarities.[78] He writes, "Every covenant, promise, and provision for Israel is earthly, and they continue as a nation with the earth when it is created new. Every covenant or promise for the Church is for a heavenly reality, and she continues in heavenly

---

74. Darby, *Collected Writings*, 2:373. He states, "[The church] is not of the world. It, as such, sits in heavenly places in Christ, where prophecy reaches not. It never will be established on earth, as the Jews. It is not its calling" (11:46).

75. Ibid., 2:376.

76. Chafer, "Dispensationalism," 448.

77. Chafer, *Systematic Theology*, 1:xiv.

78. Ibid., 4:47–53; See also 1:xiv and 1:xix, where he poses biblical questions to those who find no distinction between Israel and the church. Similar questions are asked in idem, "Dispensationalism," 444–45.

citizenship when the heavens are recreated."[79] Furthermore, classic dispensationalists reject the idea that the dispensation with Israel was a mere shadow, awaiting fuller clarity in the church. Instead, the church and Israel represent distinct dispensations in the plan of God. Applying the blessings promised to Israel requires an allegorical approach to the text. In contrast, the plain, literal reading of the Bible maintains a distinction between Israel and the church. When the consistent literal hermeneutic is abandoned, theological errors abound.[80]

How strongly this distinction is made is one of the major differences between classic and revised dispensationalism. Classic dispensationalism presents a sharp duality between Israel as *earthly* people and Christians as *heavenly* people. Concerning this distinction, Scofield comments, "In the predictions concerning the future of Israel and the church, the distinction is still more startling. The church will be taken away from the earth entirely, but restored Israel is yet to have her greatest earthly splendor and power."[81]

How Are Romans 11:26 and Galatians 6:16 Interpreted?

According to classic dispensationalists, Romans 11:26 ("And in this way all Israel will be saved") testifies that God is not done with Israel as a nation but will fulfill his promises made to her in the Old Testament. When Paul uses the term "Israel," he means ethnic Israel and not the church. This coincides with a consistent literal hermeneutic concerning prophecies related to Israel. A plain reading also understands the salvation of Israel to be a future event that follows the "fullness of the Gentiles" (11:25). God will not forget his promises to Israel but will cause the majority of Israel to believe in Jesus as the Messiah.[82] As Darby states, "Israel is blinded for the moment in part, until the fulness of the Gentiles be come in, and then Israel as

---

79. Chafer, *Systematic Theology*, 4:47.

80. Ibid., 1:xi.

81. Scofield, *Rightly Dividing the Word of Truth*, 15.

82. Scofield comments on Romans 11:1: "The Christian is of the heavenly seed of Abraham (Gen 15:5, 6; Gal 3:29), and partakes of the spiritual blessings of the Abrahamic Covenant (Gen 15, 18, *note*); but Israel as a nation always has its own place, and is yet to have its greatest exaltation as the earthly people of God" (*Scofield Reference Bible*, 1204 [Rom 11:1]).

a whole, as a nation, shall be saved."[83] Scofield explains, "According to the prophets, Israel, regathered from all nations, restored to her own land and converted, is yet to have her greatest earthly exaltation and glory."[84] Therefore, there is no reason to "spiritualize" the Old Testament promises to Israel for they will be realized literally.

Whereas dispensationalists often cite Romans 11:26 as proof that God is not yet finished with ethnic Israel,[85] covenantalists often quote Galatians 6:16 as evidence for their position. Paul states: "And as for all who walk by this rule, peace and mercy be upon them, and upon the Israel of God." Classic dispensationalists reject the notion that Paul calls the gentile congregation "the Israel of God." For example, Scofield cross-references Romans 4:12 and 9:6–8 in order to suggest that at the end of Galatians Paul is referring to ethnic Israel and is not spiritualizing. The implication is that he is not addressing gentiles at all, but merely the Jewish portion within the congregation.

4. WHAT IS THE KINGDOM OF GOD?

Classic dispensationalists often distinguish the "kingdom of heaven" from the "kingdom of God." The latter refers to God's authoritative rule, while the former refers to God's earthly rule.[86] For example, Chafer insists that Matthew's kingdom of heaven was limited to the national interests of Israel. The dispensation of grace had not been invoked.[87] Scofield suggests several distinctions between the kingdom of God and the kingdom of heaven:

---

83. Darby, *Collected Writings*, 1:319.

84. Scofield, *Scofield Reference Bible*, 1206 (Rom 11:26).

85. However, the view that God has a special plan for ethnic Israel is not necessarily unique to dispensationalism.

86. Darby, *Collected Writings*, 2:54–55; Scofield, *Scofield Reference Bible*, 996 (Matt 3:2); Chafer, *Systematic Theology*, 5:316.

87. Chafer explains that the "kingdom of heaven" refers "to the same earthly Davidic kingdom with which the Old Testament had closed its Messianic prophesying in Malachi" (*Systematic Theology*, 5:343).

- The kingdom of God is universal whereas the kingdom of heaven is the messianic and Davidic kingdom on earth.
- The kingdom of God is entered only by new birth whereas the kingdom of heaven is the sphere of a profession that may be real or false.
- The kingdom of God is chiefly that which is inward and spiritual whereas the kingdom of heaven is organic and is manifested in the glory on the earth.
- The kingdom of heaven will merge into the kingdom of God when Christ defeats all his enemies and delivers over the kingdom to God.[88]

Did Jesus Bring the Kingdom?

According to classic dispensationalists, Jesus offered the earthly, messianic kingdom to Israel during his early ministry. He was not offering the authoritative rule of God.[89] Unlike progressive dispensationalists, classic dispensationalists do not see an inauguration of the "kingdom of heaven," as defined in Christ's early ministry. Instead, Christ offered the kingdom to Israel but Israel rejected the kingdom. As a result, the establishment of the Davidic kingdom has been postponed. On the basis of the covenants with Israel, however, the kingdom-promise has not been abrogated. Each of these elements can be explained in turn.

First, Christ only announced the kingdom to Israel. Matthew records Jesus saying, "The kingdom of heaven is at hand" (Matt 3:2 KJV). This kingdom, according to Scofield, "signifies the Messianic earth [sic] rule of Jesus Christ, the son of David." He further notes, "It is called the kingdom of the heavens because it is the rule of the heavens over the earth."[90] What does Jesus mean then when he declares that the kingdom is "at hand"? Scofield explains, "'At hand' is never a

---

88. Scofield, *Scofield Reference Bible*, 1003 (Matt 6:33). The 1967 edition allows for a distinction between the phrases "in some instances" (*New Scofield Study Bible*, 1328 [Matt 6:33]).

89. Darby writes, "Israel is His people upon earth. Whilst Christ is in heaven, the Holy Ghost is gathering the Church to be His in heaven" (*Collected Writings*, 3:389).

90. Scofield, *Scofield Reference Bible*, 996 (Matt 3:2).

positive affirmation that the person or thing said to be 'at hand' will immediately appear, but only that no known or predicted event must intervene."[91] Because the kingdom had not yet come, Jesus later taught his disciples to pray for the coming of the kingdom.

Second, the kingdom is rejected by Israel and so Jesus changes his message and announces "the mysteries of the kingdom" (Matt 13:11 KJV). The seven parables in Matthew 13 "describe the result of the presence of the Gospel in the world during the present age."[92] Even though the people of Israel shouted "Hosanna" to the king, Jesus was aware of their rejection (Luke 19:36–44).

Third, because Israel rejected the King and his kingdom, the literal restoration of the national kingdom as promised by the Davidic covenant has been postponed. It will be realized in the dispensation of the kingdom. Seven signs mark the transition from the dispensation of grace to the kingdom age: (1) the removal of the church; (2) the tribulation; (3) the return of Christ; (4) the judgment of Israel; (5) the establishment of the Davidic kingdom; (6) the judgment of the nations; and (7) the binding of Satan.[93]

How Is the Kingdom Consummated?

In Acts 1:6 the disciples ask the resurrected Jesus about the restoration of the kingdom of Israel ("Lord, will you at this time restore the kingdom to Israel?"). Jesus responds by telling them that it is not for them to know the times and seasons of the Father's plans. The dispensationalist finds an implicit reality in Jesus' answer since he does not correct or rebuke their question. Indeed, it seems that the question was natural. Consequently, Jesus merely informs them that the time is God's secret.[94] The disciples' anticipation of the kingdom was correct, which demonstrates that they were basing their question

---

91. Ibid., 998 (Matt 4:17).

92. Ibid., 1014 (Matt 13:3). See also Chafer, "Dispensationalism," 428; idem, *Systematic Theology*, 1:45; 5:347. Classic dispensationalists maintain that the church was not revealed in the OT but was unforeseen (Darby, *Collected Writings*, 3:388; Chafer, "Dispensationalism," 404).

93. Chafer, *Systematic Theology*, 5:359.

94. Scofield, *Scofield Reference Bible*, 1147 (Acts 1:6). Also see idem, "The Return of Christ in Relation to the Jew and the Earth," *BSac* 108 (1951): 486; Chafer, *Systematic Theology*, 4:266–67.

on a literal fulfillment of the Davidic covenant. The manner in which Jesus answered the question marks a distinction between the realization of the Davidic fulfillment and the present dispensation. Jesus has effectively answered, "Not yet."

As Acts progresses, the commencement of the church age occurs at Pentecost. Peter then preaches his inaugural sermon and in Acts 2:17–21 he quotes from Joel. Classic dispensationalists contend that Peter is not saying Joel's prophecy is fulfilled.[95] Since Joel's message was given to Israel, Israel must still be the referent. Peter quoted Joel to show that the Spirit had come, but the signs were not fulfilled in Peter's day. The signs given in Joel are signs of God's discipline, realized in the great tribulation. These signs will lead to Israel's repentance, which will, in turn, lead to the dispensation of the kingdom, when the Davidic kingdom will be established on earth with Israel.

According to classic dispensationalists, the church age is a parenthesis in God's ultimate plan which centers on the nation of Israel.[96] Thus, Jesus announced the kingdom, but when Israel rejected the kingdom, it was postponed. During the church age, God is working his plan to redeem people from every nation, but the time will come when God removes the church so that he can once again focus his attention on Israel. Classic dispensationalists affirm the doctrine of a pretribulational rapture. That is, Christ returns secretly before the tribulation to gather his people (i.e., the church) with him in heaven. This event is then followed by a seven-year tribulation, the 70th week predicted in Daniel 9. This period will be a time of intense suffering by the people who remain on earth. It must be remembered, however, that it "is unrelated to the Church" and that it "is terminated by the glorious appearing of Christ."[97]

---

95. Scofield, *Scofield Reference Bible*, 932 (Joel 2:28), 1151 (Acts 2:18).

96. Chafer uses even stronger language: "In fact, the new, hitherto unrevealed purpose of God in the outcalling of a heavenly people from the Jews and Gentiles is so divergent with respect to the divine purpose toward Israel, which purpose preceded it and will yet follow it, that the term *parenthetical*, commonly employed to describe the new age-purpose, is inaccurate. A parenthetical portion sustains some direct or indirect relation to that which goes before or that which follows; but the present age-purpose is not thus related and therefore is more precisely termed an *intercalation*" (*Systematic Theology*, 4:41 [emphasis original]).

97. Ibid., 4:360.

What about the establishment of God's kingdom? After the church is raptured from earth, God will again focus his attention on the nation of Israel. The still unfulfilled prophecies regarding Israel will be fulfilled as many Jews will embrace Jesus as the Messiah. Jesus will reign on the physical throne of David in Jerusalem during this 1,000-year (millennial) period. As Chafer argues, "The throne of David is precisely what David believed it to be, an earthly institution which has never been, nor will it ever be, in heaven."[98] Thus, "The final form of the kingdom of heaven is that which will yet be set up in its full manifestation in the earth and in compliance with all that God has spoken."[99] But even during this period, there is not perfect peace and tranquility since this reign will not be free from evil—such will only be achieved in the eternal state. As king, Christ will judge against evil (Isa 11:3–4) and throughout his reign will be defeating his enemies (1 Cor 15:24–25). Finally, at the end of the millennial period, Satan will be released from his prison for a short time to lead a revolt against the King (Rev 20:1–9). Nevertheless, the reign of Christ will be a time characterized by righteousness and peace.

ASSESSMENT

The purpose of this section is not to argue for or against a particular viewpoint but instead to stand back and evaluate the potential strengths and weaknesses of each theological system. With each position, I will offer three strengths and three corresponding weaknesses. As we will see, the strength of a position, if not properly balanced, can result in a related weakness.

The first strength of classic dispensationalists is that they take Scripture seriously. They have great reverence for the Bible and believe it to be God's holy, infallible, and inspired word. Chafer states that "God is able to produce a book which is verbally accurate, the precise statement in every particular of His own thought."[100] If God promised something to Israel in the Old Testament, then God can and

---

98. Ibid., 4:315 (see also 4:323–24).

99. Ibid., 4:327.

100. Ibid., 1:63.

will fulfill his word precisely as prophesied. If God promises to return Israel to the land, rebuild their cities, defeat their enemies, and allow them to prosper in a manner greater than the time of Solomon, then that is what is affirmed. But this literal affirmation of Old Testament prophecies seems somewhat artificial and forced. It seems artificial because the driving force behind the "literal" hermeneutic is the distinction between Israel and the church. It seems forced because the New Testament authors don't always seem to interpret Old Testament prophecies in a literal (literalistic) manner.

A second strength of classic dispensationalists is that they tend to offer a consistent theological system. They begin with a distinction between Israel and the church and then consistently apply that distinction throughout their interpretation of the Bible. But this rigid distinction has caused them some problems (at least as perceived by some). One problem is their supposed admission that Old Testament saints and New Testament saints were saved differently (works versus grace). Although clarifying statements were later made by Chafer and others denouncing salvation by works in the Old Testament, the statements quoted earlier in this chapter are unambiguous. If we take the words at their plain or normal meaning, then it is easy to see why classic dispensationalists have been accused of teaching two ways of salvation. At the same time, it should be acknowledged that words can be taken out of context and that if a person clarifies their position, that clarification should be honored. In 1944 Chafer was censured by the General Assembly of the Presbyterian Church (USA) for teaching "a dispensational view of God's various and divergent plans of salvation for various groups in different ages."[101] In response, Chafer writes that he "never held such views" and that he fervently contends that God can deal with sin in every age only through "the blood of Christ."[102] He later added, "salvation ... is always the work of God in behalf of man and never the work of man in behalf of God. ...

---

101. See Lewis Sperry Chafer, "Editorials: Dispensational Distinctions Denounced," BSac 101 (1944): 257–60; idem, "Editorials: Inventing Heretics Through Misunderstanding," BSac 102 (1945): 1–5.

102. Chafer, "Dispensational Distinctions Denounced," 259.

There is, therefore, but one way to be saved and that is by the power of God made possible through the sacrifice of Christ."[103]

A related problem is the dismissal of Jesus' teachings, such as the Sermon on the Mount, as not directly applying to Christians. According to classic dispensationalists, Jesus' sermon relates to the kingdom ethic for Jews during the millennium but is not directly applicable for the church. Another related weakness is the claim that there are two new covenants in the New Testament. It seems that this claim is made because of a prior commitment to keep Israel and the church distinct rather than because of how the New Testament presents the material.

A third strength of classic dispensationalists is that they allow for typology. Scofield was especially keen on identifying types in the Old Testament and relating them to Christ or the church. But here we find another problem: the typological understanding of the Old Testament is not integrated into the overall hermeneutic. That is, typology is limited to elements related to the church but never to prophecy or Israel.[104] This distinction is especially difficult to maintain since the New Testament sometimes employs typology as being fulfilled in Christ and the church. Furthermore, Scofield's view that historical texts can have a dual (including a symbolic) meaning but that prophecy is to be interpreted only literally seems backwards to some. Poythress explains, "Why was an extra dimension allowed for history (which on the surface contained *fewer* figurative elements) and disallowed for prophecy (which on the surface contained *more* figurative elements)?"[105]

---

103. Chafer, "Inventing Heretics Through Misunderstanding," 1.

104. Poythress notes, "The major weakness of classic dispensationalist interpretive theory ... has been the neglecting of the integration of typological interpretation with grammatical-historical interpretation" (*Understanding Dispensationalists*, 115).

105. Ibid., 34 (emphasis original).

CHAPTER 3
REVISED DISPENSATIONALISM

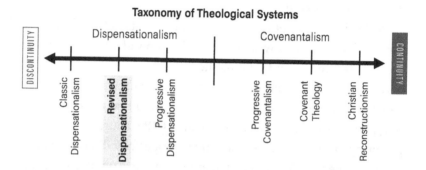

Taxonomy of Theological Systems

Revised dispensationalism is essentially a continuation—with slight adjustments—of classic dispensationalism as Chafer's influence on American dispensationalism continued to the next generation of leaders, often associated with Dallas Theological Seminary (DTS). The key proponents of this view include (1) Charles Ryrie, (2) John Walvoord, and (3) Dwight Pentecost.

Charles Caldwell Ryrie (1925–2016) was instrumental in developing and promulgating dispensational theology. Besides receiving both ThM (1947) and ThD (1949) degrees from DTS, he returned there to teach from 1953–1958 and from 1962–1981. His *Ryrie Study Bible* (1986, 1994) has sold more than 2.6 million copies. John F. Walvoord (1910–2002) is another influential dispensationalist who was also closely linked to DTS. He received a ThB, ThM, and ThD in systematic theology from DTS and became the second president of DTS (1952–1986) after his mentor Chafer. He is the author of more than thirty books, most related to eschatology. John Dwight Pentecost (1915–2014) is our third representative of revised dispensationalism and likewise received his ThM (1941) and ThD (1956) degrees from DTS. He was professor of Bible exposition at DTS from 1955–2014. Although he authored nearly twenty books, he is best known for *Things to Come* (1958).

Early revised dispensationalists did not really see themselves as affirming a different kind of dispensationalism than those who went before them. Although there were a few tweaks or adjustments, they viewed themselves essentially in agreement with their predecessors. For example, Ryrie refers to his position as "classic" or "normative" dispensationalism, often in contrast to ultra- or progressive dispensationalism. Consequently, these two systems (classic and revised dispensationalism) are very similar and represent the closest two systems that will be surveyed.

There are, however, some notable revisions that took place. Whereas the basic literal hermeneutic remained somewhat unchanged, revised dispensationalists placed less emphasis on typology. This change is most clearly demonstrated when comparing *The Scofield Reference Bible* (1909, 1917) with the *New Scofield Study Bible* (1967), which removed most of the notes that mentioned types in the Old Testament. Another change (or clarification) was the clear rejection of two ways of salvation, a revision that can also be clearly seen when comparing the notes of the 1917 version with the 1967 version.[1] A third distinction between the two systems is that revised dispensationalists typically deny that the phrases "kingdom of heaven" and "kingdom of God" are always distinct. Instead, they readily acknowledge that the two phrases can sometimes be used interchangeably. Because of these differences, Blaising and Bock contend that "revised dispensationalism is a distinctive form of the dispensational tradition."[2] Thus, this view warrants its own chapter.

---

1. *The Scofield Reference Bible* states, "As a dispensation, grace begins with the death and resurrection of Christ (Rom. 3:24–26; 4:24, 25). The point of testing is no longer legal obedience as the condition of salvation, but acceptance or rejection of Christ, with good works as a fruit of salvation" (Scofield, *Scofield Reference Bible*, 1115 [John 1:17]). The 1967 edition reads: "Prior to the cross salvation was through faith (Gen. 15:6; Rom. 4:3), being grounded on Christ's atoning sacrifice, viewed anticipatively by God" (Scofield, Gaebelein, et al., *New Scofield Study Bible*, 1477).

2. Craig A. Blaising and Darrell L. Bock, *Progressive Dispensationalism* (Grand Rapids: Baker, 1993), 46.

1. WHAT IS THE BASIC HERMENEUTIC?

Is a Literal or Symbolic Hermeneutic Employed?

Like classic dispensationalists, revised dispensationalists are firmly committed to a literal hermeneutic. Ryrie states, "Consistent literalism is at the heart of dispensational eschatology."[3] In fact, it is claimed that if the literal interpretation is applied consistently to all biblical texts, one will necessarily become a dispensationalist.[4] And what is meant by a literal hermeneutic? It "means interpretation that gives to every word the same meaning it would have in normal usage, whether employed in writing, speaking, or thinking."[5] Other words such as "plain" or "face value" are often used to describe this method, which is also labeled the historical-grammatical interpretation. The literal method of interpretation is not simplistic but accounts for the possibility of symbols, figures of speech, and types.[6] Such passages, however, will be clearly identified by the context.

But a historical-grammatical hermeneutic is in no way unique to dispensationalism. Since the Reformation, with the collapse of the fourfold sense of Scripture, a historical-grammatical hermeneutic has been employed by faithful exegetes across a wide array of theological alignments. So, what is unique to dispensational hermeneutics? It is not just the practice of a literal hermeneutic that revised dispensationalists

---

3. Charles C. Ryrie, *Dispensationalism*, rev. and exp. ed. (Chicago: Moody, 2007), 171.

4. As Ryrie boldly asserts, "If literal interpretation is the only valid hermeneutical principle and if it is consistently applied it will cause one to be a dispensationalist. As basic as one believes literal interpretation to be, to that extent he will of necessity become a dispensationalist" (Charles C. Ryrie, "The Necessity of Dispensationalism," *BSac* 114 [1957]: 250; see also idem, *Dispensationalism*, 24).

5. Ryrie, *Dispensationalism*, 91. Pentecost similarly describes the literal method as a "method that gives to each word the same exact basic meaning it would have in normal, ordinary, customary usage, whether employed in writing, speaking, or thinking" (J. Dwight Pentecost, *Things to Come: A Study in Biblical Eschatology* [Grand Rapids: Zondervan, 1964], 9). See also Elliot E. Johnson, "A Traditional Dispensational Hermeneutic," in *Three Central Issues in Contemporary Dispensationalism: A Comparison of Traditional and Progressive Views*, ed. Herbert W. Bateman IV (Grand Rapids: Kregel, 1999), 63–76.

6. See Ryrie, *Dispensationalism*, 91; John F. Walvoord, *The Millennial Kingdom* (Findlay, OH: Dunham, 1959), 130; idem, *Prophecy Knowledge Handbook*, 12–13, 15; Pentecost, *Things to Come*, 13; John S. Feinberg, "Systems of Discontinuity," in *Continuity and Discontinuity: Perspectives on the Relationship Between the Old and New Testaments*, ed. John S. Feinberg (Wheaton: Crossway, 1988), 74.

insist on, but the *consistent* practice of a literal hermeneutic. The dispensationalist subjects *every* text of Scripture to a historical-grammatical interpretation and asserts that covenantalists do not practice a *consistent* literal hermeneutic. The non-dispensationalist may *generally* (even *mostly*) utilize a historical-grammatical hermeneutic, but not *consistently*. This neglect is particularly obvious in the interpretation of prophecy.[7] Ryrie writes, "In other words, the nondispensationalist position is simply that the literal principle is sufficient except for the interpretation of prophecy."[8] Thus, with prophecy, the non-dispensationalist is often guilty of spiritualizing or even allegorizing the text. Although dispensationalists are not the sole possessors of this hermeneutic, they do affirm that they alone consistently apply it, especially when considering prophecy.

An example of this consistent literal hermeneutic can be seen in the promise of land to Abraham and his descendants (Gen 12:1, 7). The non-dispensationalist may "spiritualize" this promise or apply it to the church. The dispensationalist, however, insists that the literal promise is unaltered and thus will be literally fulfilled in the millennium kingdom. Moreover, it is claimed that a literal hermeneutic leads to a firm distinction between Israel and the church.

How can we be certain that the consistent literal approach is correct? Ryrie offers three key reasons: First, "the purpose of language itself seems to require literal interpretation."[9] God created language for the purpose of being able to communicate. Therefore, since God is the originator of language and since he created language so that he could communicate with humanity, it follows that God would use and expect people to understand it "in its literal, normal, and plain sense."[10] We must not look for some deeper or hidden meaning in Scripture but must seek to understand it as we would any form of communication.

---

7. See Ryrie, *Dispensationalism*, 47, 93; Walvoord, *Millennial Kingdom*, 129.

8. Ryrie, *Dispensationalism*, 98.

9. Ibid., 91.

10. Ibid., 92.

Second, the literal hermeneutic is confirmed by the fact that Old Testament prophecies concerning the first coming of Christ—including his birth, ministry, death, and resurrection—were all fulfilled literally.[11] Walvoord claims, "Hundreds if not thousands of prophecies have had literal fulfillment."[12] Pentecost insists that whenever a prophecy is (completely) fulfilled, it is always fulfilled literally. He explains, "Though a prophecy may be cited in the New Testament to show that a certain event is a partial fulfillment of that prophecy ... or to show that an event is in harmony with God's established program ... it does not necessitate a non-literal fulfillment or deny a future complete fulfillment, for such applications of prophecy do not exhaust the fulfillment of it."[13] Third, Ryrie adds a logical reason for embracing a literal hermeneutic: "If one does not use the plain, normal, or literal method of interpretation, all objectivity is lost."[14]

Pentecost adds another reason why a literal interpretation—especially for prophecy—must be affirmed. He claims that a literal interpretation was the prevailing method of interpretation among first-century Jews. Even though their literalism had gone to an extreme (hyper-literalism), "it can not [sic] be denied that literalism was the accepted method."[15] Their problem was not their method *per se* but simply that they misapplied it by carrying it to an extreme. Nevertheless, their basic method should be emulated. Furthermore, the apostles did not invent a new hermeneutical method but merely adapted and purified the existing literal method. Since the New Testament writers interpreted the Old Testament literally, we should too. In sum, the heart of dispensational hermeneutics is the consistent literal interpretation of Scripture for all literary genres. As Walvoord notes, "The literal method of interpretation is ... vitally related to Biblical dispensationalism."[16]

---

11. Ibid.
12. Walvoord, *Millennial Kingdom*, 131.
13. Pentecost, *Things to Come*, 11.
14. Ryrie, *Dispensationalism*, 92.
15. Pentecost, *Things to Come*, 19.
16. Walvoord, *Millennial Kingdom*, 124.

What Is the Proper Role of Typology?

It is often claimed that a non-literal hermeneutic is justified because the New Testament writers interpret the Old Testament symbolically or typologically. Thus, the New Testament use of typology is often garnered as support to reject the dispensational hermeneutic. But revised dispensationalists believe that they have an adequate response to those who approach the Bible from a non-dispensational perspective.

First, revised dispensationalists allow for the use of figurative or symbolic language as well as a controlled use of typology.[17] Though, compared with classic dispensationalists such as Scofield, revised dispensationalists give far less attention to types. For example, Ryrie argues that New Testament authors almost never use the Old Testament in any way other than the historical-grammatical sense. He contends that, at most, the New Testament contains only seven instances of New Testament authors employing a nonliteral hermeneutic to Old Testament prophecies. Instead, they interpret the Old Testament plainly, with typology being the main exception.[18] Walvoord acknowledges the legitimacy of typology but maintains that it "always involves literal interpretation first."[19] According to Pentecost, the use of typology is not the same as allegory since the typology is based on a "literal interpretation of the literal antecedent."[20] Thus, simply because Scripture allow for types does not mean it permits the use of the allegorical method.[21]

Second, revised dispensationalists affirm progressive revelation.[22] That is, God is working his purpose not only *successively* in the various dispensations but *progressively* as all the dispensations work toward a climax.[23] God chose not to reveal himself to humanity in a single act

---

17. Of course, in their view Israel is never a type of the church.

18. Charles C. Ryrie, *Basic Theology* (Wheaton: Victor, 1982), 115.

19. Walvoord, *Millennial Kingdom*, 130.

20. Pentecost, *Things to Come*, 8.

21. Ibid., 9, 15 (see also 50–53).

22. Ryrie, *Dispensationalism*, 36–39, 95–96.

23. For dispensationalists, "The entire program culminates, not in eternity but in history, in the millennial kingdom of the Lord Christ. This millennial kingdom is the climax of history and the great goal of God's program for the ages" (ibid., 108).

but progressively unfolds his will and purpose over time. According to Ryrie, "Progressive revelation views the Bible … as the continually unfolding revelation of God given by various means throughout the successive ages."[24] Thus, dispensationalists readily acknowledge that the New Testament clarifies many Old Testament texts and even reveals elements of God's message that were previously unknown (see John 1:17; Acts 17:30; Heb 1:1–2). "Dispensational and nondispensational thinkers agree that the New Testament fulfills the Old Testament and is a more complete revelation of God."[25] As we will see, however, progressive revelation does not mean that the original promise can change or be altered in any way.

So why do revised dispensationalists disagree with covenantalists regarding the use and meaning of typology? First, a key component is the dispensational system is to always maintain the distinction between Israel and the church. So, if an Old Testament prophecy or promise is made unconditionally to Israel, then it cannot be fulfilled by the church. Feinberg writes, "While a prophecy given unconditionally to Israel has a fulfillment for the church if the NT *applies* it to the church, it must also be fulfilled to Israel."[26]

Second, revised dispensationalists affirm the priority of the Old Testament. Although dispensationalists affirm progressive revelation and may affirm the priority of the New Testament for Christian doctrine,[27] they support the notion that the New Testament cannot alter the meaning of an Old Testament passage. Instead, the Old Testament must mean what it meant to the original audience and cannot be reinterpreted through the message of the New Testament. In fact, they accuse covenantalists of reading (or forcing) the teachings of the New Testament back into the Old.[28] But when this method of interpretation is practiced, it ends up distorting the original meaning, which can never change. Whatever the New Testament does with

---

24. Ibid., 39.

25. Feinberg, "Systems of Discontinuity," 75.

26. Ibid., 76.

27. For example, Ryrie claims to support the priority of the New Testament since it has "greater priority as the source of doctrine" (*Basic Theology*, 17).

28. See, for example, Ryrie, *Dispensationalism*, 37–38.

the Old Testament, it can never change or alter its original message. Feinberg explains, "Nondispensationalists begin with New Testament teaching as having priority, and then go back to the Old Testament. Dispensationalists often begin with the Old Testament, but wherever they begin they demand that the Old Testament be taken on its own terms rather than reinterpreted in light of the New Testament."[29]

Third, it is incorrect to think that the New Testament antitype necessarily does away with the Old Testament type. In other words, revised dispensationalists do not think that all types are shadows and thus become irrelevant when the antitype appears. They maintain that it is wrong to assume that the New Testament "fulfillment" is a completion of the Old Testament. The Old Testament type does not fade away and is not a mere "shadow" if it is tied to an unconditional promise. Thus, the application of the passage by the New Testament does not eliminate or cancel the passage's original meaning.

Fourth, the use of fulfillment language sometimes indicates an "application" (or "partial fulfillment") of the original text but not an ultimate fulfillment. Because the New Testament fulfillment can never change the Old Testament type (or prophecy), it can only be "fulfilled" in a partial sense, but is not the full or final fulfillment. Even if the New Testament uses the word "fulfill," this is only an application (or "this is like that") of the text to the New Testament context. Pentecost prefers to speak of a "double reference" whereas Feinberg prefers "double fulfillment."[30] Feinberg summarizes the revised dispensationalism view:

> NT application of the OT passage does not necessarily eliminate the passage's original meaning. No NT writer claims his new understanding of the OT passage cancels

---

29. Feinberg, "Systems of Discontinuity," 75. Ladd makes a similar point: "Here is the basic watershed between a dispensational and a nondispensational theology. Dispensationalism forms its eschatology by a literal interpretation of the Old Testament and then fits the New Testament into it. A nondispensational eschatology forms its theology from the explicit teaching of the New Testament" (George E. Ladd, "Historic Premillennialism," in *The Meaning of the Millennium: Four Views*, ed. Robert G. Clouse [Downers Grove, IL: InterVarsity, 1977], 27).

30. Pentecost, *Things to Come*, 63 (see also Walvoord, *Prophecy Handbook*, 14); Feinberg, "Systems of Discontinuity," 77.

the meaning of the OT passage in its own context or that the new application is the only meaning of the OT passage. The NT writer merely offers a different application of an OT passage that the OT might have foreseen; he is not claiming the OT understanding is now irrelevant. Double fulfillment, then, is necessitated by the NT's application of the passage to the church and by maintaining the integrity of the OT's meaning, especially in view of the unconditional nature of the promises to Israel.[31]

By way of illustration, Walvoord maintains that in Acts 2:14–21 when Peter quotes from Joel 2:28–32, "it was quite clear that the entire prophecy was not fulfilled."[32] According to dispensationalists, this prophecy awaits complete fulfillment which will only occur at the second coming of Christ.

How Are Old Testament Restoration Prophecies Fulfilled?

Besides Acts 2:14–21, a helpful example to consider is Amos 9:11–15, where Amos predicts the restoration of Israel. Whereas non-dispensational interpreters typically view this promise as being fulfilled in the church with the inclusion of the gentiles, dispensational interpreters fervently disagree. They insist that the final fulfillment cannot relate to the church since it is a prophecy about the future of the nation of Israel. In addition, God has unconditionally promised Israel the land and so such a promise must be fulfilled precisely as promised.

Walvoord, for example, maintains that the "tabernacle of David" (Amos 9:11 KJV) "is an expression referring to the whole nation of Israel" which is in contrast to the gentile nations and certainly cannot refer to the New Testament church.[33] This interpretation is certain because the blessings mentioned "are *earthly, territorial,* and *national,* and have nothing to do with a spiritual church to which none of these

---

31. Feinberg, "Systems of Discontinuity," 77. Most revised dispensationalists prefer to speak of an application rather than a partial fulfillment.

32. Walvoord, *Prophecy Handbook,* 289.

33. Walvoord, *Millennial Kingdom,* 205.

blessings has been promised."[34] The explanation offered by Walvoord is that James is declaring that it was God's intention to visit the gentiles *first* and that the period of Jewish blessing and triumph would only occur *after* the gentile period. He claims, "Instead of identifying the period of Gentile conversion with the rebuilding of the tabernacle of David, it is carefully distinguished by the *first* (referring to Gentile blessing), and *after* this (referring to Israel's coming glory)."[35] Finally, when the text says that "I [God] will return," this is a reference to the second coming of Christ. Thus, Amos 9 was partially fulfilled when the people of Israel returned to the land in the fourth and fifth centuries BC, and partially fulfilled when Israel again returned to the land in the twentieth century.[36] It was applied to the church by James in Acts 15 but it still awaits full and final fulfillment, which will take place only when Christ returns.

2. WHAT IS THE RELATIONSHIP BETWEEN THE COVENANTS?

In dispensationalism, a proper understanding of the covenants plays a crucial role. But to speak of covenants is not the same as speaking of dispensations. According to revised dispensationalists, a dispensation is "a distinguishable economy in the outworking of God's purpose."[37] What is it that differentiates one dispensation from another? Ryrie states that the answer is threefold: (1) a change in God's governmental relationship with man; (2) a resultant change in man's responsibility; and (3) a corresponding revelation necessary to effect the change. The usual characteristics of a new dispensation are: a test, a failure, and a judgment.[38] Ryrie, as well as most other revised dispensationalists,

---

34. Ibid.

35. Ibid., 205–6.

36. Walvoord, *Prophecy Handbook*, 295–96.

37. Ryrie, *Dispensationalism*, 33. Ryrie notes, "A dispensation is basically the arrangement involved, not the time involved; and a proper definition will take this into account" (ibid.).

38. Ryrie, *Dispensationalism*, 40.

affirms the same seven dispensations as Scofield.[39] Within certain dispensations we find the biblical covenants.

Are the Covenants Conditional or Unconditional?

Dispensationalists typically divide the biblical covenants into two different types: conditional and unconditional. Pentecost explains that in "a conditional covenant that which was covenanted depends for its fulfillment upon the recipient of the covenant, not upon the one making the covenant," whereas in "an unconditional covenant that which was covenanted depends upon the one making the covenant alone for its fulfillment."[40] But this does not rule out the possibility that an unconditional covenant contains conditional elements as well. An unconditional covenant "may have blessings attached to that covenant that are conditional upon the response of the recipient of the covenant ... but these conditioned blessings do not change the unconditional character of the covenant."[41]

For revised dispensationalists, the Abrahamic, Palestinian, Davidic, and new covenants are all unconditional.[42] The Abrahamic covenant is the basis of the other unconditional covenants and (along with the Palestinian covenant) provides the basis on which Abraham will be blessed with descendants and inherit the land. Because this covenant involves Israel (the seed of Abraham), it means that Israel as a nation will be preserved, converted, and restored. And because this covenant is unconditional, the blessings of the covenant are certain to occur.

Some amillennialists argue that the Abrahamic covenant is conditional,[43] whereas dispensationalists contend that it is unconditional. And yet, dispensationalists readily acknowledge that there

---

39. Ibid., 59–65.

40. Pentecost, *Things to Come*, 68.

41. Ibid. (see also 79).

42. For texts related to the Palestinian covenant, see Deuteronomy 30:1–9; Jeremiah 32:36–44; Ezekiel 11:16–21; 36:21–38. For dispensational arguments concerning the covenants, see J. Dwight Pentecost, *Thy Kingdom Come: Tracing God's Kingdom Program and Covenant Promises Throughout History* (Grand Rapids: Kregel, 1995), 72–123, 137–56, 164–77; Elliot E. Johnson, "Covenants in Traditional Dispensationalism," in *Three Central Issues in Contemporary Dispensationalism*, 121–55.

43. See Oswald Allis, *Prophecy and the Church* (Grand Rapids: Baker, 1947), 32–36.

is one (and only one) condition in this covenant. The condition is simply, "Go" ("Go out from your land, your relatives, and your father's house to the land that I will show you," Gen 12:1 CSB). But Walvoord explains, "The one condition having been met, no further conditions are laid upon Abraham; the covenant having been solemnly established is now dependent upon divine veracity for its fulfillment."[44] Similarly Pentecost writes, "When once this act was accomplished, and Abraham did obey God, God instituted an irrevocable, unconditional program."[45] The Abrahamic covenant is expressly declared to be "eternal" and therefore it is unconditional (Gen 17:7, 13, 19; 1 Chr 16:17; Ps 105:10). It is possible, however, for disobedience to deprive someone of the immediate blessings of the covenant, but the final fulfillment of the covenant is certain because it is ultimately based on God's promise.

Dispensationalists take the provisions made in the covenant literally. That is, the covenant will be fulfilled by Abraham and his literal seed in a literal land (Palestine). This covenant is the foundation of the other unconditional covenants. Pentecost summarizes: "Since [the Abrahamic covenant] was unconditional and eternal, and has never yet been fulfilled, it must await a future fulfillment, Israel must be preserved as a nation, must inherit her land, and be blessed with spiritual blessings to make this inheritance possible."[46]

The same could be said for the other unconditional covenants. The Davidic covenant is considered an unconditional covenant that contained a conditional element—that is, whether or not a descendent of David would continually occupy the throne. Disobedience or unfaithfulness might cause chastening but could never nullify the covenant.[47]

Finally, the new covenant is unconditional since it is the outworking of earlier promises of God originating in the Abrahamic covenant. It is an eternal covenant (Isa 24:5; 61:8; Jer 31:36, 40; 32:40; 50:5) that "depends entirely upon the 'I will' of God for its fulfillment" and "does

---

44. Walvoord, *Millennial Kingdom*, 149.

45. Pentecost, *Things to Come*, 74.

46. Ibid., 93.

47. Ibid., 103.

not depend upon man."[48] This covenant will be accomplished after the second coming of Christ. Following classic dispensationalists such as Chafer, revised dispensationalists view the new covenant prophesied in the Old Testament as not being fulfilled by the church; it can be fulfilled only by the nation of Israel. Walvoord comments, "The new covenant in force in the present age is not claimed to fulfill the new covenant with Israel at all."[49] This is because there are two distinct new covenants—one for Israel and a distinct one for the church—or there is one new covenant that has application to the church but will be fulfilled in Israel in the future.[50] It would be wrong, however, to assume that the church does not benefit from the new covenant. Just as the church receives the blessings of the Abrahamic covenant without being under (or fulfilling) that covenant, so also the church receives blessings from the new covenant without being under (or fulfilling) the new covenant.[51]

Revised dispensationalists affirm that all of the covenants to Israel are unconditional (except the Mosaic covenant). Because these covenants are unconditional, they will be fulfilled by God. Since they have yet to be fulfilled, in the future God will again turn his attention to Israel in order to stay true to his promises. As Feinberg notes, "The unconditionality of the promises to Israel guarantees that the NT does not even implicitly remove those promises from Israel."[52]

How Were Old Testament Saints Saved?

Revised dispensationalists adamantly deny that dispensationalists teach (or ever taught) that salvation was by works in the Old Testament. They contend that those places where Scofield and Chafer appeared to teach that salvation was based on works in the Old Testament were merely "unguarded statements" that should be judged in light of everything else they said on the topic.[53] Ryrie clar-

---

48. Ibid., 118.

49. Walvoord, *Millennial Kingdom*, 217.

50. Ryrie contends that there are at least two new covenants (*Dispensationalism*, 204).

51. Pentecost, *Things to Come*, 127.

52. Feinberg, "Systems of Discontinuity," 76.

53. Ryrie, *Dispensationalism*, 123.

ifies, "Neither the older nor the newer dispensationalists teach two ways of salvation, and it is not fair to attempt to make them appear so to teach."[54]

Ryrie maintains that different dispensations do not amount to different ways of salvation. He states, "The basis of salvation is always the death of Christ; the means is always faith; the object is always God (though man's understanding of God before and after the Incarnation is obviously different); but the content of faith depends on the particular revelation God was pleased to give at a certain time."[55] Thus, in the Old Testament, saints were saved by faith through Jesus' work on the cross. The place where revised dispensationalists disagree with covenantalists relates to the *content* of faith. Whereas covenant theologians usually maintain that the content Old Testament saints' faith was in the coming Messiah, Ryrie maintains that for Old Testament saints, "Jesus Christ was not the conscious object of their faith."[56] Instead, "they were saved by faith in God as He had revealed Himself principally through the sacrifices that He instituted as a part of the Mosaic Law."[57] Due to the progress of revelation, the Old Testament saints did not see with clarity what can be seen today. Therefore, the conscious content of faith differs in dispensations, but the basis of salvation remains the same. Thus, although God is gracious in every dispensation, he does not always reveal grace in the same way or in the same amount in every age.[58]

---

54. Ibid., 244.

55. Ibid., 140. He similarly writes, "The basis of salvation in every age is the death of Christ; the *requirement* for salvation in every age is faith; the *object* of faith in every age is God; the *content* of faith changes in the various dispensations" (134). See also Walvoord, who claims, "In every dispensation salvation is by grace through faith, made possible by the death of Christ" (John F. Walvoord "Reflections on Dispensationalism," *BSac* 158 [2001]: 137).

56. Ryrie, *Dispensationalism*, 139. Later he writes that "it is impossible to say that Old Testament saints under the law exercised personal faith in Jesus Christ" (ibid.).

57. Ibid.

58. Allen P. Ross, "The Biblical Method of Salvation: A Case for Discontinuity," in *Continuity and Discontinuity: Perspectives on the Relationship Between the Old and New Testaments*, ed. John S. Feinberg (Wheaton: Crossway, 1988), 161–78.

How Is the Old Testament Law to Be Applied Today?

According to revised dispensationalists, Old Testament law does not apply to the church because it belongs to a previous dispensation.[59] Because each dispensation represents a distinct way in which God relates to his people, it is illegitimate to apply the law of the Mosaic dispensation to the current dispensation. But the Old Testament law is not the only "law" that applies to a distinct dispensation; some of the teaching of Jesus also falls into a category that does not apply directly to the church. For example, Jesus' teaching in the Sermon on the Mount portrays an ethic specifically for the people of Israel during the millennial kingdom (a view also taught by Scofield). Ryrie, however, argues that it is obvious that the Sermon on the Mount is not *exclusively* for that time. For he asks, what would be the purpose of someone praying "Thy kingdom come" during the millennium if it had already come? His solution is that the Sermon on the Mount relates not only the future kingdom, but any time the kingdom is offered (such as during Jesus' ministry or the future tribulation).[60]

What is clear is that the text does not relate *directly* to the church. When considering the allegation that dispensationalists teach that the Sermon on the Mount is all law and no gospel, his response is, "Where can one find a statement of the gospel in the Sermon?"[61] His answer to that question is that "a straightforward statement of the gospel cannot be found in the Sermon."[62] Furthermore, neither the Holy Spirit nor praying in the name of Christ is ever mentioned. Consequently, the Sermon on the Mount directly applied to the Jews during Jesus' ministry and will again apply to the Jews during the tribulation, but does not apply directly to the church. And yet, the church can still glean *principles* from the message, similar to finding legitimate principles in the Old Testament. Here, Ryrie is similar to Scofield, who writes

---

59. However, there is not consensus here among all revised dispensationalists since some affirm the Sermon on the Mount as a kingdom ethic for this age.

60. Ibid., 113. Pentecost writes, "In its primary interpretation the Sermon on the Mount is directly applicable to those of our Lord's own day who ... were anticipating the coming of the King and the kingdom" (J. Dwight Pentecost, "The Purpose of the Sermon on the Mount," *BSac* 115 [1958]: 317).

61. Ryrie, *Dispensationalism*, 115.

62. Ibid.

that in the Sermon on the Mount "there is a beautiful moral application to the Christian."[63]

3. WHAT IS THE RELATIONSHIP BETWEEN ISRAEL AND THE CHURCH?

Does the Church Replace or Fulfill Israel, or Are the Two Distinct?

When answering the question as to what marks off a person as being a dispensationalist, Ryrie famously responded with his *sine qua non* of dispensationalism, that is, the absolutely indispensable parts that qualify someone as a bona fide dispensationalist. Tellingly, Ryrie's first *sine qua non* is, "A dispensationalist keeps Israel and the church distinct."[64] This distinction, then, becomes the essence or touchstone of what it means to be a dispensationalist. In fact, it is "the most basic theological test of whether or not a person is a dispensationalist, and it is undoubtedly the most practical and conclusive."[65] Ryrie adds, "The one who fails to distinguish Israel and the church consistently will inevitably not hold to dispensational distinctions; and one who does will."[66]

The church is completely distinct from Israel because the church is the body of Christ whereas the Old Testament people of God (Israel) was an ethnic group promised physical blessings. The church is distinct because, as the body of Christ, it is composed of both Jews and

---

63. Scofield, *Scofield Reference Bible*, 1000 (Matt 5:2). Chafer similarly writes, "A secondary application to the Church means that lessons and principles may be drawn from it" (Lewis Sperry Chafer, *Systematic Theology*, 8 vols. [Dallas: Dallas Seminary Press, 1947], 5:97).

64. Ryrie, *Dispensationalism*, 46. Later, he claims that this distinction is "the essence of dispensationalism" and that "the clear and consistent distinction between Israel and the church ... is a vital part of dispensationalism" (48, 172). The second *sine qua non* is that a Dispensationalist is committed to "a system of hermeneutics that is usually called literal interpretation" (47). Third, a dispensationalist understands God's glory as "the underlying purpose of God in the world" (48).

65. Ibid., 46.

66. Ibid. Toussaint adds, "If the church and Israel become so blurred in dispensationalism that there is no separation between them, dispensationalism will become as extinct as the pitied dodo bird" (Stanley D. Toussaint, "Israel and the Church of a Traditional Dispensationalist," in *Three Central Issues in Contemporary Dispensationalism*, 227).

gentiles. It is also distinct in that Christians have a relationship with Christ, being indwelt by his Spirit.[67] This new mysterious relationship was not experienced by God's people in the Old Testament (or during the ministry of Jesus) and was unpredicted in the Scriptures. Ryrie summarizes: "The church as a living organism in which Jew and Gentile are on an equal footing is the mystery revealed only in New Testament times and able to be made operative only after the cross of Christ. It is the distinct character of the church—a character that was not true of the body of Old Testament saints."[68]

Not only does the church have a distinct *character* as the body of Christ, it also has a distinct *time*. The church age represents a parenthesis in God's plan and thus should not be confused with the times that occur before or after this age. The church, consisting of Jews and gentiles, is a "new man" (Eph 2:15), only made possible after the death and resurrection of Christ. Furthermore, gifts given to the church are given after the ascension of Christ (Eph 4:7–12). Finally, the baptizing work of the Holy Spirit did not begin until Pentecost (Acts 2). All of this evidence suggests that the church did not come into existence until the day of Pentecost.[69]

Consequently, the promises made to Israel must apply to Israel and cannot be fulfilled by the church. Ryrie explains: "The Church is not fulfilling in any sense the promises to Israel. ... The church age is not seen in God's program for Israel. It is an intercalation. ... The Church is a mystery in the sense that it was completely unrevealed in the Old Testament and now revealed in the New Testament."[70] For revised dispensationalists, Israel and the church must remain completely separate. This position is what it means to be a dispensationalist.

---

67. Ryrie, *Dispensationalism*, 144.

68. Ibid., 145.

69. Ibid., 146–47.

70. Charles C. Ryrie, *The Basis of the Premillennial Faith* (1954; Dubuque, IA: ECS Ministries, 2005), 112; see also Pentecost, *Thy Kingdom Come*, 268–69.

How Are Romans 11:26 and Galatians 6:16 Interpreted?

How do revised dispensationalists interpret Romans 11:26 and Galatians 6:16? These two texts are important because the former is often cited in favor of a dispensational viewpoint whereas Galatians is often cited against it. Romans 9–11 demonstrate that Israel is still distinct from the church. Throughout these three chapters Paul consistently uses the term "Israel" to refer to natural (not spiritual) Israel. The term "Israel" occurs 66 times in the New Testament and is never used of the church. In Romans 9:3–4 Paul laments over the spiritual condition of his "kinsmen according to the flesh." This text "is proof that the church does not rob Israel of her blessings."[71]

Romans 11:26 ("And in this way all Israel will be saved") is often cited as evidence that although God has temporarily removed Israel from the place of blessing, when Christ returns and God has terminated his program with the church, he will restore them to their place of blessing.[72] Because the unconditional promises God made to Israel in the Old Testament are still unfulfilled, the time will come when that will all change. When Paul states that "a partial hardening has come upon Israel," it signifies that the blindness experienced by Jews is not universal so that no Jews can believe. It is possible for *individuals* to be saved but not the nation as a whole. But when Christ returns, the blindness will be removed.[73] "All Israel" refers to those Jews who believe at the second advent of Christ.[74] This text is referring not merely to individual salvation (which is offered now), but to a group or national deliverance—that is, the time when the nation of Israel (i.e., the people as a whole) will be restored.[75] At the second coming, Christ will deliver Israel and usher in the millennial kingdom ("The Deliverer will come from Zion, he will banish ungodliness from

---

71. Ryrie, *Dispensationalism*, 148.

72. Pentecost, *Things to Come*, 88–89, 267; John F. Walvoord, "Israel's Blindness," *BSac* 102 (1945): 287–88.

73. Pentecost, *Things to Come*, 303.

74. Ibid., 294–95.

75. Walvoord, *Millennial Kingdom*, 173, 190. Walvoord argues that this text does not refer to spiritual salvation but merely physical salvation: "The reference to Israel being saved is not in respect to freedom from the guilt of sin or the redemptive truth, but rather that Israel will be delivered from their enemies at the time of the Second Coming" (*Prophecy Handbook*, 453).

Jacob," Rom 11:26b, quoting Isa 59:20). The fulfillment of the Old Testament covenants will take place after the fullness of the gentiles comes in (Rom 11:25).

In Galatians 6:16, Paul concludes his correspondence with the Galatian Christians by stating, "And as for all who walk by this rule, peace and mercy be upon them, and upon the Israel of God." Is Paul here equating the church with "the Israel of God"? Revised dispensationalists universally reject such an interpretation. Instead, they claim that Paul is singling out *Christian Jews* for special recognition in the benediction.[76] That is, Jewish believers are distinguished from gentile believers and only the Jewish believers are called "the Israel of God."

One of the main arguments in favor of this position is that every other time the term "Israel" is referenced in Scripture, it refers to the natural seed of Abraham and never to gentiles. Why would Paul make this distinction in an epistle where he is demonstrating that the law cannot save and that one's Jewish background is not necessarily an advantage? Ryrie explains, "Paul had strongly attacked the Jewish legalists; therefore, it would be natural for him to remember with a special blessing those Jews who had forsaken this legalism and followed Christ."[77] Thus, in Galatians Paul does not use the term "Israel" to refer to the church but to Jewish Christians who are physical descendants of Abraham.

4. WHAT IS THE KINGDOM OF GOD?

Whereas classic dispensationalists clearly distinguished the "kingdom of God" from the "kingdom of heaven," revised dispensationalists have backed away from it. For example, Ryrie insists, "Within the ranks of dispensationalists there are those who hold to the distinction and

---

76. See Ryrie, *Dispensationalism*, 149; Walvoord, *Millennial Kingdom*, 169–70; Pentecost, *Things to Come*, 89; idem, *Thy Kingdom Come*, 80, 290; S. Lewis Johnson Jr., "Paul and the 'Israel of God': An Exegetical and Eschatological Case-Study," *MSJ* 20.1 (2009): 41–55 (also found in *Essays in Honor of J. Dwight Pentecost*, ed. Stanley D. Toussaint and Charles H. Dyer [Chicago: Moody, 1986], 181–96).

77. Ryrie, *Dispensationalism*, 149; see also idem, *Basic Theology*, 399.

those who do not. It is not at all determinative."[78] He continues by asserting that it is "minor league and unimportant stuff."[79] Likewise, Walvoord maintains, "As far as affecting the premillennial or dispensational argument, [in my] opinion ... it is irrelevant."[80] Pentecost admits that the two phrases "while not synonymous" are sometimes "used interchangeably."[81] The context must determine the precise meaning. Yet, Walvoord does claim that the *kingdom of God* refers to believers who have genuine faith and never includes unbelievers, whereas the *kingdom of heaven* is "concerned with the outward display of God's government and appearance rather than reality."[82] Consequently, the kingdom of God is not to be identified with the millennial kingdom. The millennial kingdom is the rule of God on earth, which is different from the rule of God in the hearts of his people.[83]

Did Jesus Bring the Kingdom?

Dispensationalists affirm that Jesus offered the kingdom to Israel but that because they rejected it, the kingdom has been postponed (offered→ rejected→ postponed).[84] When Jesus declared that the kingdom of heaven was "at hand," this statement is "not a guarantee that the kingdom will be instituted immediately, but rather that all impending events have been removed so that it is now imminent."[85] When the Jewish nation rejected Jesus (and thus his kingdom), God delayed the messianic kingdom and instituted the church age. The kingdom "is totally future, awaiting fulfillment in the Millennium and eternity."[86] Based on a literal interpretation of prophecy which sees

---

78. Ryrie, *Dispensationalism*, 180.

79. Ibid., 181.

80. John F. Walvoord, "A Review of *Crucial Questions about the Kingdom of God* by George Eldon Ladd," *BSac* 110 (1953): 6.

81. Pentecost, *Things to Come*, 144.

82. Walvoord, *Millennial Kingdom*, 171.

83. Ibid., 297.

84. Pentecost, *Things to Come*, 142, 446–66; Ryrie, *Basic Theology*, 397–99. Ryrie argues, "It is one's understanding of the Davidic/Messianic kingdom that differentiates various theologies" (*Dispensationalism*, 182).

85. Pentecost, *Things to Come*, 449–50.

86. Toussaint, "Israel and the Church of a Traditional Dispensationalist," 231.

Christ as reigning on earth as the seed of David, Walvoord asserts that "the present session of Christ is *not* a fulfillment of the covenant" and so the fulfillment must be sometime in the future.[87] He continues, "The inference is plain that Christ is seated on the Father's throne, but that is not at all the same as being seated on the throne of David."[88] Jesus' assumption of the Davidic throne and consequent reign are both future. Thus, the present age is a parenthesis in God's plan since it is an unexpected age that was not specifically predicted in the Old Testament. The church age did not replace but merely interrupted God's program for Israel.

In Matthew 13 Jesus essentially outlines God's program for the development of the theocratic kingdom during the period of the King's absence. Thus, he proclaims the beginning of an entirely new, previously unannounced program—the church.[89] During this dispensation of grace, the church should not be focused on a social agenda since there are no commands to improve society as a whole. Walvoord states that the dispensational (premillennial) view "presents no commands to improve society as a whole. The apostles are notably silent on any program of political, social, moral, or physical improvement of the unsaved world." He continues, "The program of the early church … was a matter of saving souls out of the world rather than saving the world. It was neither possible nor in the program of God for the present age to become the kingdom of God on earth."[90] Thus, the focus of the church should be on gospel ministry rather than having a social agenda to transform life here on earth. Ryrie offers the following succinct summary:

> We recognize a universal kingdom over which God
> rules the entire world (1 Chron. 29:11; Ps. 145:13). We

---

87. Walvoord, *Millennial Kingdom*, 199; see also Pentecost, *Things to Come*, 109.

88. Walvoord, *Millennial Kingdom*, 203.

89. Pentecost, *Things to Come*, 464, 467. It should be noted that Toussaint takes a different view than most revised dispensationalists. He believes that the kingdom in Matthew 13 refers to the promised future fulfillment of Israel's OT covenants and prophecies (Stanley D. Toussaint, *Behold the King* [Portland: Multnomah, 1980]; idem, "Israel and the Church of a Traditional Dispensationalist," 237–41).

90. Walvoord, *Millennial Kingdom*, 134.

recognize the Davidic/Messianic kingdom over which our Lord will rule in the present-earth Millennium. … We understand a mystery form of the kingdom as announced and illustrated in Matthew 13. And there is the kingdom of His dear Son (Col. 1:13) into which believers enter by the new birth.[91]

Acts 1:6 portrays the kingdom as a future physical reign of Jesus over the earth. Because Jesus did not yet inaugurate the kingdom (and thus fulfill Old Testament promises to restore Israel), the disciples (rightly) expect that to occur. So, the disciples ask Jesus, "Lord, will you at this time restore the kingdom to Israel?" Jesus did not tell the disciples they were in error that the kingdom would be restored to Israel, only that it was not for them to know when that would occur.[92] Thus, the disciples' question "was a completely logical inference."[93] Jesus' response was ambiguous regarding the *timing* in which he would restore the kingdom to Israel. The response does not mean that they had an incorrect view of the kingdom. It was simply not for them to know the time of Jesus' return. What the disciples learned was that the time of Jesus' coming was going to be separate from the giving of the promised Holy Spirit.

How Is the Kingdom Consummated?

The church is first raptured from the earth before the seven-year tribulation. At the end of the seven years, Christ will return and establish the millennial kingdom where God is once again focused on Israel. In the millennium, Israel will be a glorious nation, protected from all her enemies and exalted above other nations. Ryrie remarks,

> If the yet unfulfilled prophecies of the Old Testament made in the Abrahamic, Davidic, and New Covenants are to be literally fulfilled, there must be a future period,

---

91. Ryrie, *Dispensationalism*, 182.

92. Walvoord, *Millennial Kingdom*, 117–18, 187.

93. Toussaint, "Israel and the Church of a Traditional Dispensationalist," 242. See also Pentecost, *Thy Kingdom Come*, 268–69.

the Millennium, in which they can be fulfilled, for the church is not now fulfilling them. In other words, the literal picture of Old Testament prophecies demands either a future fulfillment or a nonliteral fulfillment. If they are to be fulfilled in the future, then the only time left for that fulfillment is the Millennium.[94]

Because of the complete separation between Israel and the church, the earthly kingdom, which concerns the unfulfilled national promises, does not relate to those Israelites who die before the millennium begins.[95] That is, those Jews who had faith but died before the second coming of the Messiah, and are therefore members of the church, do not inherit the promises made to Israel during the millennium.[96] Rather, it applies only to those who become believers after the rapture.

During the millennial reign of Jesus on the earth, Israel will be blessed above all nations. During the end of this period, Satan (who had been bound at Christ's return) will be released for a short season and incite a rebellion against God and his people. But when the thousand years have ended, Satan and his followers will be defeated and thrown into the lake of fire. After this follows the resurrection of unbelievers as well as those who have become believers during the millennium. Finally, there is the "great white judgment" followed by the eternal state.

ASSESSMENT

The first strength relates to the hermeneutic of revised dispensationalism which offers more clarity than its predecessors regarding the literal interpretation. Whereas classic dispensationalists claimed to affirm a literal hermeneutic, because of their eternal dualism of the earthly (Jewish) and the heavenly (gentile) people, they often embraced a spiritual interpretation of texts which were applied to

---

94. Ryrie, *Dispensationalism*, 172.

95. Ibid., 159.

96. See Pentecost, *Things to Come*, 546.

the church. In contrast, revised dispensationalists more consistently apply a literal hermeneutic.

But this strength also reveals some weaknesses. For example, one of the arguments that revised dispensationalists use to justify their literal hermeneutic (especially with prophecy) is that "No prophecy which has been completely fulfilled has been fulfilled any way but literally."[97] This statement, however, reveals a caveat that makes it impossible to disprove. By adding the word "completely," a dispensationalist always has a way of escape. If it is claimed that an Old Testament prophecy is fulfilled nonliterally in the New Testament, the dispensationalist can simply claim that the prophecy is only partially fulfilled. This argument is also circular: one knows that a prophecy must have a literal fulfillment because all other instances are literal. And one knows that all other instances are literal because all exceptions are excluded as being only "partial fulfillments."[98]

Another argument that revised dispensationalists use in support of their literal hermeneutic is that such was the practice of first-century Jews.[99] But this argument could easily be turned on its head since it could be claimed that it was their literal hermeneutic that caused them to miss Jesus as the Messiah and ultimately reject him. Pentecost calls their method a "decadent literalism" which caused them to "warp Scripture of all meaning." He argues, "Misuse of the method does not militate against the method itself" since "it was not the method that was at fault, but rather the misapplication of it."[100] But it is difficult to see how Pentecost's hermeneutic is essentially different than what he claims about first-century Jewish interpretation.

Finally, sometimes revised dispensationalists unnecessarily impugn the motives of those who do not embrace a strict literal interpretation. Pentecost contends that all other methods of interpretation are "introduced to promote heterodoxy."[101] He later adds, "The reason

---

97. Pentecost, *Things to Come*, 10–11.

98. See Poythress, *Understanding Dispensationalists*, 54–55.

99. It should be noted that Pentecost does not seek to prove or argue for the Jewish hermeneutic, he simply asserts it.

100. Pentecost, *Things to Come*, 19.

101. Ibid., 33.

a non-literal method of interpretation is adopted is, almost without exception, because of a desire to avoid the obvious interpretation of the passage."[102] *Ad hominem* arguments might prove effective with those who are already convinced of one's position but they do not actually offer a convincing argument.

The second strength is that revised dispensationalists see more continuity between the covenants, especially the idea that the new covenant relates to the church. And although some have modified their views (Ryrie and Walvoord), the two (new)-covenant view is endorsed by Pentecost. He argues that when Jesus inaugurated the new covenant, "these to whom it was primarily and originally made [i.e., the disciples] will not receive its fulfillment nor its blessings until it is confirmed and made actual to them at the second advent of Christ."[103] He continues by claiming that there is a difference between the "institution" of a covenant and the "realization" of its benefits. The death of Christ laid the foundation but the true benefits are realized only after the second coming. Blaising, a progressive dispensationalist, confesses that the two-covenant view "is really a defenseless position."[104] Ware similarly states, "It thus seems clear that this earlier dispensational proposal for understanding the relation of the new covenant to Israel and the church as distinct peoples of God under distinct new covenants is thereby rendered unacceptable."[105]

The third strength of revised dispensationalism is the willingness to back off the rigid distinction between the terms the "kingdom of heaven" and "kingdom of God." Exegetically it is difficult to defend such a position, and most revised dispensationalists have rightly acknowledged that at least sometimes the terms are used interchangeably.[106] But a difficulty arises with their view regarding the cur-

---

102. Ibid., 60.

103. Ibid., 126.

104. Craig A. Blaising, "Development of Dispensationalism by Contemporary Dispensationalists," *BSac* 145 (1988): 278.

105. Ware, "The New Covenant and the People(s) of God," 92.

106. Matthew often uses the phrase "kingdom of heaven" in the parallel accounts in which Mark and/or Luke use "kingdom of God" (cf. Matt 4:17 with Mark 1:14–15; Matt 5:3 with Luke 6:20; Matt 8:11 with Luke 13:28; Matt 10:7 with Luke 9:2; Matt 11:11 with Luke 7:28; Matt 11:12 with Luke 16:16; Matt 13:33 with Luke 13:20; Matt 13:11 with Mark 4:11 and Luke 8:10; Matt

rent reign of Jesus. They maintain that the fulfillment of the Davidic covenant only comes when Jesus leaves his throne at his Father's side to occupy David's earthly throne. One wonders how the climax of redemptive history could involve Jesus leaving his Father's throne to occupy the earthly throne of David. Furthermore, progressive dispensationalists make a good case that according to the New Testament, Jesus' current reign is a fulfillment of the Davidic covenant.[107]

Finally, regarding the parable of the hidden treasure (Matt 13:44), Pentecost claims that the purpose of this parable "is to depict the relationship of Israel to this present age." He seems to offer an allegorical interpretation when he claims that the individual who finds the treasure is the Lord Jesus Christ. He purchases this treasure through his death on the cross. Pentecost summarizes the meaning: "The parable is showing that Christ has laid the foundation for Israel's acceptance in this age, even though the age ends without His having appropriated His treasure. The treasure will be unearthed when He comes to establish His kingdom."[108] Is that really the most "plain" or "natural" reading of the text, especially in light of the fact that the vast majority of scholars reject such an interpretation?

13:31 with Mark 4:30–31 and Luke 13:18–19; Matt 19:14 with Mark 10:14 and Luke 18:16; Matt 19:23 with Mark 10:23 and Luke 18:24). Even more compelling is where Matthew uses the terms interchangeably in the same context: "Truly, I say to you, only with difficulty will a rich person enter the *kingdom of heaven*. Again I tell you, it is easier for a camel to go through the eye of a needle than for a rich person to enter the *kingdom of God*" (Matt 19:23–24, emphasis added).

107. Blaising and Bock, *Progressive Dispensationalism*, 175–87; Darrell L. Bock, "The Reign of the Lord Christ," in *Dispensationalism, Israel and the Church: The Search for Definition*, ed. Craig A. Blaising and Darrell L. Bock (Grand Rapids: Zondervan, 1992), 47–55; Robert L. Saucy, *The Case for Progressive Dispensationalism: The Interface Between Dispensational and Non-Dispensational Theology* (Grand Rapids: Zondervan, 1993), 59–80.

108. Pentecost, *Things to Come*, 148–49.

CHAPTER 4
PROGRESSIVE
DISPENSATIONALISM

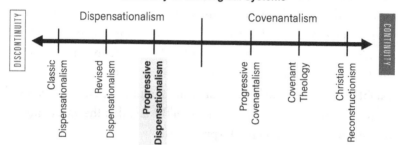

Taxonomy of Theological Systems

Dispensationalism — Covenantalism

DISCONTINUITY — CONTINUITY

Classic Dispensationalism · Revised Dispensationalism · **Progressive Dispensationalism** · Progressive Covenantalism · Covenant Theology · Christian Reconstructionism

During the middle part of the 1980s, a redefinition of the traditional dispensational interpretation of Scripture began to emerge.[1] Led by prominent dispensational theologians Robert Saucy, Craig Blaising, and Darrell Bock, this redefinition reflected an increasing willingness to engage in dialogue with covenantalists, partly in an effort to promote greater harmony but also to refine their dispensational heritage in light of advances in the study of hermeneutics.[2] Reflecting upon such

---

1. See Ron J. Bigalke Jr. and Thomas D. Ice, "History of Dispensationalism," in *Progressive Dispensationalism: An Analysis of the Movement and Defense of Traditional Dispensationalism*, ed. Ron J. Bigalke Jr. (Lanham, MD: University Press of America, 2005), xxx–xxxii.

2. For an overview of the emergence of progressive dispensationalism, see Craig A. Blaising and Darrell L. Bock, *Progressive Dispensationalism* (Grand Rapids: Baker, 1993), 9–56; Craig A. Blaising, "Dispensationalism: The Search for Definition," in *Dispensationalism, Israel and the Church: The Search for Definition*, ed. Craig A. Blaising and Darrell L. Bock (Grand Rapids: Zondervan, 1992), 31–32; and Blaising and Bock, "Dispensationalism, Israel and the Church: Assessment and Dialogue," in *Dispensationalism, Israel and the Church*, 377–80.

advancements, these theologians began to question and revise the *sine qua non* of dispensationalism as Charles Ryrie had defined it.[3] By 1991, the resulting revisions to traditional dispensationalism had become so extensive that they adopted the name "progressive dispensationalism" at the annual meeting of the Evangelical Theological Society.[4]

Blaising explains that the label "progressive dispensationalism" was used "because of the way in which this Dispensationalism views the interrelationship of divine dispensations in history, their overall orientation to the eternal kingdom of God (which is the final, eternal dispensation embracing God and humanity), and the reflections of these historical and eschatological relations in the literary features of Scripture."[5] In other words, as Saucy adds, progressive dispensationalism emphasizes a "greater continuity within God's program of historical salvation" than does traditional dispensationalism. For example, the church is no longer considered a parenthesis in the fulfillment of Old Testament messianic kingdom prophecies, but rather represents "a first-stage partial fulfillment of these prophecies."[6]

Thus, progressive dispensationalism seeks a balanced approach between continuity and discontinuity.[7] In relation to classic or revised dispensationalism, there are similarities but also some noted differences. The similarities include: (1) a distinction between Israel and the church; (2) a future pre-tribulational rapture; (3) a seven-year tribulation; and (4) a future millennial kingdom. The differences are: (1) a complementary hermeneutic (which allows for some expansion of the original meaning); (2) Israel and the church refer to two

---

3. Blaising, "Dispensationalism: The Search for Definition," 23–34.

4. Blaising and Bock, *Progressive Dispensationalism*, 23.

5. Blaising and Bock, "Dispensationalism, Israel and the Church: Assessment and Dialogue," 380. Elsewhere Blaising adds, "Its major distinctive is found in its conception of the progressive accomplishment and revelation of a holistic and unified redemption" which "is revealed in a succession of dispensations which vary in how they stress the aspects of redemption, but all point to a final culmination in which all aspects are redeemed together" (*Progressive Dispensationalism*, 56).

6. Robert L. Saucy, *The Case for Progressive Dispensationalism: The Interface Between Dispensational and Non-Dispensational Theology* (Grand Rapids: Zondervan, 1993), 9.

7. Saucy comments, "To my mind, a study of Scripture discloses greater unity between the church and Israel than traditional dispensationalists allow, but does not eradicate all distinction for Israel as non-dispensationalists generally contend" (ibid., 143).

dimensions of the one people of God; (3) the present age is not a parenthesis in God's plan; (4) Christ has inaugurated the eschatological kingdom from heaven; and (5) there is a unified kingdom plan in both Testaments.

Progressive dispensationalism will be represented primarily through three key proponents: (1) Robert Saucy, (2) Craig Blaising, and (3) Darrell Bock. Robert Saucy (1930–2015) received his ThM (1958) and ThD (1961) degrees from Dallas Theological Seminary (DTS). He taught at Biola's Talbot School of Theology from 1961 until his death in 2015. Craig Blaising received both his ThM (1976) and ThD (1979) degrees from DTS. He completed a second doctorate (PhD) at the University of Aberdeen in 1988. He has taught at DTS, Southern Baptist Theological Seminary, and is currently Distinguished Research Professor of Theology at Southwestern Baptist Theological Seminary. Darrell Bock received his ThM from Dallas Theological Seminary (1979) and his PhD from the University of Aberdeen (1983). He is currently senior professor of New Testament studies at Dallas Theological Seminary, where he has taught since 1982.

1. WHAT IS THE BASIC HERMENEUTIC?

Is a Literal or Symbolic Hermeneutic Employed?

Progressive dispensationalists view themselves as having a similar interpretative approach as revised dispensationalists in that they claim to embrace a "literal" hermeneutic (and reject a "spiritual" or "allegorical" hermeneutic).[8] Likewise, progressive dispensationalists describe their hermeneutic as a grammatical-historical approach.[9] They are careful, however, to distinguish their definition of "literal"

---

8. Bock writes, "There are differences between progressives and earlier expressions of dispensationalism, but they are not a dispute over spiritualizing, nor are they about serious deviations in the historical-grammatical method" (Darrell L. Bock, "Hermeneutics of Progressive Dispensationalism," in *Three Central Issues in Contemporary Dispensationalism: A Comparison of Traditional and Progressive Views*, ed. Herbert W. Bateman IV [Grand Rapids: Kregel, 1999], 85–86).

9. See Saucy, *The Case for Progressive Dispensationalism*, 30; Blaising and Bock, *Progressive Dispensationalism*, 76–77.

from that of traditional dispensationalists. While they affirm that it is a literal approach, they reject as inadequate the traditional dispensational definition of literal as "clear, plain, normal," arguing that earlier dispensationalism has a tendency to interpret key terms in isolation, "often without indicating any of [their] contextual, conceptual connections."[10] They explain instead that a true grammatical-historical approach is multidimensional, involving three interactive components: the historical, the grammatical, and the literary-theological.[11] Bock elaborates, "First, the historical level seeks to be sensitive to the message as it came to its initial audience, understanding original terms and ideas. Second, the grammatical level considers how the terminology of that message is laid out. Terms are not understood in isolation from each other but in conjunction with one another. Third, the literary-theological level highlights the fact that there is an abiding message and unity in the text, which is laid out literarily in various ways called genres."[12]

Although some traditional dispensationalists decry this as "a shift away from literal interpretation," Blaising responds that "progressive dispensationalism is a development of 'literal' interpretation into a more consistent historical-literary interpretation" that reflects advances in grammatical-historical interpretation among evangelical scholars as a whole.[13]

Progressive dispensationalists claim that subsequent texts can develop the meaning of original texts, even beyond the understanding of the human author, though the original texts retain their original meaning.[14] Some critics of progressive dispensationalism have

---

10. Bock, "Hermeneutics of Progressive Dispensationalism," 86–87, 107.

11. Blaising and Bock, *Progressive Dispensationalism*, 77. In a subsequent paragraph, Bock calls this the "historical-grammatical-literary-theological" method, but explains that this is what most evangelicals really mean by the term "historical-grammatical."

12. Ibid. Elsewhere Bock states that the differences with revised dispensationalism are "over how to read the Bible in a normal literary-theological manner as a canonical whole" ("Hermeneutics of Progressive Dispensationalism," 86).

13. See the critique by Robert L. Thomas, "The Hermeneutics of Progressive Dispensationalism," *MSJ* 6.1 (1995): 79–95 and response by Blaising and Bock, *Progressive Dispensationalism*, 52.

14. Darrell L. Bock, "The Son of David and the Saints' Task: The Hermeneutics of Initial Fulfillment," *BSac* 150 (1993): 445–46.

accused its hermeneutic of having an "affinity for New Testament priority in the interpretation of the canon."[15] Such a statement, however, would likely not find agreement among progressive dispensationalists.[16] Rather, their understanding of the historical-grammatical hermeneutic yields what Bock calls a "complementary hermeneutic."[17] Such a hermeneutic "argues that we should continue to read the Old Testament as still telling us something about Israel in God's plan, while being sensitive to how the New Testament *complements* that hope by expressing fulfillment today in Christ."[18] This means that, while the New Testament may develop the meaning of Old Testament texts, the expansion of meaning does not change the original meaning unless the New Testament explicitly states otherwise.[19] Indeed, Bock explicitly cautions against reading New Testament texts back into the Old Testament such that "what the second text means is what the first text always meant."[20] Likewise, he warns against reading New Testament texts solely on the terms of the Old Testament texts. Consequently, he argues that each text must be interpreted in its own setting before the message of subsequent texts is integrated with it.[21] According to Bock, this "complementary" hermeneutic means that "one can make points from a 'both-and' perspective without denying either side of

---

15. Roy E. Beacham, "Progressive Dispensationalism: An Overview and Personal Analysis," *Detroit Baptist Seminary Journal* 9 (2004): 15. Saucy comes close when he states that we must "use all the Bible with the recognition that the principle of progressive revelation obviously gives the New Testament writers the last word" (*The Case for Progressive Dispensationalism*, 33).

16. Bock comments, "In my view, the New Testament does not have a priority. Rather, it has a place, a competing (complementary) one" (Darrell L. Bock, "Response," in *Three Central Issues in Contemporary Dispensationalism*, 157).

17. See Blaising and Bock, *Progressive Dispensationalism*, 100–3; Bock, "Hermeneutics of Progressive Dispensationalism," 89–101; idem, "The Son of David and the Saints' Task," 447.

18. Bock, "Hermeneutics of Progressive Dispensationalism," 92–93.

19. Blaising and Bock explain their hermeneutic: "the New Testament does introduce change and advance; it does not merely repeat Old Testament revelation. In making complementary additions, however, it does not jettison old promises. The enhancement is not at the expense of the original promise" (Blaising and Bock, "Dispensationalism, Israel and the Church: Assessment and Dialogue," 392–93). See also Blaising and Bock, *Progressive Dispensationalism*, 81; Darrell L. Bock, "Current Messianic Activity and OT Davidic Promise: Dispensationalism, Hermeneutics, and NT Fulfillment," *TrinJ* 15.1 (1994): 72; Saucy, *The Case for Progressive Dispensationalism*, 244–45.

20. Blaising and Bock, *Progressive Dispensationalism*, 96–97.

21. Saucy notes that simply because the OT is designated as "Old," does not mean that it is superseded historically by the NT (*The Case for Progressive Dispensationalism*, 30).

the present-future relationship. It is possible to get fulfillment 'now' in some texts, while noting that a 'not yet' fulfillment exists in other passages."[22] The "now" fulfillment may be initial or partial, without being complete or final.

Another aspect related to a literal hermeneutic is what Blaising calls a performative language interpretation of divine promise.[23] Here, Blaising applies speech-act theory to the promises of God given to Israel in the Bible. The idea of speech-act theory is that language does not merely communicate information, but it also does something— especially when it is God making a promise to his people. Thus, the promise creates an obligation on God's part since he cannot lie (Heb 6:18). Thus, cautions Blaising, we ought to be careful not to take God's promises and treat them as "shadowy type correspondences" that "somehow mean that the Lord's explicit speech acts promising a nation and a land have somehow been dissolved, replaced, or transformed in their meaning."[24] In the end, such a hermeneutical approach which does seek to alter God's performative language "calls into question the integrity of God."[25]

What Is the Proper Role of Typology?

This complementary hermeneutic is integral to the way in which progressive dispensationalists understand the way the New Testament uses the Old Testament. To read a text from this "both/and" perspective is to read it in both its "historical-exegetical" context, preserving the original author's intent, and its "theological-canonical" context, perceiving its "eventual significance … in the light of [its] theological-canonical development" through the course of Scripture.[26] With

---

22. Blaising and Bock, *Progressive Dispensationalism*, 97–98.

23. See Craig Blaising, "A Critique of Gentry and Wellum's, *Kingdom Through Covenant*: A Hermeneutical-Theological Response," *MSJ* 26.1 [2015]: 118–20; idem, "Israel and Hermeneutics," in *The People, the Land, and the Future of Israel: Israel and Jewish People in the Plan of God*," ed. Darrell Bock and Mitch Glaser (Grand Rapids: Kregel, 2014), 160–62; idem, "Biblical Hermeneutics: How Are We to Interpret the Relation between the Tanak and the New Testament on This Question?" in *The New Christian Zionism: Fresh Perspectives on Israel and the Land*, ed. Gerald R. McDermott (Downers Grove, IL: IVP Academic, 2016), 97.

24. Blaising, "A Critique of Gentry and Wellum's, *Kingdom Through Covenant*," 119.

25. Ibid., 120.

26. Darrell L. Bock, "Single Meaning, Multiple Contexts and Referents: The New

regard to Old Testament prophecies, Bock notes that "this kind of both/and referent in the progress of revelation shows the kind of multi-layered possibilities that exist" for their fulfillment, such that one must allow for their partial fulfillment, even as the prophecies retain their original features.[27]

In contrast to revised dispensationalists, progressive dispensationalists more readily embrace typology since they view "typology as an aspect of historical-literary interpretation."[28] They also see their version of typology as distinct from that embraced by classic dispensationalists, which often consisted of a "spiritual" interpretation (e.g., oil was a *type* of the Holy Spirit). In contrast, their use of typology is more historical (e.g., the Davidic-Solomonic kingdom is a *type* of the eschatological kingdom).[29] Thus, progressive dispensationalists reject any approach to typology that attempts to find hidden meanings or to reinterpret material objects in the Old Testament as spiritual entities in the New Testament. Rather, typology simply indicates "patterns of resemblance between persons and events in earlier history to persons and events in later history."[30] As noted in chapter 1, Edward Glenny identifies four criteria necessary to establish such typological-prophetic connections between the Old and New Testaments: (1) the type must be linked to an historical fact (person, event, etc.); (2) the link to the antitype must be identifiable within Scripture; (3) a pattern must exist between the type and antitype; and (4) there must be an escalation or progression from the type to the antitype.[31]

Bock specifies several ways in which the New Testament can use the Old Testament: (1) directly-prophetic; (2) typological-prophetic;

Testament's Legitimate, Accurate and Multifaceted Use of the Old," in *Three Views on the New Testament Use of the Old Testament*, ed. Kenneth Berding and Jonathan Lunde (Grand Rapids: Zondervan, 2008), 115–17.

27. Bock, "Current Messianic Activity and OT Davidic Promise," 72.

28. Blaising and Bock, *Progressive Dispensationalism*, 52.

29. Ibid., 52–53.

30. Ibid., 52.

31. W. Edward Glenny, "The Israelite Imagery of 1 Peter 2," in *Dispensationalism, Israel and the Church*, 157–58. Blaising disputes the idea that escalation is an essential component of typology. In particular, he is concerned about the way progressive covenantalists use this idea to suggest that previous covenants are fulfilled in the new covenant (see Blaising, "A Critique of Gentry and Wellum's, *Kingdom Through Covenant*," 115–18).

(3) analogical; (4) cancellation; and (5) substitution.[32] Therefore, "promise and prophecy are not always a matter of exclusively direct prophetic texts, where the Old Testament passage refers only to one event or person in one setting."[33] Often, he explains, the Old Testament establishes a pattern of God's redemptive activity that, in the progress of revelation, repeats (sometimes more than once) in escalated fashion. As such, the force of God's earlier activity "becomes clearer and more developed ... in later events and texts."[34] This leads to the identification of new or expanded referents that fulfill the earlier events in the sense that they show the ultimate significance of those events. Thus, progressive dispensationalists acknowledge that sometimes a promise is expanded beyond its original scope in the New Testament. Yet, Bock adds that the "additional inclusion of some in the promise does not mean that the original recipients are thereby excluded. *The expansion of promise need not mean the cancellation of earlier commitments God has made.*"[35] So, regardless of what the New Testament adds to Old Testament promises, the Old Testament promises must be fulfilled as originally stated to the group to whom they were promised (i.e., Israel). Bock refers to this as *inaugurated eschatology* since it allows for partial fulfilment in the church which does not preclude ultimate fulfillment in the future kingdom.[36]

Acts 2:16–20 provides an appropriate example of progressive dispensationalism's use of typology. Bock points to three features of the text that indicate Peter is announcing the first stage of new covenant fulfillment.[37] First is the introductory formula ("this is that which is spoken through the prophet Joel" [Acts 2:28–32]), a phrase which was commonly used in in the Second Temple period to denote fulfillment. Second is Peter's use of "the last days," compared to Joel's, "after these things," which indicates Peter's understanding that the eschaton

---

32. Blaising and Bock, *Progressive Dispensationalism*, 102–3.

33. Ibid., 102.

34. Bock, "Single Meaning, Multiple Contexts and Referents," 114.

35. Blaising and Bock, *Progressive Dispensationalism*, 103 (emphasis original).

36. Ibid., 98.

37. Darrell L. Bock, "The Reign of the Lord Christ," in *Dispensationalism, Israel and the Church*," 47–48.

has arrived. Third, and most importantly, is the emphasis on the out-pouring of the Holy Spirit which is connected to the new covenant promises in Jeremiah 31 and Ezekiel 36. In other words, the outpour-ing of the Spirit is not only a fulfillment of Joel's prophecy, but also a fulfillment of the new covenant promises.

Bock qualifies his interpretation, however, by stating that the ful-fillment is only partial.[38] Two features of the Acts text confirm this partiality: (1) the reference to the coming day of the Lord in Acts 2:20 and (2) the absence of any of the cosmic signs referenced in Joel, which are repeated in Acts 2:19–20. Thus, Bock explains, while the coming of the Spirit is a sign of initial fulfillment, it is also "a sign that drives toward the Day of the Lord and its accompanying judgment."[39] Similarly, Saucy insists, "Peter did not mean that all of Joel's prophecy was fulfilled at Pentecost."[40] Contrary to traditional dispensationalism, however, he does acknowledge that Peter is affirming that the escha-tological era (including promises related to the Davidic covenant) was inaugurated with the work of Christ at his first coming.

How Are Old Testament Restoration Prophecies Fulfilled?

Progressive dispensationalists maintain that the New Testament authors never offered a radical reinterpretation (i.e., a purely sym-bolic interpretation) of Old Testament prophecies where the origi-nal prophecy is jettisoned for a more Christological interpretation. Instead, they insist that New Testament authors establish a legitimate link to the Old Testament text but the New Testament "fulfillment" is not the complete or final fulfillment.

According to Saucy, when James cites the prophecy of Amos 9:11–15 in Acts 15:16–17, he is doing so "in support of gentile salvation."[41]

---

38. Ibid., 48–49. Barker maintains that it is not merely an analogy or illustration but that the prophecy was at least partially fulfilled. Because the physical phenomenon did not occur, however, we know it is not completely fulfilled (Kenneth L. Barker, "The Scope and Center of Old and New Testament Theology and Hope," in *Dispensationalism, Israel and the Church*, 326). He summarizes: "Acts 2, then, is a direct, initial, partial fulfillment of Joel 2, but it is not the final and complete fulfillment" (327).

39. Darrell L. Bock, "The Reign of the Lord Christ," 49.

40. Saucy, *The Case for Progressive Dispensationalism*, 33.

41. Ibid., 78. See also Blaising and Bock, *Progressive Dispensationalism*, 267; Barker, "The

But James is not simply indicating that God's redemptive plan ultimately includes the gentiles; he is also indicating that the salvation of the gentiles is a direct result of the work of Christ, who is the restored Davidic king prophesied in Amos 9.[42] In other words, had James not understood Jesus to be the fulfillment of the restored Davidic dynasty, he would not have explicitly connected the salvation of the gentiles to this prophecy. In addition, Blaising opines that the issue is not simply that gentiles are saved, but that they are saved without needing to become Jews. He writes, "God's cleansing of the hearts of Gentile believers in Jesus by the Holy Spirit without requiring them to become Jews was seen to be in accord with the plan to have *Gentiles as Gentiles* in the messianic kingdom."[43]

At the same time, Saucy notes that James is not intending to comment on the prophecy's ultimate fulfillment and that elements of Amos' prophecy, particularly in Amos 9:13–15, remain unfilled (e.g., cities have yet to be rebuilt and occupation of the land has yet to be permanent).[44] Thus, while the prophecy has been initially fulfilled in the first coming of Christ, it awaits its ultimate fulfillment at Christ's second coming. Barker concurs, "What happened in Acts 15 constitutes a stage in the progressive fulfillment of the entire prophecy of Amos 9. ... It is an instance of direct fulfillment, but not the final and complete fulfillment, as the following verses in Amos (9:13–15) plainly indicate."[45]

Scope and Center of Old and New Testament Theology and Hope," 327.

42. Saucy, *The Case for Progressive Dispensationalism*, 78–79.

43. Craig Blaising, "A Theology of Israel and the Church," in *Israel, the Church and the Middle East: A Biblical Response to the Current Conflict*, ed. Darrell L. Bock and Mitch Glaser (Grand Rapids: Kregel, 2018), 97.

44. Saucy writes, "According to the New Testament, this prophetic picture was not completely fulfilled in the first coming of Christ. Instead, only an initial or partial fulfillment occurred, with the rest awaiting the second appearance of the Messiah" (ibid., 79). He later adds that the apostles affirmed the inauguration of the messianic promises but "they never went to the extent of saying that the experience of the church is the complete fulfillment of the prophecies" (211).

45. Barker, "The Scope and Center of Old and New Testament Theology and Hope," 327.

2. WHAT IS THE RELATIONSHIP BETWEEN THE COVENANTS?

In comparison to its dispensational predecessors, progressive dispensationalists espouse a more unified understanding of the biblical covenants since the progress of revelation reveals these covenants are linked together.[46] Furthermore, they hold that the Abrahamic, Davidic, and new covenants are unconditional, each taking the form of a grant covenant in which God promises future blessings and unilaterally declares his intent to fulfill those promises. The Abrahamic covenant is viewed as the foundational covenant for the subsequent covenants (especially the Davidic and new covenants).[47] Indeed, the covenant with Abraham provides the framework for interpreting the history of redemption as this covenant is confirmed, clarified, and expanded. These covenants are not now being *fulfilled* by the church, though the church's participation in the spiritual blessings offered in the covenants is an inaugural fulfillment of covenant blessings. The fullness of the blessings will only occur at the return of Christ.

Of course, the various dispensations directly relate to the biblical covenants that God ratified throughout history. Blaising defines a dispensation as "a particular arrangement by which God regulates the way human beings relate to Him."[48] Progressive dispensationalists "understand the dispensations not simply as *different* arrangements between God and humankind, but as *successive* arrangements in the *progressive* revelation and accomplishment of redemption."[49] Each successive dispensation reveals a qualitative advancement of different aspects of the final redemption. As such, this view is markedly different from covenantalism, which sees the various dispensations (or epochs in history) as different historical expressions of the same overarching covenant of redemption. Another noted difference is the tendency of progressive dispensationalists to keep the political

---

46. See Blaising and Bock, *Progressive Dispensationalism,* 132, 163; Saucy, *The Case for Progressive Dispensationalism,* 42, 65–66.

47. See Blaising and Bock, *Progressive Dispensationalism,* 130–40.

48. Ibid., 14.

49. Ibid., 48 (emphasis original).

(cultural/social) purpose of God somewhat distinct from the spiritual purpose of God. While the latter does not replace the former, they are also not completely separate but complement each other. The new dispensation, which began with the church, is distinct from the previous (Mosaic) dispensation—but it is not *wholly* different. This dispensation is a progression from the previous dispensations in partial fulfillment of the divine plan to which both are pointing and in which both are fulfilled.[50] Thus, "The present arrangement is not the culmination of the divine plan, but it is both the revelation and the guarantee that that plan will yet be realized."[51]

Blaising recognizes four main dispensations:[52]

- Patriarchal (to Sinai)
- Mosaic (to Messiah's ascension)
- Ecclesial (to Messiah's return)
- Zionic (millennial and eternal)

These dispensations are progressive phases of salvation history, which culminates in the eschatological kingdom of God. As with previous dispensationalists, progressive dispensationalists maintain that God's plan for Israel and the nations in the past dispensation points forward to the redemption of humanity in its political and cultural dimensions. And yet, they affirm that the church is a key part of the same plan of redemption. The church is *not* a secondary plan, a parenthesis, or an intercalation, but is a revelation of all the spiritual blessings that are shared by all the redeemed of God in the eschatological kingdom.

Are the Covenants Conditional or Unconditional?

The Abrahamic covenant is a grant covenant, which is a type of unconditional covenant that "guarantees the gift to the master's servant and his heirs."[53] The unconditional nature of the covenant is supported by the way in which the covenant was given to Abraham and,

---

50. Ibid., 101.
51. Ibid., 115.
52. Ibid., 123.
53. Ibid., 132.

secondly, the way in which Abraham received it. That is, he *believed in* the Lord and his belief was reckoned as righteousness (Gen 15:18). A grant covenant, however, does not exclude certain demands from the recipient, and failure to comply with such demands could result in the removal of certain benefits. Simply because God commands Abraham to "Go" or "Walk blameless" does not change the nature of the covenant (i.e., it is still a grant covenant and not a bilateral covenant). As Blaising explains, "Abraham's obedience to God's commandments does function as *the means* by which he experiences God's blessing on a day to day basis. ... But these obligations do not condition the fundamental intention to bless Abraham. They condition the *how* and the *when* of the blessing."[54] God will fulfill his promises to Abraham in spite of Abraham's disobedience. Such a view does not mean that God's commands are irrelevant or inconsequential since some of the blessings are tied to obedience, demonstrating that God is concerned about righteousness and holiness.[55]

In contrast to the Abrahamic covenant (i.e., a grant covenant), the Mosaic covenant was a *conditional* covenant based on the suzerain-vassal treaty of the ancient Near East.[56] The latter was a bilateral agreement between a king and his subjects where the king promises to provide for his subjects if they remain loyal to him. Obedience brings about blessings whereas disobedience results in punishment (curses of the covenant). Thus, the blessings of the treaty were conditioned on the compliance to the stipulations. The Mosaic covenant, however, was dependent on the Abrahamic covenant. As a result, disobedience to the former does not ultimately affect the latter. Regarding the progress of redemptive history, the Mosaic dispensation marks a

---

54. Ibid., 133–34 (emphasis original). They add that "the unconditional nature of the grant covenant guarantees the legal possession of the gift even during the period of such punishment" (132–33).

55. Saucy adds that because the land was promised to Abraham and his descendants as "an everlasting possession," this promise cannot be interpreted "as only temporary or as a type of something 'spiritual' or 'heavenly'" (*The Case for Progressive Dispensationalism*, 45).

56. See Darrell L. Bock, "Covenants in Progressive Dispensationalism," in *Three Central Issues in Contemporary Dispensationalism*, 169.

progression as it "sets up a *national* religious cult for the relationship between God and His people."[57]

The Davidic covenant is connected to the Abrahamic covenant in that it both repeats key elements of the Abrahamic covenant and identifies the Davidic king as the mediator of its blessings. Accordingly, the Davidic covenant not only becomes a part of the Abrahamic covenant but also becomes the means by which it will be fulfilled.[58] Similar to the Abrahamic covenant, the Davidic covenant was an unconditional grant covenant, which is frequently described as "eternal" (2 Sam 7:13, 16; 23:5; Ps 89:4, 28, 36–37). As such, there were no conditions when the covenant was revealed to David (2 Sam 7; 1 Chr 17). It was only when the covenant was transferred to Solomon that a condition was added. The conditional promise of never lacking a king on the throne of Israel is given the condition of obedience to God's ordinances. Blaising clarifies: "God's promise to raise up a descendent is unconditional. But a continuous, uninterrupted reign is not. That is conditioned upon the faithfulness of the Davidic kings."[59] The conditional portions of the promise only related to personal and individual forfeiture of the covenant. The final fulfillment of the Davidic covenant will take place when Jesus reigns as king over Israel during the millennium.

Finally, the new covenant will bring the blessings and promises of the Abrahamic covenant to fulfillment.[60] At the same time, these promised blessings are expanded to include the promise of forgiveness of sins, the resurrection, and a transformed heart that desires obedience to God. The dispensation of the new covenant again shows progress and advancement over the previous (Mosaic) dispensation. As Blaising notes, "It is indisputable that the New Testament views the new covenant predicted by Jeremiah and Ezekiel as established in the death of Jesus Christ with some of its promised blessings now

---

57. Blaising and Bock, *Progressive Dispensationalism*, 151.

58. Ibid., 166–68.

59. Ibid., 164.

60. Saucy writes, "The Davidic and the new covenants ... are basically elaborations of provisions of the Abrahamic promises and therefore partake of the perpetuity of the original Abrahamic covenant" (*The Case for Progressive Dispensationalism*, 59n1).

being granted to Jews and Gentiles who are believers in Jesus."[61] As a result, the final fulfillment of both the Abrahamic and Davidic covenants is ultimately tied to the fulfillment of the new covenant.

Progressive dispensationalists affirm that all of these covenants find their initial fulfillment in the first coming of Christ and thus the church.[62] The reason for this is that all the covenants find their final fulfillment in the kingdom of God and that the church is an inaugural form of that kingdom. At the same time, they explain that certain covenantal blessings (particularly the national/political blessings promised to Israel) remain unfulfilled. These promises await a more complete fulfillment which will take place when Christ returns to reign on the earth from Israel. As a result, because the covenants are unconditional, progressive dispensationalists assert that, as a matter of God's faithfulness, the unfulfilled promises must be literally fulfilled.[63] That is, just as the New Testament affirms that spiritual blessings (including the resurrection and the full transformation of the heart) promised in the new covenant await ultimate fulfillment upon Christ's return, material blessings also await ultimate fulfillment at his return.[64]

How Were Old Testament Saints Saved?

Progressive dispensationalists affirm that the blessings of the new covenant (based on the Abrahamic covenant) are received on the basis of faith in Christ (Gal 3:7).[65] At the heart of these blessings is the guarantee of salvation. But how did God's people in the previous dispensation of the Mosaic covenant receive salvation, since its blessings were

---

61. Blaising and Bock, *Progressive Dispensationalism*, 202. Ware comments that "Israel and the church share theologically rich and important elements of commonality while at the same time maintaining distinct identities" (Bruce A. Ware, "The New Covenant and the People[s] of God," in *Dispensationalism, Israel and the Church*, 92). See also Saucy, *The Case for Progressive Dispensationalism*, 126.

62. Bock states, "All of the covenants of promise are initially realized in the church" ("Covenants in Progressive Dispensationalism," 171). This affirmation is contrary to the position of traditional dispensationalism which "does not view any promissory covenant fulfilled at the First Advent" (Elliot E. Johnson, "Response," in *Three Central Issues in Contemporary Dispensationalism*, 206).

63. Bock, "The Reign of the Lord Christ," 65; idem, "Covenants in Progressive Dispensationalism," 173.

64. Blaising and Bock, *Progressive Dispensationalism*, 174–211.

65. Ibid., 192–93.

conditioned on obedience to the Mosaic law? The answer resides in the connection of the Mosaic covenant to the Abrahamic covenant.

According to Blaising, the Mosaic covenant is dependent upon the Abrahamic covenant. As such, the granting of blessing under the Mosaic covenant is still on the basis of faith.[66] Indeed, obedience is a manifestation of faith. Of course, on this point, dispensationalists and covenantalists generally agree. They differ, however, in regard to the object of faith. Covenantalists identify Jesus Christ as the object of faith, even among Old Testament saints, whereas progressive dispensationalists assert, "the Old Testament saints could not have expressly placed their faith in Christ and the saving work of his death and resurrection in the same way believers could after those events took place."[67]

How Is the Old Testament Law to Be Applied Today?

If the Old Testament saints and the New Testament people of God are all saved by faith, to what do progressive dispensationalists attribute the purpose of the law, and what is its role for New Testament believers now that it has been fulfilled in Christ? With regard to its purpose, Barker explains that the law was never intended as a means of salvation. Rather, God gave it to the people of Israel as a display of his grace, as evidenced by the fact that he gave it only after he redeemed them from their bondage in Egypt. It was intended to serve for Israel "as a means of expressing their love to God [and] ... governing their relationship to God and to each other."[68] Barker sees the law functioning in a similar capacity for new covenant believers. For them, the law "is the gracious revelation of God's righteous will and is to be followed as the grateful and joyful expression of that faith."[69] Thus, while the ceremonial laws, which function as types and shadows pointing to Christ, are no longer applicable, the moral and ethical part of the law remains very much authoritative for new covenant believers.[70]

---

66. Ibid., 145.

67. Saucy, *The Case for Progressive Dispensationalism*, 16.

68. Kenneth Barker, "False Dichotomies between the Testaments," *JETS* 25.1 (1982): 7.

69. Barker, "The Scope and Center of Old and New Testament Theology and Hope," 296.

70. Ibid., 301–2. See also David K. Lowery, "Christ, the End of the Law," in *Dispensationalism,*

One of the issues that some dispensationalists have with classic or revised dispensationalism relates to their view of the relevance and applicability of the Sermon on the Mount for Christians today. For example, Ryrie claims, "If the Sermon is directly for the church, it will be difficult if not impossible to interpret all of it completely and in a consistently literal manner."[71] According to Ryrie, because no one interprets the Sermon in a consistently literal manner, this demonstrates that the Sermon is not for Christians today. But progressive dispensationalists often reject such a strict literalness in interpreting Jesus' words in the Sermon on the Mount. Saucy acknowledges, "Most scholars suggest that Jesus used some extreme examples designed to teach fundamental principles rather than offering strict, actual cases that are to be interpreted absolutely."[72] If this is the case, "then the argument for the impossibility of a primary application for the present age loses its force."[73] Progressive dispensationalists often contend that the application of Jesus' words continues throughout the present age and is not limited to the original disciples. Saucy notes that this view "would appear to be becoming more popular within dispensationalism, thus excluding this issue as a point of distinction vis-à-vis non-dispensationalists."[74]

3. WHAT IS THE RELATIONSHIP BETWEEN ISRAEL AND THE CHURCH?

Does the Church Replace or Fulfill Israel, or Are the Two Distinct?

Like previous dispensationalists, progressive dispensationalists see the church as a part of the new dispensation in the history of redemption. The church is not found in the Old Testament since it did not

---

Israel, and the Church, 230–47; and John A. Martin, "Christ, the Fulfillment of the Law in the Sermon on the Mount," in *Dispensationalism, Israel, and the Church*, 248–63.

71. Charles C. Ryrie, *Dispensationalism*, rev. and exp. ed. (Chicago: Moody, 2007), 111.

72. Saucy, *The Case for Progressive Dispensationalism*, 18.

73. Ibid.

74. Ibid.

exist prior to Pentecost. And like earlier dispensationalists, progressive dispensationalists view the church as a *new manifestation* of grace. But unlike traditional dispensationalists, they do not see it as a completely new or distinct type of redemption. Instead, "this grace is precisely *in keeping with* the promises of the Old Testament, particularly the promises of the new covenant in Isaiah, Jeremiah, and Ezekiel."[75] Barker asserts that, given the progressive nature of God's plan of redemption, "the old sharp distinction between Israel and the church begins to become somewhat blurred."[76] Yet, at the same time, some distinction does exist. As Ware explains, "between the two extremes of a strict distinction between Israel and the church ... and a strict identity of Israel and the church ... a middle position would suggest that Israel and the church share theologically rich and important elements of commonality while at the same time maintaining distinct identities."[77] In other words, there is unity and distinction; continuity and discontinuity. For Blaising, the kingdom is the key connection between Israel and the church. Israel is an ethnic, national, territorial aspect of the kingdom alongside of other ethnic, national, and territorial aspects, whereas the church refers to the unity of all peoples—of whatever ethnic or national identity or territorial location—in Christ, unity with him by the indwelling Holy Spirit.[78]

The continuity between Israel and the church reflects the common salvation presently available under the new covenant, which Saucy writes, "provides for the ultimate unity of all God's people."[79] Thus,

---

75. Blaising and Bock, *Progressive Dispensationalism*, 49 (emphasis original). More recently, Blaising has coined the phrase "Redemptive Kingdom Theology" as a synonym for progressive dispensationalism. He explains: "Redemptive Kingdom Theology sees the presence of the kingdom in the application of redemption to the peoples of the world who believe in Christ forming them into a spiritual communion which as such constitutes a present inaugural form of the coming Kingdom of God" ("A Theology of Israel and the Church," 88n10). Thus, the church neither replaces or supersedes Israel in God's plan nor does the church constitute a distinct people group, separate from Israel and the Gentiles. Consequently, inclusion in the church does not mean exclusion from the inheritance of Israel for Jewish believers nor exclusion from the blessings promised to Gentiles for Gentile believers (88–89).

76. Barker, "The Scope and Center of Old and New Testament Theology and Hope," 303.

77. Ware, "The New Covenant and the People(s) of God," 92.

78. See Blaising, "A Theology of Israel and the Church."

79. Saucy, *The Case for Progressive Dispensationalism*, 112; see also Ware, "The New Covenant and the People(s) of God," 93.

Israel and the church "share a similar identity as the people of God enjoying equally the blessings of eschatological salvation."[80] He qualifies that statement, however, by explaining that this unity in salvation does not erase Israel's distinction as a national, political entity. He states that "it is the lack of national characteristics that distinguishes the church from Israel."[81]

To explain this distinction, Ware observes that the new covenant includes both spiritual aspects (forgiveness of sins, indwelling Holy Spirit, and a renewed relationship with God) and territorial/political aspects (restoration of Israel as a nation to the land God promised).[82] While the New Testament clearly teaches that the spiritual aspects have been inaugurated and applied to the church by means of the indwelling Holy Spirit, the territorial/political aspects have not yet been fulfilled. They must be fulfilled, however, for "neither Old Testament nor New Testament teaching would allow us to understand the territorial and political aspects of God's new covenant promise to Israel in anything other than a literal fashion."[83] Because they cannot be applied to the church, since the church is not a national entity, Ware therefore maintains that there must be "a future action of God whereby he will bring 'all Israel' (Rom 11:26) ... under the provision of forgiveness of sin and Spirit-indwelling as well as territorial and political restoration that it will surely enjoy in their fullness when Christ comes again."[84] Jew and gentile are one *spiritually*, but not one *physically*. Or, to put it differently, *positional* unification does not rule out *functional* distinctions.[85]

---

80. Saucy, *The Case for Progressive Dispensationalism*, 210. Ware explains his position: "Israel and the church are in one sense *a united people* of God (they participate in the same new covenant), while in another sense they remain separate in their identity and so comprise *different peoples* of God" since "Israel is given territorial and political aspects of the new-covenant promise not applicable to the church" ("The New Covenant and the People[s] of God," 96–97).

81. Saucy, *The Case for Progressive Dispensationalism*, 210.

82. Ware, "The New Covenant and the People(s) of God," 93–96; see also Saucy, *The Case for Progressive Dispensationalism*, 114–17.

83. Ware, "The New Covenant and the People(s) of God," 94. Saucy maintains that the "blessings promised to Israel are nowhere reinterpreted as presently belonging to the church" (*The Case for Progressive Dispensationalism*, 58).

84. Ware, "The New Covenant and the People(s) of God," 96.

85. See Robert L. Saucy, "The Church as the Mystery of God," in *Dispensationalism, Israel*

In his study of 1 Peter 2, Glenny affirms a correlation between Israel and the church. He writes, "Peter is teaching that the church represents a pattern and thus is a fulfillment of the promises made to Israel in these Old Testament passages."[86] Yet, he adds that Peter "is not saying the church equals Israel; instead he is saying that as Israel in the Old Testament was the people of God by virtue of its relationship with Yahweh, so the church is the present people of God by virtue of its relationship with Jesus, the elect Messiah of God."[87] Thus, although the church fulfills certain Old Testament prophecies, it does not exhaust them. There still remains a future (literal) fulfillment related specifically to the nation of Israel. Thus, the church does not replace Israel but Israel does provide a pattern of the church's relationship with God. Again, the spiritual promises given to the church do not exhaust the physical (national, political, and geographical) promises given to Israel.[88]

How Are Romans 11:26 and Galatians 6:16 Interpreted?

Progressive dispensationalists, like *all* dispensationalists, affirm that, based on Old Testament prophecy, the nation of Israel will someday be restored to the land and receive the full blessings that God has promised them. This promise of restoration is not only mentioned in the Old Testament but is also referenced in the New Testament (e.g., Acts 3:20–21)—and the clearest prediction is found in Romans 9–11. Indeed, Romans 11:26 contains a new covenant prediction that at the return of the Messiah to earth, the salvation of the nation as a whole will be fulfilled.[89] Progressive dispensationalists insist that the Old Testament promises to Israel still exist because in Romans 9–11 Paul singles out ethnic Israel.[90]

---

and the Church, 155.

86. Glenny, "The Israelite Imagery of 1 Peter 2," 183.

87. Ibid.

88. Ibid., 186–87.

89. Blaising and Bock, *Progressive Dispensationalism*, 205, 210.

90. See Barker, "The Scope and Center of Old and New Testament Theology and Hope," 322–23.

Regarding Romans 11, Burns explains that verses 1–24 confirm God's abiding commitment to Israel, as seen in his preserving of the believing remnant. These verses also reveal the temporal nature of Israel's hardening.[91] Though they are presently hardened, he explains that the unbelieving majority will ultimately be driven to jealousy by the gentiles' "special covenantal relationship with their 'root,'" which will then lead to the salvation of all Israel (referring to the nation as a whole, not to every member) after the full number of elect gentiles have attained salvation.[92] As a result, he concludes, "Ethnic Israel has a future, because God will accomplish salvation for Israel according to his new-covenant promise."[93]

In Galatians 6:16 Paul states, "And as for all who walk by this rule, peace and mercy be upon them, *and* upon the Israel of God" (emphasis added). The word "and" is a gloss of the Greek term *kai*, which is typically translated as "and," "even," or "also." If it is translated as "even," then the implication is that the church (i.e., the addressees of the letter, a group that includes gentiles) is equated with "the Israel of God." For example, the NIV 84 renders the verse: "Peace and mercy to all who follow this rule, *even* to the Israel of God" (NIV 84, emphasis added).[94] The NLT offers a similar interpretation: "May God's peace and mercy be upon all who live by this principle; they are the new people of God."

Representatives of progressive dispensationalism vigorously deny that the church is called "the Israel of God," offering the following reasons: (1) the explicative sense of *kai* (i.e., translated as "even") is not common in Paul's writings; (2) this would be the only place where Paul gives "Israel" the meaning of "church"; and (3) such an

---

91. See J. Lanier Burns, "The Future of Ethnic Israel," in *Dispensationalism, Israel and the Church*, 188–229. See also idem, "Israel and the Church of a Progressive Dispensationalist," in *Three Central Issues in Contemporary Dispensationalism*, 263–91.

92. Burns, "The Future of Ethnic Israel," 216. See also Blaising, "A Theology of Israel and the Church," 94; Darrell Bock, "Biblical Reconciliation between Jews and Arabs," in *Israel, the Church and the Middle East*, 179–82.

93. Burns, "The Future of Ethnic Israel," 216.

94. The NIV (2011) offers a similar meaning: "Peace and mercy to all who follow this rule—to the Israel of God."

interpretation does not fit the context of Galatians.[95] Consequently, progressive dispensationalists insist that Paul is merely singling out Jewish Christians in this final benediction.

4. WHAT IS THE KINGDOM OF GOD?

The theme of God's kingdom is central to progressive dispensationalism.[96] Instead of dividing up the progression of redemptive history into distinct *kingdoms*, they view a single eschatological kingdom that contains both *spiritual* and *political* dimensions. The Old Testament portrayal of the kingdom will occur as predicted but the New Testament clarifies the outworking of the kingdom during this age and in the age to come. The church today is an inaugural aspect of the eschatological kingdom. Although there are political and social implications for this present inaugural phase of the kingdom, that does not mean that the political and social aspects of the kingdom are here today since they await the coming of Christ. Thus, the inauguration of the kingdom does not mean that all aspects of the eschatological reality are here today, but only those aspects that are specifically said to be inaugurated.[97]

Progressive dispensationalists insist that God's plan unfolding in history is one unified plan. Thus, the present dispensation is *not* a parenthesis unrelated to past or future purposes of God. Instead, the current age "is an integrated phase in the development of the mediatorial kingdom. It is the beginning of the fulfillment of the eschatological promises."[98] At the same time, Israel remains a unique entity in God's redemptive plan since many Old Testament promises are yet to be fulfilled regarding the nation. Unlike earlier dispensationalists,

---

95. Saucy, *The Case for Progressive Dispensationalism*, 198–200.

96. Saucy defines the kingdom as "that program through which God effects his lordship on the earth in a comprehensive salvation within history" (ibid., 27–28). He posits that "the kingdom of God is one of the grand themes, if not *the* theme, of Scripture" (81).

97. See Blaising and Bock, *Progressive Dispensationalism*, 288–90. Saucy's view is somewhat different: "God's kingdom, which today may be said to be *over* the earth, will one day be established *on* the earth" (*The Case for Progressive Dispensationalism*, 28 [emphasis original]).

98. Saucy, *The Case for Progressive Dispensationalism*, 28.

progressive dispensationalists "make no substantive distinction between the terms kingdom of heaven and kingdom of God."[99]

Did Jesus Bring the Kingdom?

In distinction to earlier dispensationalists, progressive dispensationalists affirm the idea that the kingdom was present in Jesus' earthly ministry. Blaising writes that the Gospel writers portray "Jesus speaking of the kingdom being present in His own day by virtue of the fact that He Himself, the Christ, is present ministering by the power of the Holy Spirit, manifesting in His works characteristics belonging to the eschatological kingdom of God."[100] Revised dispensationalists maintain Jesus offered the kingdom to Israel but when they rejected the offer, it was withdrawn and so the kingdom never came. In contrast, Bock asserts, "The offer of the kingdom came. ... The offer was not withdrawn," although he acknowledges that it did contain some previously unannounced elements.[101]

Another distinction from traditional dispensationalism is that progressive dispensationalism affirms that the New Testament applies Davidic authority and power to Jesus as he now is seated at the right hand of God. Thus, Jesus is not seated on the throne of David now; that will occur during the millennial kingdom when Jesus rules from Jerusalem on the physical throne of David. It does indicate, however, that the New Testament recognizes Jesus as the Messiah from the house of David as he now rules from heaven. Blaising argues that "every New Testament description of the present throne of Jesus is drawn from Davidic covenant promises."[102] But this does not mean that they deny the necessity of a literal reign of Jesus in Jerusalem on the physical throne of David to fulfill the physical blessings promised in the Old Testament. Thus, progressive dispensationalists affirm the

---

99. Blaising and Bock, *Progressive Dispensationalism*, 54; See also Saucy, *The Case for Progressive Dispensationalism*, 19.

100. Blaising and Bock, *Progressive Dispensationalism*, 249.

101. Bock, "The Reign of the Lord Christ," 60–61.

102. Blaising and Bock, *Progressive Dispensationalism*, 182 (emphasis original). Bock adds, "Jesus' resurrection-ascension to God's right hand is put forward by Peter as a fulfillment of the Davidic covenant" ("The Reign of the Lord Christ," 49). See also Saucy, *The Case for Progressive Dispensationalism*, 72.

existing presence of the kingdom which was inaugurated with the coming of Jesus, especially his resurrection and ascension. But the kingdom has not yet been fully restored; it is *inaugurated*, but not *consummated*. Ultimate consummation only takes place when Jesus returns and establishes a physical kingdom over Israel.[103] Christ's return will be accompanied by a full restoration not only of the spiritual aspects of salvation, but also of the material and political aspects promised specifically to the nation of Israel and all the nations.[104]

Saucy takes a similar view as Blaising and Bock but rejects the idea of Jesus actually *reigning* over his kingdom on earth. He suggests that the kingdom as initially proclaimed by Jesus did not come in its totality but certain dimensions did come through Christ's first coming.[105] So whereas the salvation blessings of the kingdom have arrived, Christ is not *reigning* over his kingdom on earth and the church is not currently building this kingdom.[106] He clarifies, "although Christ has been exalted to receive kingly authority over the entire universe and all its contexts, he is not presently exercising that kingship in the sense of 'reigning,' nor are we as believers doing so."[107] The full eschatological sense of the kingdom will occur during the millennium.

As we've seen, a key passage that dispensationalists often cite in support of their view of the kingdom is Acts 1:6–7. In this passage Jesus responds to the disciples' question, "Lord, will you at this time restore the kingdom to Israel?" The lack of any correction or rebuke by Jesus indicates that their expectation of a future, political, and national restoration is correct.[108] Blaising insists that disciples were

---

103. Bock states, "There is no indication that earthly and Israelitic elements in Old Testament promises have been lost in the activity of the two stages. In the 'not yet,' visible, consummative kingdom, Jesus will rule on earth" ("The Reign of the Lord Christ," 66).

104. See Blaising, "A Theology of Israel and the Church," 85–100.

105. Saucy, *The Case for Progressive Dispensationalism*, 97–98.

106. Ibid., 101.

107. Ibid., 106. Saucy also claims that Peter's sermon in Acts 2 indicates that although the eschatological era has begun, it would be premature to state that actual kingdom *reign* has begun. Such a reign will not take place until Christ returns. Thus, Peter is not reinterpreting Old Testament prophecies to teach that Christ is currently *reigning* over the kingdom. Christ has been exalted to the right hand of God in fulfillment of Old Testament promises to David, but that promise, while inaugurated, still awaits consummation in the next dispensation (74–76).

108. Ibid., 268–69.

on the right track in asking such a question since they had received forty days of post-resurrection instruction. Thus, this passage "is a most significant testimony to the continuity of Jesus' teaching with that of the Old Testament prophets. The notion of a political, earthly kingdom has not dropped out or been resignified."[109]

Blaising adds that Acts 3:21 supports this interpretation by saying, "heaven must receive [Jesus] until the period of restoration of all things, about which God spoke by the mouth of His holy prophets from ancient time."[110] Referencing these same verses, Bock summarizes: "The last days of fulfillment have two parts. There is the current period of refreshing, which is correlated to Jesus' reign in heaven and in which a person shares, if he or she repents. Then at the end of this period Jesus will come to bring the restoration of those things promised by the Old Testament. Peter does not predict when Jesus will come, but with his return will come the second period of fulfillment, the times of restoration. This is a time when the promises made to Israel are completed."[111]

How Is the Kingdom Consummated?

Precisely how will this future kingdom be fully realized? The answer, according to progressive dispensationalists, resides in Revelation 20–22, where both an initial millennial phrase and then the everlasting consummation of the eschatological kingdom are presented.[112] With respect to the millennium, as Blaising explains, Revelation 20:4–5a identifies two resurrections that are divided by a literal thousand-year reign of Christ. During this thousand-year reign, Christ rules the nations of the earth from Jerusalem with his resurrected saints, who receive advanced fulfillment of the covenant promises while much of humanity still lives under the condition of mortality. It is during this time that, "as Messiah of Israel, Jesus will fulfill for that nation the promises covenanted to her, and He will rule over all nations so

---

109. Blaising and Bock, *Progressive Dispensationalism*, 237 (see also 268).

110. Ibid., 240; see also Saucy, *The Case for Progressive Dispensationalism*, 271.

111. Bock, "The Reign of the Lord Christ," 57; see also Blaising and Bock, *Progressive Dispensationalism*, 268.

112. See Blaising and Bock, *Progressive Dispensationalism*, 270–83.

that through Him all nations might be blessed."[113] At the end of the millennium, the second resurrection will occur and the devil will be released, leading a rebellion against Jesus and the saints. Christ will then defeat the rebellion, at which time the final judgment will come and usher in the full eschatological kingdom of God, manifested in an eternal new heaven and new earth, over which God will rule forever as Father, Son, and Holy Spirit.[114] Blaising explains that, while this two-phased realization of the kingdom is not explicitly revealed in the Old Testament, it is compatible with Old Testament prophecies (esp. Isa 65:17–25), as they seem to describe the eschatological kingdom as both containing sin and mortality while at the same time characterizing righteousness and immortality.[115]

ASSESSMENT

A strength of progressive dispensationalists is their willingness to adjust their hermeneutic, even amidst fierce criticism from revised dispensationalists who have accused them of being unfaithful to the essence of dispensationalism.[116] They have developed a complementary hermeneutic, allowing for an expansion to the original prophecy.

But it seems that progressive dispensationalists could also be charged with being inconsistent in following their stated hermeneutic. For example, based on their understanding of typology, one wonders why certain Old Testament promises could not be fulfilled in the new earth. Indeed, as Anthony Hoekema observes, "Prophecies about the restoration of Israel may be fulfilled *antitypically*—that is, as finally fulfilled in the possession by all of God's people of the new earth of which [the land of] Canaan was a type" since Jesus expanded the referent of land to include the earth in his citation of Psalm 37:11

---

113. Ibid., 283. He also states, "The Old Testament prophets ... predict that God will establish a world-wide kingdom on the earth centered at Jerusalem in which He and His Messiah, a descendent of David, will rule Israel and all nations" (228).

114. Ibid., 283.

115. See Craig A. Blaising, "Premillennialism," in *Three Views on the Millennium and Beyond*, ed. Darrell Bock (Grand Rapids: Zondervan, 1999), 202–4.

116. See, e.g., Thomas, "The Hermeneutics of Progressive Dispensationalism," 79–95.

(Matt 5:5).[117] This application of typology appears consistent with both Bock's and Glenny's permitted use of typology.[118]

Saucy addresses this objection by saying, "placing the fulfillment of these promises in the time of the new earth puts them beyond the pale of the history of this present earth and the messianic age of Christ's reign."[119] In other words, he insinuates that the promises must be fulfilled prior to the coming of the new earth. For some, this objection might prove unconvincing since the New Testament affirms several aspects of the new covenant that will only be fulfilled in the new earth, including the permanent removal of sin and the dwelling of God with humanity. Accordingly, if the spiritual aspects of the new covenant await their ultimate fulfillment in the new heaven and new earth, then it seems reasonable to conclude the same with regard to the physical aspects, including the restoration of land. Indeed, later in the same book Saucy states, in reference to the ultimate fulfillment of the new covenant, that "God will finally make his people perfect and bring them into the relationship with him for which they were originally created. *This perfected spiritual relationship will then issue in a fullness of material blessing.*"[120] He appears to affirm that the fulfillment of the physical aspects is dependent upon the ultimate fulfillment of the spiritual aspects, which according to Revelation, awaits consummation in the new heaven and new earth.

In addition, some may question the legitimacy of their understanding of inaugurated eschatology, particularly in relation to their application of the "already/not yet" schema. In order to apply the new covenant to both the church and Israel, progressive dispensationalists maintain the church is fulfilling the new covenant promises in a preliminary and partial manner (already) whereas Israel

---

117. Anthony A. Hoekema, *The Bible and the Future* (Grand Rapids: Eerdmans, 1979), 211 (emphasis original).

118. Progressive dispensationalists, however, do not usually consent that Canaan is a type of the new earth nor do they agree that escalation from type to antitype is required.

119. Saucy, *The Case for Progressive Dispensationalism*, 22. It should be noted that Blaising disagrees with Saucy here. Instead, Blaising insists that the promises are primarily fulfilled in the new earth.

120. Ibid., 119 (emphasis added).

will experience them in a full and complete manner (not yet).[121] But such an application seems to misconstrue the meaning or intention of the already not-yet schema. Typically, this schema affirms that the church is experiencing the *already* portion now and that *the same group* will experience the *not-yet* portion later. For example, according to Ephesians 1:13–14, Christians now have been sealed with the Holy Spirit (already) which is a guarantee of their future inheritance (not yet). Progressive dispensationalists, however, insist that the church now receives the initial deposit (already) whereas a different entity (Israel) receives the future consummation (not yet).[122] It seems that they have taken a legitimate theological concept and misapplied it to fit their theological system.

A second strength of progressive dispensationalists is their willingness to see more continuity between the Old Testament people of God and the New Testament people of God. Although Israel and the church are still considered distinct, they recognize some overlap and even see the church as partially fulfilling promises to Israel.

But progressive dispensationalists also insist that Old Testament promises to Israel, especially those regarding the land, must ultimately be fulfilled with the nation of Israel. When questioned as to why the New Testament says so little about the land promise,[123] progressive dispensationalists use the same argument as covenant theologians regarding the continuity of the covenants. That is, they suggest that there is no reason to assume a change unless the New Testament declares it so. Silence assumes continuity (at least regarding Old Testament restoration prophecies regarding Israel). Saucy explains his view: "Why should we think it necessary that the prophecies be reiterated in the New Testament? If they desired to teach their

---

121. See, e.g., Ware, who states that "only the spiritual aspects of new-covenant promise are now inaugurated in this age; the territorial and political aspects, though part of God's new-covenant promise, await future fulfillment. The fulfillment of God's new covenant ... is best seen as partially realized now (spiritual aspects of forgiveness and the indwelling Spirit for all covenant participation) and later to be realized in its completeness (when all Israel is saved and restored to its land)" ("The New Covenant and the People[s] of God," 94–95).

122. It should be noted, however, that some of the future kingdom-blessings impact the nations as well. Yet, some elements are reserved only for Israel (e.g., a specific land and a status as a distinct nation).

123. Though see Acts 1:6; 3:20–21; Rom 11:26.

continued validity, it would seem sufficient for the apostles to simply affirm this fact without repeating all the prophecies. ... [Therefore,] we should consider the prophecies valid unless there is explicit teaching to the contrary."[124] This argument from silence is precisely what dispensationalists charge covenant theologians of doing. That is, covenant theologians insist that because the Abrahamic covenant included blessings to the children of believers, we should expect this feature in the new covenant as well since there is no explicit verse to say otherwise.

Additionally, the progressive dispensationalist interpretation of the "fullness of the Gentiles" in Romans 11:25 is unconvincing. Saucy argues that this phrase cannot be the end of gentile salvation since many gentiles will be saved during the millennium as prophesied in the Old Testament.[125] Thus, he is arguing that this is only a "partial" fulfillment of "fullness." But one must ask if that is the "clear, plain, or normal" meaning of "fullness."

A third strength of progressive dispensationalists is that they offer a more unified understanding of God's kingdom. The strong affirmation of the progressive nature of revelation leads them to see the biblical dispensations not as fragmented, but as building upon one another in a unified plan of redemption. The result is that progressive dispensationalism does not view the church as a parenthesis in God's plan, thereby placing greater emphasis on God's sovereignty. Because older dispensationalism affirmed a strict dichotomy between Israel and the church, those who were part of the church (including Jewish believers) do not enjoy the blessings of the millennium as promised specially to the nation of Israel. But for progressive dispensationalists, Jews converted before the return of Christ do not forfeit their participation in Israel's future millennial blessings but still participate in the earthly kingdom. Earlier dispensationalists excluded Jewish Christians from that future promise since the church was viewed anthropologically as a people group and thus distinct from Israel.

---

124. Saucy, *The Case for Progressive Dispensationalism*, 34–35.

125. Ibid., 259–61.

Blaising comments, "A Jew who becomes a Christian today does not lose his or her relationship to Israel's future promises."[126]

But a weakness here regarding their view of the kingdom can also be highlighted. For example, Saucy's view that Jesus is exalted to the throne, but is not reigning, seems contradictory.[127] Is it exegetically sound to claim that the exalted Jesus, who is now sitting on the throne in heaven, is *not* reigning as the Davidic king? What about Hebrews, which speaks of Christ on his throne (Heb 1:3; 8:1; 12:2), and Ephesians or Colossians, where he has subdued every power (Eph 1:20–22; Col 2:10, 15)? How is the reigning king of the universe not also reigning as the Davidic king?

---

126. Blaising and Bock, *Progressive Dispensationalism*, 50.

127. See, e.g., Saucy, *The Case for Progressive Dispensationalism*, 106. Although Saucy's view is not necessarily normative of progressive dispensationalism, it represents a potential pitfall of that view.

CHAPTER 5
PROGRESSIVE COVENANTALISM

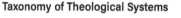

Taxonomy of Theological Systems

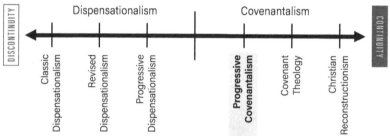

Progressive covenantalism represents the first view on the "continuity" side of the spectrum, as this position affirms more continuity than discontinuity between the Old Testament and New Testament. Those who hold to this position view themselves as being non-dispensational. Because this theological system is somewhat new, this position may be the least familiar to the reader. In their book *Kingdom through Covenant*, Peter Gentry and Stephen Wellum offer a substantial defense of what they label "progressive covenantalism."[1] Wellum explains why they embrace this terminology: "*Progressive* seeks to underscore the unfolding nature of God's revelation over time, while *covenantalism*

---

1. In a footnote they give credit to Richard Lucas for suggesting this term to them, though they later found that it was previously used by Dan Lioy, "Progressive Covenantalism as an Integrating Motif of Scripture," *Conspectus* 1 (2006): 81–107 (Peter J. Gentry and Stephen J. Wellum, *Kingdom through Covenant: A Biblical-Theological Understanding of the Covenants*, 2nd ed. [Wheaton: Crossway, 2018], 35n8). Unless noted otherwise, all references to *Kingdom through Covenant* are to this second edition.

emphasizes that God's plan unfolds *through* the covenants and that *all* of the covenants find their fulfillment, *telos*, and terminus in Christ."[2] They argue for continuity and unity in God's plan, which culminates in the new covenant. In sum, "Progressive covenantalism argues that the Bible presents a *plurality* of covenants that *progressively* reveal our triune God's *one* redemptive plan for his *one* people, which reaches its fulfillment and terminus in Christ and the new covenant."[3]

Progressive covenantalism was officially launched in 2012 with the publication of *Kingdom through Covenant*; a second edition was released in 2018.[4] This view is not content with the way both dispensational and covenant theologies articulate the relationship between the covenants and their ultimate fulfillment in Christ. As a result, Gentry and Wellum view their position as a mediating view, one that learns from others but, in the end, offers an alternative to the two dominant views of dispensationalism and covenant theology.

Although they initially viewed their work as a subset or species of "new covenant theology,"[5] because of significant differences, they prefer to see themselves as a distinct view.[6] As opposed to progressive covenantalists, *some* new covenant theologians: (1) deny a creation

---

2. Stephen J. Wellum, "Introduction," in *Progressive Covenantalism: Charting a Course between Dispensational and Covenant Theologies*, ed. Stephen J. Wellum and Brent E. Parker (Nashville: B&H, 2016), 2 (emphasis original). See also Gentry and Wellum, *Kingdom through Covenant*, 35n8. Wellum further explains that *"progressive* emphasizes the idea that God's redemptive plan did not occur all at once but was gradually disclosed in redemptive history as God entered into covenant relationships with his people and brought his plan to fulfillment in Christ" (ibid., 116n18 [emphasis original]).

3. Gentry and Wellum, *Kingdom through Covenant*, 35 (emphasis original).

4. The new edition sought to address matters that required correction and clarification. Reflecting on this process, Gentry and Wellum write, "But as we learned in writing the first edition, no matter how carefully one states one's position—especially when it centers on key differences between theological systems—it is difficult to hear exactly what the other person is saying" (ibid., 16).

5. "If we were to label our view and to plot it on the map of current evangelical discussion, it would fit broadly under the umbrella of what is called 'new covenant theology'" (Peter J. Gentry and Stephen J. Wellum, *Kingdom through Covenants: A Biblical-Theological Understanding of the Covenants*, 1st ed. [Wheaton: Crossway, 2012], 24). See also Wellum, "Introduction," 2. More recently, Meyer adds, "Progressive covenantalism has affinity with the theological movement that has been called 'new covenant theology'" (Jason C. Meyer, "Mosaic Law, Theological Systems, and the Glory of Christ," in *Progressive Covenantalism*, 73).

6. Wellum laments that some of their critics have labeled and dismissed their view as new covenant theology (Gentry and Wellum, *Kingdom through Covenant*, 34n9).

covenant; (2) deny Christ's active obedience and the imputation of Christ's righteousness; (3) reject the instructive value of the Mosaic law in the life of the church; (4) maintain a distinction between conditional and unconditional covenants; and (5) fail to appreciate the progression of the covenants from creation to new creation. Consequently, in this chapter we will deal primarily with the thought of progressive covenantalism, interacting occasionally with new covenant theology, especially in the footnotes.[7]

Whereas new covenant theology began as a grassroots pastor-led movement beginning in the 1980s, progressive covenantalism began as a scholar-driven movement similar to progressive dispensationalism. In the rest of this chapter, we will discuss progressive covenantalism, primarily using the work of (1) Stephen Wellum, (2) Peter Gentry, and (3) various new covenant theologians. Stephen Wellum received his PhD from Trinity Evangelical Divinity School and is professor of Christian theology at Southern Baptist Theological Seminary in Louisville, Kentucky. He previously taught at the Associated Canadian Theological Schools and Northwest Baptist Theological College and Seminary. Peter Gentry received his PhD from the University of Toronto and is professor of Old Testament interpretation at Southern Baptist Theological Seminary. He previously taught at Toronto Baptist Seminary and Bible College, the University of Toronto, Heritage Theological Seminary, and Tyndale Theological Seminary. The new covenant theologians that I will interact with include John Reisinger, Gary Long, Steve Lehrer, Tom Wells, Fred Zaspel, and A. Blake White.

---

7. New covenant theology can be defined as "God's eternal purpose progressively revealed in the commandments and promises of the biblical covenants of the OT and fulfilled in the New Covenant of Jesus Christ" (Gary D. Long, *New Covenant Theology: Time for a More Accurate Way* [www. CreateSpace.com, 2013], 2). For a history of new covenant theology, see Heather A. Kendall, *One Greater Than Moses: A History of New Covenant Theology* (Orange, CA: Quoir, 2016), 177. Kendall maintains that new covenant theology affirms three major tenets: (1) a Christ-centered biblical storyline, (2) a believers-only church, and (3) the doctrines of grace (i.e., Calvinism) (35, 39).

1. WHAT IS THE BASIC HERMENEUTIC?

Is a Literal or Symbolic Hermeneutic Employed?

The hermeneutical approach of progressive covenantalism cannot be tagged as either "literal" or "symbolic" since it affirms elements of both. In fact, they would argue that such casting of the issue is misguided since progressive covenantalists do not merely choose one or the other but seek to interpret the Bible according to the author's intention, which is conveyed in various literary forms. Thus, it could be said that they affirm a literal hermeneutic in the sense that the Reformers understood it. That is, they interpret the Bible according to the original intention of the author (*sensus literalis*) as opposed to an allegorical interpretation which seeks a deeper, spiritual meaning that was perhaps unknown to the author. And yet, when the literal sense includes symbols and types as part of the feature of divine revelation, they seek to interpret Scripture accordingly. Thus, it is not a question of choosing a literal or symbolic method of interpreting Scripture. Rather, their hermeneutic involves seeking to understand the intention the author, who (sometimes) seeks to convey meaning through the use of metaphors, symbols, figurative language, and types.

Wellum maintains that a proper approach to interpreting Scripture is to "take seriously what Scripture claims to be" and to "interpret Scripture in light of what it actually is as God's unfolding revelation across time."[8] Consequently, because Scripture is God's word, "we expect *an overall unity and coherence* between the Testaments," which means we should interpret the Bible as a unified revelation.[9] Wellum concludes, "given our view of Scripture, we will *not* view the covenants as independent and isolated from each other, but as together, in all of their diversity, unfolding the one plan of God centered in our Lord Jesus Christ."[10] Though a bit hesitant, Wellum also affirms *sensus plenior*. By this term he simply means that the biblical authors, though

---

8. Gentry and Wellum, *Kingdom through Covenant*, 109.

9. Ibid., 110 (emphasis original).

10. Ibid., 110–11 (emphasis original).

inspired by God, did not fully grasp the meaning and implications of what they wrote. He explains:

> As authors who wrote under divine inspiration, what they wrote was God-given, true, and authoritative. However, they might not, and probably did not, understand where the entire revelation was going, given the fact that God had not yet disclosed all of the details of his eternal plan. Thus, as more revelation was given over time and through later authors, we discover more of God's plan and where that plan is going.[11]

Furthermore, Wellum maintains that "the New Testament's interpretation of the Old Testament becomes definitive, since later texts bring with them greater clarity and understanding. In other words, we must carefully allow the New Testament to show us how the Old Testament is brought to fulfilment in Christ."[12] Because revelation was given by God progressively, later revelation helps clarify what God intended in the earlier revelation. He notes, however, that although the New Testament author may expand the implications or applications of Old Testament authors, the "later texts do *not* contravene the integrity of the earlier texts" but develop them in a manner consistent with the original intent of the Old Testament authors.[13]

Progressive covenantalism follows a grammatical-historical-literary method of interpreting Scripture which then seeks to interpret each text in light of its place in the canon of Scripture. Following Richard Lints,[14] Wellum suggests that we should interpret the biblical texts according to three horizons: textual, epochal, and canonical.[15]

---

11. Ibid., 111–12.

12. Ibid., 112. He adds, "The effect of this is not to downplay the authority of the Old Testament prophetic revelation; rather the point is that the previous revelation was incomplete and by its very nature was intended by God to point beyond itself to God's full self-disclosure in his Son" (116).

13. Ibid., 112 (emphasis original).

14. Richard Lints, *The Fabric of Theology: A Prolegomenon to Evangelical Theology* (Grand Rapids: Eerdmans, 1993), 259–311.

15. See Gentry and Wellum, *Kingdom through Covenant*, 118–29.

The *textual horizon* involves understanding a text in its immediate context. It seeks to comprehend God's intent as communicated through the human author by knowing and analyzing the (1) historical setting, (2) rules of language and grammar, (3) syntax, (4) textual variants, and (5) literary features including the literary form/genre and structure. The *epochal horizon* seeks to interpret a text "in light of where they are located in God's unfolded plan" in redemptive history.[16] Thus, later authors build on earlier authors so that we gain greater understanding of the earlier revelation in light of the later. These later authors are not changing the original meaning but are clarifying and expanding the original intent of the earlier author. The *canonical horizon* examines the text in relation to the entire canon. This method of interpretation allows Scripture to interpret itself in light of the progressive nature of revelation which finds its fulfillment in Jesus Christ. Consequently, "As texts are placed along the storyline of Scripture and ultimately interpreted in light of the culmination of God's plan in Christ, we begin to read Scripture in the way God intended and thus 'biblically.'"[17]

Because they affirm progressive revelation, progressive covenantalists read in the Old Testament in light of the New Testament.[18] Yet, such a statement must be carefully nuanced. That is, they insist that they are not simply giving hermeneutical priority to the New Testament and running roughshod over the Old Testament. In fact, Wellum agrees that there is danger in reading new covenant realities

---

16. Ibid., 120.

17. Ibid., 127.

18. As their very name suggests, new covenant theology gives hermeneutical preference to the New Testament. In other words, because the New Testament is God's full and final revelation (Heb 1:1–2), it should be the lens through which the OT is read. In contrast to most dispensationalists (and, at some points, covenant theologians) who give hermeneutical priority to the Old Testament, new covenant theology gives priority to the New Testament. See John G. Reisinger, *Abraham's Four Seeds: A Biblical Examination of the Presuppositions of Covenant Theology and Dispensationalism* (Frederick, MD: New Covenant Media, 1998), 53, 99; idem, *New Covenant Theology and Prophecy* (Frederick, MD: New Covenant Media, 2012), 8, 20, 69; Tom Wells and Fred Zaspel, *New Covenant Theology: Description, Definition, Defense* (Frederick, MD: New Covenant Media, 2002), 1, 7, 33; Tom Wells, *The Priority of Jesus Christ: Why Do Christians Turn to Jesus First?* (Frederick, MD: New Covenant Media, 2005), 71; A. Blake White, *What Is New Covenant Theology? An Introduction* (Frederick, MD: New Covenant Media, 2012), 9; Long, *New Covenant Theology*, 2.

too quickly into the old era which prioritizes the New Testament without first doing justice to the Old Testament.[19] Instead, we must seek to carefully analyze all three horizons mentioned above, giving serious attention to where each text falls within redemptive history, how it relates to its particular covenantal administration, and how it relates to creation and ultimately to Christ. When this is carefully done, "the New Testament does have priority over the Old Testament."[20] Wellum concludes, "The New Testament's interpretation of the Old is definitive in interpreting the details of the Old but *not* in such a way that contravenes the earlier texts."[21]

Thus, progressive covenantalism affirms a literal hermeneutic, seeking to interpret the text according to the intention of the author. But they maintain that such an approach, by itself, is insufficient since we must also follow the progress of revelation and relate each text to its place in redemptive history which culminates in Christ. And, as we will see, for progressive covenantalists, typology plays a key role in properly understanding the theological connection between Old Testament realities and New Testament fulfillments.

What Is the Proper Role of Typology?

Progressive covenantalism carefully differentiates typology from allegory.[22] These are distinct literary features that should not be confused or lumped together as if they are synonymous. According to Wellum, "The major difference is that typology is grounded in *history*, the *text*, and *interbiblical/intertextual development*" where the various types "are intended by God to correspond to teach other, while allegory assumes none of these."[23] Parker helpfully clarifies how progressive covenantalists define typology: "Typology is the study of how Old Testament historical persons, events, institutions, and settings

---

19. Gentry and Wellum, *Kingdom through Covenant*, 144–45.

20. Ibid., 145. He later writes, "Jesus and the new covenant, then, become the hermeneutical lens by which we interpret the fulfillment of the types/patterns of the Old Testament" (658).

21. Ibid., 145.

22. See Brent E. Parker, "Typology and Allegory: Is There a Distinction? A Brief Examination of Figural Reading," *SBJT* 21.1 (2017): 57–83.

23. Gentry and Wellum, *Kingdom through Covenant*, 129 (emphasis original).

function to foreshadow, anticipate, prefigure, and predict the greater realities in the new covenant age."[24] He continues, "Typological patterns are prospective in that God has designed and intended certain Old Testament figures, institutions, settings, and events to serve as advance presentations, which are then transcended and surpassed by the arrival of the New Testament antitype."[25] Typology, then, is a legitimate literary feature that is used by the biblical authors to communicate divine truth whereas an allegorical interpretation is illegitimate since the meaning is not intended by the author and thus not found in the text.

Thus, as Wellum notes, "typology is a feature of divine revelation rooted in *history* and the *text*."[26] Something in one epoch of redemptive history prefigures another reality in another epoch—an organic relationship that can be demonstrated from the text. In addition, "typology is *prophetic* and *predictive* and thus divinely intended."[27] It is prophetic because the type is designed by God to anticipate a future greater reality in a later period in redemptive history. Such types are forward-pointing and culminate first in Christ and then the church. Although typology is not an overt verbal prediction, it is predictive in the sense that types are patterns intended by God which become clear as later authors identify such patterns and clarify how they are fulfilled in Christ.

Wellum also notes three key characteristics of typology.[28] First, typology involves repetition. A person, event, or institution is repeated in a later epoch revealing a divinely intended pattern. Second, typology involves escalation. That is, the antitype is something greater in God's divine plan than the initial type. In fact, "the antitype is *always*

---

24. Brent E. Parker, "The Israel-Christ-Church Relationship," in *Progressive Covenantalism*, 47–48.

25. Ibid., 48. Wellum defines typology as "the study of the Old Testament redemptive-historical realities or 'types' (persons, events, institutions) that God has specifically designed to correspond to, and predictively prefigure, their intensified antitypical fulfilment aspects (inaugurated, appropriated, and consummated) in New Testament redemptive history" (Gentry and Wellum, *Kingdom through Covenant*, 130).

26. Gentry and Wellum, *Kingdom through Covenant*, 130 (emphasis original).

27. Ibid., 131 (emphasis original).

28. Ibid., 133–37. See also Parker, "The Israel-Christ-Church Relationship," 48–52.

greater than the previous types."[29] The full escalation thus occurs with Christ's coming. Consequently, typology includes an eschatological escalation or heightening with the arrival of the New Testament antitype. With the coming of the antitype, the text must dictate whether the type is completely fulfilled in Christ's first advent ("already"; e.g., the Old Testament sacrificial system) or whether an additional final fulfillment still awaits his second advent and the new creation ("not yet"; e.g., the temple). Third, typology develops through the covenants. Key types are linked with the various biblical covenants. Thus, types develop along with the biblical covenants and will have textual indicators that the Old Testament person, event, or institution functions as a type. It should also be noted that a typological relationship does not include every aspect of a person, event, or institution, but usually focuses on one or a few key elements (e.g., David as a type of Christ).[30]

The clearer or more explicit types in the Old Testament include Adam, Melchizedek, David, the exodus, and the Passover. But the study of typology should not be limited to those only explicitly referenced in the Bible. Other types include the nation of Israel, the promised land, the seed theme, circumcision, and the Sabbath.[31] The most common (and most important) types are fulfilled in Jesus.

For progressive covenantalism, typology is not merely something that is permitted. Rather, typology is a feature of divine revelation that is intended by the biblical authors and is interpreted therefore according to *sensus literalis*. Typology is also seen fundamental to understanding the storyline of the Bible and how the Old Testament

---

29. Gentry and Wellum, *Kingdom through Covenant*, 134 (emphasis original).

30. Parker, "The Israel-Christ-Church Relationship," 52.

31. For defenses of the typological function of these themes, see the following: (1) the nation of Israel as a type (Parker, "The Israel-Christ-Church Relationship," 39–68); (2) the land as a type (Oren R. Martin, "The Land Promise Biblically and Theologically Understood," in *Progressive Covenantalism*, 255–74); (3) the seed as a type (Jason S. DeRouchie, "Father of a Multitude of Nations: New Covenant Ecclesiology in OT Perspective," in *Progressive Covenantalism*, 7–38); (4) circumcision as a type (John D. Meade, "Circumcision of Flesh to Circumcision of Heart: The Typology of the Sign of the Abrahamic Covenant," in *Progressive Covenantalism*, 127–58); and (5) the Sabbath as a type (Thomas R. Schreiner, "Good-bye and Hello: The Sabbath Command for New Covenant Believers," in *Progressive Covenantalism*, 159–88).

and New Testament relate to each other. Indeed, understanding how Jesus is the typological fulfillment of the Old Testament is a central component to understanding the overarching message of the Bible.[32]

How Are Old Testament Restoration Prophecies Fulfilled?

Progressive covenantalism interprets restoration prophecies given to the nation of Israel as being fulfilled in Christ, the true Israelite. In Acts 15:16–18, James quotes Amos 9:11–12: "After this I will return, and I will rebuild the tent of David that has fallen; I will rebuild its ruins, and I will restore it, that the remnant of mankind may seek the Lord, and all the Gentiles who are called by my name, says the Lord, who makes these things known from of old." Because James applies this text to the ingathering of God's elect, both Jews *and* gentiles, progressive covenantalists affirm that believing gentiles are equally part of God's people as believing Jews. The rebuilding of the tent of David is fulfilled in the ingathering of the gentiles into the church.[33] Wellum comments, "James appeals to the words of the Prophets to warrant the fact that God in his plan has always intended to form *one* people that would include believing Jews and Gentiles."[34] Thus, James offers a Spirit-inspired interpretation of the Old Testament indicating that in the Messiah, the house of David is being rebuilt—a house that includes both Jews and gentiles. What James is saying is that what Amos predicted has now come to pass.

In the following verses in the Amos 9 passage, the promised restoration includes the land of Israel: "'I will restore the fortunes of my people Israel, and they shall rebuild the ruined cities and inhabit them; they shall plant vineyards and drink their wine, and they shall make gardens and eat their fruit. I will plant them on their land, and they shall never again be uprooted out of the land that I have given them,' says the LORD your God" (Amos 9:14–15). But since the land functions typologically, the fulfillment should not be taken literally.

---

32. Parker states, "Progressive covenantalism argues that the biblical covenants and typological structures converge and climax in Christ with entailments for the eschatological people of God—the church" ("The Israel-Christ-Church Relationship," 44).

33. See White, *What Is New Covenant Theology?*, 17–18.

34. Gentry and Wellum, *Kingdom through Covenant*, 763 (emphasis original).

Indeed, Abraham realized that, although he was living in the promised land, the land did not represent the full or final promise but was only a pledge of something greater: "By faith he went to live in the land of promise, as in a foreign land, living in tents with Isaac and Jacob, heirs with him of the same promise. For he was looking forward to the city that has foundations, whose designer and builder is God" (Heb 11:9–10).[35]

By appealing to Amos 9:11–12, James indicates that the fulfillment of God's promise to bless his people and restore their land is being fulfilled in Christ and the new covenant. Specifically, the restoration of David's house is occurring in Christ and his new covenant people. "Yet what Amos anticipates, and James says has now occurred in the church, is that the Messiah's people will include believing Jews and Gentiles together as inheritors of the Davidic kingdom."[36] God has united Jews and gentiles who believe in the Davidic king together in the new covenant.

Progressive covenantalism affirms the overall unity of the Bible. It maintains that God's revelation in Scripture is progressive in nature and it develops according to the biblical covenants. Furthermore, following the author's intent, it recognizes typological patterns in Scripture which are fulfilled in Jesus Christ. As such, prophecies to the nation of Israel should not be interpreted in a literalistic manner but should be understood as fulfilled in Christ, though the full consummation of some prophecies await the new heavens and new earth.

---

35. Reisinger concludes, "Abraham obviously realized, while his feet were actually standing in the promised land itself, that the land was not the full or real promise, but only a pledge of something greater" (*Abraham's Four Seeds*, 93).

36. Gentry and Wellum, *Kingdom through Covenant*, 763.

2. WHAT IS THE RELATIONSHIP BETWEEN THE COVENANTS?

The importance of the relationship between the covenants is evidenced by the label "progressive covenantalism" as well as the title of Gentry and Wellum's book, *Kingdom through Covenant.*[37] Progressive covenantalism affirms six biblical covenants: Adamic, Noahic, Abrahamic, Mosaic, Davidic, and the new covenant.[38] As Wellum points out, "The *progression* of the covenants is the primary means by which God's plan is unveiled, and God's promises *and* intended typological patterns are given, developed, and fulfilled in Christ and his people. Given this fact, it is best to view *all* covenants as interrelated and mutually dependent."[39] He also states that "the biblical covenants form the backbone of the Bible's metanarrative, and apart from understanding each covenant in its immediate context *and* then in relation to its fulfillment in Christ, we will potentially misunderstand the Bible's overall message and misapply Scripture to our lives."[40] This view embraces neither radical discontinuity nor radical continuity, but sees the progression in God's purpose through the covenants, culminating in the new covenant which is fulfilled in Jesus Christ.[41]

---

37. The abbreviated version of this book is entitled *God's Kingdom through God's Covenants: A Concise Biblical Theology* (Wheaton: Crossway, 2015).

38. See, e.g., Gentry and Wellum, *Kingdom through Covenant*, 674.

39. Ibid., 656 (emphasis original).

40. Ibid., 32n2 (emphasis original).

41. The label "new covenant theology" emphasizes the distinctive nature of the new covenant in contrast to the old (Mosaic) covenant. This view acknowledges two distinct covenants: a legal covenant at Sinai and a gracious new covenant that replaces it. The Mosaic covenant (or the covenant at Sinai) is a covenant made with the nation of Israel and has no direct bearing on the church today. And yet, God has one distinct and unchanging purpose which he is working out according to the election of grace. Reisinger contrasts new covenant theology with dispensationalism and covenant theology: "Dispensationalism cuts the Bible in half and never the twain shall meet. Covenant Theology does the exact opposite and merges two distinctly different covenants (the Old and the New) into one covenant with two administrations. Dispensationalism cannot get the OT into the NT in any sense, and Covenant Theology does not even have a really *New* Covenant. They have a *newer* and *older* version of the same covenant. Dispensationalism cannot get the two *together*, and Covenant Theology cannot get them *apart!*" (*Abraham's Four Seeds*, 47 [emphasis original]).

Progressive covenantalism affirms the covenant with creation (i.e., the Adamic covenant).[42] Wellum offers the following reasons as to why progressive covenantalism insists on a covenant with creation:[43] First, the absence of the word "covenant" in Genesis 1–2 does not necessitate that there is no covenant. Second, the context of Genesis 1–2 reveals "all the elements of a lord-vassal agreement are in the context, including conditions of obedience with sanctions for obedience."[44] Thus, Adam functioned as a representative of the human race (cf. Rom 5:12–21; 1 Cor 15:20–21). Third, the main storyline of Scripture is centered on two individuals: Adam and Christ. Just as Christ is head of the new covenant, so also Adam is head of the original covenant that God made with mankind. Finally, various typological patterns are established in God's covenant with creation that are foundational to subsequent covenants. Thus, the covenants start at creation with Adam and then culminate in Christ and the new covenant.

In the biblical storyline, then, the covenant with Adam is key, serving as the foundation of all other covenants. "*All* subsequent covenant heads function as the subsets of Adam, who, in God's plan points forward to Christ, the last Adam, who by his obedience ushers in a new covenant."[45] Adam's pre-fall situation was temporary, which the tree of life implies. If Adam would have been fully obedient to God, he would have been granted eternal life. Wellum concludes, "as we move through the covenants, the only way back to the presence of God is through God's provision, which eventually is seen through the covenants and through the provision of the tabernacle, the temple, and ultimately the one who is the fulfillment of the temple, our Lord Jesus Christ."[46] Progressive covenantalism sees this is a major distinction between them and various forms of dispensationalism, which all focus

---

42. Some new covenant theologians oppose labeling something a "covenant" that is not labeled as such in Scripture. Consequently, they reject the covenant with creation. But see Long, *New Covenant Theology*, 9–19, for an example of a new covenant theologian who accepts the covenant with creation.

43. Gentry and Wellum, *Kingdom through Covenant*, 666–85 (see also 211–58 for an exegetical defense).

44. Ibid., 667.

45. Ibid., 672 (emphasis original).

46. Ibid., 679.

on the Abrahamic covenant as the foundation for the other biblical covenants. But in doing so, dispensationalists fail to fully appreciate the bigger picture of God's plan to redeem humanity from the beginning.

Are the Covenants Conditional or Unconditional?

In contrast to dispensational and covenant theologies, progressive covenantalism rejects the notion that some covenants (e.g., Abrahamic, Davidic, and new) are unconditional (or royal grant) covenants whereas the Mosaic covenant is a conditional (suzerain-vassal) covenant.[47] Instead, this position claims that every covenant has conditions:[48] "The covenants consist of unconditional (unilateral) and conditional (bilateral) elements blended together. In fact, it is precisely due to this blend that there is a deliberate *tension* within the covenants—a tension which is heightened as the Bible's storyline unfolds through the progression of the covenants and is only resolved in Christ."[49] Thus, all biblical covenants are both unconditional (since they are guaranteed by the power and grace of God) and conditional (since they demand an obedient partner).[50] The conditional component is even true of the new covenant since obedience was demanded of Christ, the mediator of the covenant, who perfectly obeyed the conditions of the covenant in both his life and death.

---

47. Wellum argues that dividing up the biblical covenants into categories of conditional and unconditional is "incorrect," "inadequate," "problematic," and "reductionistic" (ibid., 149, 662, 663).

48. Caneday comments, "The difference between old and new covenants is not that the former is conditional and the latter is not. Rather, because the old was purposefully temporary in anticipation of its fulfillment and completion in the new covenant, it stipulated obedience that featured earthly shadows of God's heavenly kingdom" (Ardel B. Caneday, "Covenantal Life with God from Eden to the Holy City," in *Progressive Covenantalism*, 103).

49. Gentry and Wellum, *Kingdom through Covenant*, 663–64 (emphasis original; see also 149, 662–66).

50. Although the covenants reveal the gracious God who makes and keeps his promises, "*all* the biblical covenants also demand an obedient, human covenant partner" (Gentry and Wellum, *Kingdom through Covenant*, 664 [emphasis original]). New covenant theologians typically affirm the unconditional nature of the new covenant and the conditional nature of the Mosaic covenant. Reisinger notes, "The New Covenant that established the church as the Body of Christ *guarantees* that every covenant obligation will be met in the Surety. ... The nation of Israel was never promised such guarantees under the Old Covenant simply because it was a legal covenant based on works" (*Abraham's Four Seeds*, 29 [emphasis original]).

Because the Abrahamic covenant is often viewed as being unconditional, many have drawn unbiblical conclusions. For example, dispensationalists infer that because the covenant with Abraham is
unconditional and eternal, the land promise given to the nation of
Israel is still unfulfilled. Similarly, covenant theologians infer that the
promise to Abraham's seed (offspring) relates to the (covenant) children of believers who have a special status in the covenant. Reisinger
writes, "It is rather amazing … to hear a dispensationalist plead the
unconditional covenant made with Abraham and his seed as the foundation of his belief in a separate and future purpose for the nation
of Israel, and then hear a Paedobaptist plead the *very same unconditional covenant made with Abraham and his seed* as the foundation for
his infant baptism."[51]

How Were Old Testament Saints Saved?

Progressive covenantalism teaches that Old Testament saints were
saved by grace through faith in the promises of God in Christ.
Although the church as the body of Christ is not found in the Old
Testament but was birthed after the giving of the Spirit at Pentecost,
"in no sense whatsoever does this mean that the believer living prior
to Christ's coming was not just as saved and secure as we are, or that
he was not saved in exactly the same way that we are today."[52] Against
most dispensationalists, however, they maintain that there is only one
people of God. The difference with people under the covenants of the
Old Testament is that they had inferior knowledge and understanding
of how the Messiah would fulfill God's promises. Wellum explains:
"under the Old Testament covenants, God's people were saved by grace
through faith in the promises of God, and the same is true under
the new covenant, yet now there is greater knowledge and clarity
regarding how God's promises reach their terminus and fulfillment

---

51. Reisinger, *Abraham's Four Seeds*, 5 (emphasis original; see also 94, 99–100).

52. Ibid., 111. Steve Lehrer states, "Acceptance comes from trusting in the promises of God
and having God apply the work of Christ on the cross to the individual. So Abraham, David,
and all Old Testament saints were saved by grace through faith, in just the same way believers
living in the New Covenant era are saved" (*New Covenant Theology*, 207).

in Christ."[53] Now that the Old Testament promises have given way to New Testament fulfillment, it is not possible for one to know God in a saving way without having faith in Christ.

Nevertheless, the Old Testament believer's personal experience will be different since such experience cannot exceed the revelation or covenant under which he lived. Thus, although the new covenant includes the promise of inward transformation (new hearts, law written on hearts, the Holy Spirit), this does not mean that "old covenant believers did not experience regeneration or that the Spirit of God was inactive during that time in terms of his inward transforming work."[54]

Against covenant theologians, progressive covenantalists stress that Old Testament Israel and the New Testament church are not the same type of community. Although there is only one people of God and therefore continuity between the Old Testament and New Testament, there is also some distinction. That is, unlike Israel, the church is not a mixed community of believers and unbelievers but consists of only regenerate people. Within Israel, there was an elect remnant who had saving faith. Although all of Israel was God's people in a covenantal sense, not all of them were regenerate, being united to Christ. Thus, regeneration, justification, and union with Christ are not different in the New Testament, only the fact that now *all* members of the covenant community are truly redeemed.

How Is the Old Testament Law to Be Applied Today?

Although they have been accused of being antinomian, progressive covenantalists ardently reject such a claim. Unlike covenant theologians who divide the Old Testament law into three parts and then claim the moral law is applicable today, progressive covenantalists have a different approach. Wellum, for example, offers several truths that must be taken into account when applying Old Testament law.[55]

---

53. Gentry and Wellum, *Kingdom through Covenant*, 748.

54. Fred Zaspel, *The New Covenant and New Covenant Theology* (Frederick, MD: New Covenant Media, 2008), 14.

55. See Gentry and Wellum, *Kingdom through Covenant*, 782–98; Stephen J. Wellum, "Progressive Covenantalism and the Doing of Ethics," in *Progressive Covenantalism*, 215–33.

First, all Scripture is authoritative and thus provides the norm for Christian ethics. As Paul states in 2 Timothy 3:16, all Scripture (including the Old Testament) is God's breathed-out word which is the authoritative standard for Christians. Thus, "although Christians are not 'under the law' *as a covenant,* it still functions *as Scripture* and demands our complete obedience."[56] All Scripture is given for our ethical instruction even if it does not all apply to us in exactly the same way.

Second, the tripartite division of the law is not the means of determining what is morally binding on Christians.[57] Many theologians divide the law into three different types (civil, ceremonial, and moral) and then claim that the civil and ceremonial laws are abrogated since they are fulfilled in Christ, but that the moral (or ethical) law must still be kept since it reflects God's character. Wellum rejects such an approach for three reasons.[58] First, Old Testament law should be viewed as a covenantal package. All the laws under the old covenant form a unit and cannot be separated from the covenant under which they were given. Because Scripture does not appeal to a tripartite distinction of the law as the means of determining which laws are applicable today, neither should we. This does not mean some distinction between laws can be made but that "Scripture views the law-covenant as a covenant package that serves a specific role in God's plan for the life of Israel, and as an entire covenant, it is brought to fulfillment in Christ and the new covenant."[59] Unlike covenant theologians who maintain that

---

56. Gentry and Wellum, *Kingdom through Covenant,* 784 (emphasis original).

57. See ibid., 697, 783, 785–88.

58. Jason Meyer also offers four reasons why such a division of the law is unhelpful: "First, the NT does not explicitly establish a tripartite division" of the Old Testament law. Second, the division is artificial since laws cannot easily be divided into such categories. For example, all Old Testament law can be considered moral since it would have been morally wrong for an Israelite to disobey any of the old covenant commands. Third, "even the Ten Commandments are not automatically binding because many see the Sabbath command as abrogated under the new covenant." Fourth, relegating non-binding laws (e.g., civil or ceremonial) "can inadvertently cause us to turn a deaf ear to the wise guidance certain commands give us today." That is, although certain laws are not binding on believers, they can still function as Scripture. The entire Bible is still completely authoritative as revelation, though we are dependent on the New Testament as to how to now apply past revelation ("The Mosaic Law, Theological Systems, and the Glory of Christ," 88).

59. Gentry and Wellum, *Kingdom through Covenant,* 785.

unless the New Testament explicitly changes or repeals the Mosaic law, it is still applicable today, progressive covenantalists view the entire old covenant as a package that is fulfilled in Christ. Second, the law-covenant was temporary and pointed toward fulfillment in Christ. We must always apply the law through the lens of the new covenant. Thus, Christians are no longer under the covenant with Israel *as a covenant*.[60] The Mosaic law, as part of the Mosaic covenant, is no longer directly binding on the Christian. Third, the New Testament teaches that believers are no longer "under the law." Because the New Testament affirms that Christians are no longer under the law as a covenant, it has no "direct authority" for them.

Third, in order to determine what is morally binding on Christians today, we must appeal to the entirety of Scripture viewed through the new covenant. All of the Bible still functions as Scripture for the Christian. Even the book of Leviticus still applies to believers—not directly but in light of Christ and his sacrifice. Thus, "all Scripture's moral teaching is binding on us only in light of its fulfillment in Christ."[61] Although the Ten Commandments represent God's moral law, we cannot simply go to the Old Testament and directly apply such laws as if that is all there is to say about moral law. Often, the way Old Testament laws apply to us is in an even greater way in light of their fulfillment in Christ. According the progressive covenantalism, the law of Christ is all of Scripture but now seen in light of its fulfillment in Christ and the new covenant.[62]

---

60. See ibid., 694, 696–97. White argues that "one cannot pull the Ten Commandments out of the covenant and make them eternal moral law, transcending the covenant in which they were given" (*What Is New Covenant Theology?*, 29).

61. Gentry and Wellum, *Kingdom through Covenant*, 789 (emphasis original).

62. New covenant theologians claim that Christians are bound to follow the laws of Christ which consist of: (1) Jesus' own moral character which is the brightest and best exposition of the character of God; (2) Jesus' implicit demands laid out in his ideal descriptions of Christian character; (3) Jesus' explicit demands clearly set out as law for Christians to follow; (4) the demands laid out for Christians by the apostles and writers of the New Testament; (5) the summary demands of Christ and his apostles for love of God and neighbor; (6) acts of judgment we must make in light of those summary demands; and (7) acts of judgment we must make on situations analogous to things he demands or forbids (Wells, *The Priority of Jesus Christ*, 138). White comments, "The law of Christ can be defined as those prescriptive principles drawn from the example and teaching of Jesus and his apostles (the central demand being love), which are meant to be worked out in specific situations by the guiding influence and empowerment of the Holy Spirit" (*What Is New Covenant Theology?*, 38).

In the Sermon on the Mount (esp. Matt 5:21–48), Jesus demonstrates that he fulfills the old covenant. He fulfills Old Testament law and the prophecies since they point to him and he alone brings them to their intended end. But Jesus' teaching in the Sermon on the Mount also fulfills Old Testament law. "If this is so, it is important to see that in his *teaching*, Jesus *fulfills* the law not simply by extending, annulling, or merely intensifying it" but by showing that the Old Testament law actually pointed to him.[63] Thus, Jesus is the authoritative interpreter of the Old Testament and the one who alone gives the Old Testament its validity and significance for today.

In opposition to covenant theology, Wellum argues, "even if the new covenant does not explicitly forbid [a sin such as] bestiality, this does not entail that the Mosaic law is still in force unless the New Testament explicitly modifies/abrogates it."[64] And in opposition to dispensationalism and new covenant theology, he contends that it is wrong to teach "that we are only bound to that which is clearly repeated in the New Testament."[65] Instead, we must consider a "whole Bible" reading of Scripture that moves across the covenants beginning with creation and ending with the new creation, and all done in view of how Christ is the fulfillment of the new covenant. Additionally, the Bible's own structure of creation, fall, and redemption become important for developing ethics. Many of the commands and prohibitions in Scripture are based on creation and creation order. Therefore, it is necessary to first ground our ethics in creation.

Fourth, by way of example, the Sabbath command is applied differently under the new covenant. Are Christians required to obey the Sabbath law? No, if by that it means simply applying the law today as if one still lived under the Mosaic covenant. As Christians under the new covenant, such laws do not *directly* apply. And yet, this command is still applicable to believers as Scripture. It must, however, be filtered through the fact that Christ is the fulfillment of the law. Because the Sabbath command was a sign of the Sinai covenant and because

---

63. Gentry and Wellum, *Kingdom through Covenant*, 791 (emphasis original).

64. Ibid., 793.

65. Ibid.

believers are not under that covenant, they are no longer obligated to keep that command. Instead, that command was a type that looked forward to the eschatological Sabbath rest which believers possess in Christ now and will fully enjoy in the heavenly city.[66]

Schreiner offers three reasons how Sabbath observance can be one of the Ten Commandments and still not be normative for a Christian today.[67] First, the Decalogue includes the covenant stipulations for the Sinai covenant for the nation of Israel (of which the Sabbath was a sign of the covenant). Christians are not under the Sinai covenant since the new covenant has been inaugurated by the coming of the Messiah. Second, the other nine commandments are still applicable to Christians, not because they are part of the Decalogue but because they are part of the law of Christ. Third, elsewhere in the Old Testament we find laws that are applicable today (since they are cited in the New Testament as authoritative) in the same context as laws that are no longer applicable (e.g., Lev 19:18–19).

Thus, the Sabbath is no longer applicable since it typologically pointed to the rest that believers have in Christ.[68] It simply will not do to divide the law into three parts (moral, civil, and ceremonial), lift the Ten Commandments out of that context, and then apply them to us without asking how they function in the old covenant. Furthermore, it is not simply a matter of rejecting the certain Old Testament laws because we are no longer under the old covenant. Rather, we are to obey the Sabbath, *but we do so in light of Christ*. That is, the Sabbath was not only tied to God's rest in creation, but it also pointed forward to recovering the covenantal rest lost in Genesis 3—a rest that is brought to fulfillment in Christ.

---

66. Schreiner, "Good-bye and Hello," 160.

67. Ibid., 170. See also D. A. Carson, ed., *From Sabbath to Lord's Day: A Biblical, Historical, and Theological Investigation* (Grand Rapids: Zondervan, 1982).

68. Wells and Zaspel, *New Covenant Theology*, 236; Long, *New Covenant Theology*, 7, 135.

3. WHAT IS THE RELATIONSHIP BETWEEN ISRAEL AND THE CHURCH?

For progressive covenantalists, Israel and the church are related but not wholly the same. Israel was the people of God in the sense that God chose them and made a covenant with them. Nevertheless, Israel was a nation that included regenerate and unregenerate people. It was a mixed congregation of believers and unbelievers alike. The church, as the body of Christ, however, consists of only regenerate members and is not a mixed congregation. As Parker maintains, "The church is a new redemptive-historical reality—the heavenly, eschatological, Spirit-empowered, new covenant community, which is the new creation (2 Cor 5:17; Gal 6:15) and new humanity in Christ (Eph 2:15)."[69] Wellum similarly writes, "The church is something *new* in God's plan, not ontologically (against dispensationalism) but redemptive-historically. God's plan of salvation has now reached its fulfillment in Christ. ... The church is *not* simply an extension of Israel. It is related to Israel and the covenants of promise, but it is a *new* humanity, part of the new creation."[70]

And yet, both Israel and the church represent the one people of God.[71] That is, there is both unity and diversity in the relationship between Israel and the church. The diversity relates to their places in redemptive history and accompanying covenants. In this sense, then, the church is new. The unity relates to the fact that both represent

---

69. Parker, "The Israel-Christ-Church Relationship," 45–46. Reisinger remarks, "The Church, as the Body of Christ, became the *true holy nation* of God on the day of Pentecost" (*Abraham's Four Seeds*, 116 [emphasis original]). Commenting on Matthew 16:18 ("I will build my church ..."), Wells reasons that the use of the future tense ("I will") suggests that the church was still a future reality when Jesus originally made that statement (Wells and Zaspel, *New Covenant Theology*, 51). He continues, "The church of Jesus Christ was a product of the age of the New Covenant" (52). See also Long, *New Covenant Theology*, 8, 155.

70. Gentry and Wellum, *Kingdom through Covenant*, 757, 760 (emphasis original). Later Wellum adds, "The church is *new* in a redemptive-historical sense precisely because she is the community of the *new* covenant and thus *different* from Israel in her structure and nature" (801 [emphasis original]).

71. Wellum states, "there is only *one* people of God (elect) across time" (ibid., 748 [emphasis original]). Similarly, Long asserts, "NCT sees only one redemptive purpose for the one people of God, which is represented in the good olive tree (Rom. 11)" (*New Covenant Theology*, 8).

the people of God who are saved by grace through the atoning work of Christ, the Messiah.

Does the Church Replace or Fulfill Israel, or Are the Two Distinct?

Progressive covenantalists believe that the church neither replaces Israel nor is to be equated with Israel. Rather, Christ is the typological fulfillment of Israel, and the church, by means of her union with Christ, is the recipient of all the promises given to Israel.

First, Christ is the typological fulfillment of Israel. That is, the nation of Israel was a type that is eschatologically fulfilled in the person and work of Jesus the Messiah.[72] Throughout the Gospels, Jesus is portrayed as the "true Israel" who accomplished what Israel was called to do but consistently failed. Parker explains:

> The NT presents Jesus as the fulfillment of Israel and all the OT covenant mediators, for he ushers in the promises to Israel (restoration and return from exile, the land, etc.), embodies their identity, and completes Israel's role, calling, and vocation. All the institutions (the sacrificial system, tabernacle, temple, Sabbath, feasts, the law), identity markers (e.g., circumcision), office (prophet, priest, king), and key events (e.g., the exodus) of Israel find their culmination in the life, death, resurrection, and ascension of Christ. ... Jesus is the "true Israel" in that he typologically fulfills all that the nation of Israel anticipated and hoped for; Jesus is the one who brings to completion the covenants, inaugurates the kingdom, and establishes the prophesied new covenant with his blood.[73]

---

72. Wellum writes, "Israel functions as a type that is fulfilled in Christ, the true Israel and King" (Gentry and Wellum, *Kingdom through Covenant*, 142). He continues, "Our view is that Christ is the last Adam, true Israel, and Davidic king who, in himself, fulfills Israel's role and who reconstitutes a people composed of believing Jews and Gentiles into a new humanity, the church. In Christ, *all* God's promises are fulfilled and applied to the church, including the land promise" (142n92 [emphasis added]).

73. Parker, "The Israel-Christ-Church Relationship," 44–45.

Second, Israel and the church are related indirectly. In other words, the church does not *replace* Israel because the church does not *directly* fulfill the promises given to Israel.[74] Instead, all such promises are fulfilled in Christ.[75] Jesus is the direct fulfillment of the promises to Israel, and the church has access to these promises because of its union with Christ. "The church, then, is *not* directly the 'new Israel' or her replacement. Rather, in Christ, the church is God's new creation, composed of believing Jews and Gentiles, because Jesus is the last Adam and true Israel, the great Davidic king, who inherits *all* God's promises by his person and work."[76] Thus, Israel is directly related to Christ and not the church. The church is only secondarily related to Israel through its relationship with Christ. The church does not displace Israel, but is the restored new covenant community which is anticipated in the Old Testament.[77]

Third, it is through its union with Christ that the church has access to the Old Testament promises given to Israel. There is a real sense that the new covenant is made with Israel ("I will establish a new covenant with the house of Israel and with the house of Judah," Heb 8:8) since it is fulfilled first and foremost in Jesus. Gentiles now have access to the promises given to Abraham because Christ, the physical seed of Abraham, has fulfilled the Old Testament promises, ushered in the kingdom of God, and inaugurated a new covenant through his blood.[78]

---

74. Because "replacement" is a loaded word, Wellum makes the following plea: "This is an unhelpful way of describing nondispensational views since covenant theology and our view of progressive covenantalism do *not* affirm such a view. Our recommendation is that such pejorative language be dropped from our polemics since it simply clouds the real debate" (Gentry and Wellum, *Kingdom through Covenant*, 56n18 [emphasis original]).

75. As Wellum notes, "In Christ Jesus, the church is God's new creation, composed of believing Jews and Gentiles, *because Jesus* is the last Adam and the true Israel, the faithful seed of Abraham who inherits the promises by his work. Thus, in union with Christ, the church is God's *new* covenant people, in continuity with the elect in all ages but *different* from Israel in its nature and structure" (Gentry and Wellum, *Kingdom through Covenant*, 36 [emphasis original]).

76. Ibid., 150 (see also 801). Parker likewise comments, "Progressive covenantalism understands the Israel-church relationship as *indirect*—the church is the fulfillment of Israel *only* in Christ, the true Israel" ("The Israel-Christ-Church Relationship," 63).

77. Reisinger declares, "God did not cast off a physical *nation* and then replace it with a physical *church*. He fulfilled the true promise to Abraham by creating a *spiritual **regenerate** nation*, the Body of Christ" (*Abraham's Four Seeds*, 97n32 [emphasis original]).

78. White summarizes his view: "New Covenant Theology does not teach that the church replaces Israel but that the church is the *fulfillment* of Israel by virtue of its union with the

The church is the true people of God because Christ perfectly kept the covenant and earned the blessings given to her. According to the analogy that Paul uses in Romans 11,[79] believing gentiles are grafted into the same tree as believing Israel and form the one people of God.

How Are Romans 11:26 and Galatians 6:16 Interpreted?

There is no unified interpretation in progressive covenantalism regarding Romans 11:26. That is, when Paul declares "And in this way all Israel will be saved," the salvation of all Israel can refer to (1) the church, (2) the elect among ethnic Israel throughout history, or (3) a future mass conversion of ethnic Israel.[80] In a chapter devoted to Romans 11, Richard Lucas maintains that many (though not all) progressive covenantalists affirm a future salvation of ethnic Israel.[81] He also notes, however, that they all reject the idea that the restoration of Israel includes physical features such as the land and the temple.[82] Lucas claims that dispensationalists wrongly apply inaugurated-consummated eschatology when they claim that the spiritual blessings of the new covenant have been inaugurated now whereas the material blessings (land and temple) will be consummated in the future (millennium). In order to affirm their approach, however, dispensationalists must reject the land promise as typological of the new creation. Instead, Lucas argues that it is better to affirm that both blessings are

---

Jewish Messiah. ... It is not that Israel equals the church, as Covenant Theology teaches, but that Jesus is the climax and fulfillment of Israel and the church is the end-time Israel *because it is united to Jesus Christ, her covenant head.* ... The church is the eschatological Israel by virtue of her union with Israel's Messiah" (*What Is New Covenant Theology?*, 45, 49 [emphasis original]).

79. Gentry argues that the olive tree in Romans 11, consisting of both Jews and gentiles, signifies that "the new humanity and restored Israel is based on faith and covenant relationship to the Lord rather than on ethnicity" (Gentry and Wellum, *Kingdom through Covenant*, 546).

80. Zaspel contends that Romans 11:26 provides the grounds for the future redemption of Israel (*The New Covenant and New Covenant Theology*, 11, 23). Similarly, Reisinger acknowledges, "Romans 11 convinces me there will be many Jews saved in the future, but they will be part of the church" (*Abraham's Four Seeds*, 44). In contrast, White leans away from this position when he admits, "I read the chapter differently" (*What Is New Covenant Theology?*, 59n20).

81. Richard J. Lucas, "The Dispensational Appeal to Romans 11 and the Nature of Israel's Future Salvation," in *Progressive Covenantalism*, 235–53.

82. According to Reisinger, "we must realize that there is not a single repetition, or mention, of the land promise in any passage in the NT Scriptures including Romans 11 and the entire book of Revelation" (*Abraham's Four Seeds*, 92). Gentry asserts, "There is no separate future for physical Israel outside of the church" (Gentry and Wellum, *Kingdom through Covenant*, 546).

here now but not yet fully realized. He writes, "Nothing in these verses proves the anticipation of a future restoration of Israel as a distinct fulfillment of the new covenant apart from the Gentiles or as a separate stage (subsequent to the church age) of new covenant fulfillment."[83] He later concludes, "Romans 11 does not provide support for dispensationalism's distinctive teachings concerning a restored national Israel mediating blessings to Gentile nations in the millennial kingdom."[84]

How is Galatians 6:16 understood by progressive covenantalists? Or, more pointedly, when Paul addresses the Galatians believers as "the Israel of God," is Paul using the term non-literally so that it includes gentiles? Whereas dispensationalists answer that question with a resounding "no" (in order to maintain a distinction between Israel and the church), progressive covenantalists answer that question with a qualified "yes."[85] Consequently, this verse demonstrates the close theological connection between Israel and the church, a connection that comes via the church's relationship with Jesus. "Through Jesus, the last Adam and true Israel, the church may be viewed as the 'Israel of God' (Gal. 6:16)."[86] That is, in relationship to Christ, the church becomes the "Israel of God." Yet, there are significant redemptive-historical differences between ethnic Israel and the church as the "Israel of God." Namely, "The church is covenantally *new* and constituted as a believing, regenerate people and not a mixed community."[87]

---

83. Lucas, "The Dispensational Appeal to Romans 11," 242.

84. Ibid., 252. Wellum likewise contends that "there is no warrant from [Romans 11:26] to think that national Israel will receive an outstanding promise in the millennium or consummated state *distinct* or *different* from believing Gentiles. Nothing in Romans 9–11 speaks of the 'restoration' of Israel as a nation in her land with a specific identity and role of service to the nations apart from believing Jews and alongside believing Gentles" (Gentry and Wellum, *Kingdom through Covenant*, 765 [emphasis original]; see also 805–6).

85. Explaining the relationship between Israel and the church, Reisinger states, "The nation of Israel was not the 'Body of Christ,' even though the Body of Christ is indeed the true 'Israel of God'" (*Abraham's Four Seeds*, 19). He notes that the first part of this is rejected by covenant theology (since Israel is the OT church) whereas the second part is rejected by dispensationalism (since Israel and the church have separate futures).

86. Gentry and Wellum, *Kingdom through Covenant*, 749. DeRouchie similarly asserts that "God regards both Jew and Gentiles as part of the *true* 'Israel of God' (Gal 6:16; cf. 3:28–29) if they are joined by faith to Christ Jesus, the *true* Israel (Isa 49:3, 5) and Abraham's *true* 'seed' (Gal 3:16)" ("Father of a Multitude of Nations," 27 [emphasis original]).

87. Gentry and Wellum, *Kingdom through Covenant*, 749 (emphasis original; see also 134, 758; Parker, "The Israel-Christ-Church Relationship," 53–56).

4. WHAT IS THE KINGDOM OF GOD?

Wellum specifies four affirmations regarding the kingdom of God.[88] *First, as Creator, God is the sovereign King and ruler of the universe.* There is a sense in which the entire universe is God's kingdom. He alone is the Creator and thus is the sovereign ruler of all his creation. He would establish a proper habitation for his kingdom people and would establish his reign over his image-bearers based on his covenantal love and faithfulness.

Second, because of the entrance of sin and rebellion into the world, God's rightful rule (i.e., kingdom) over his creation has been rejected. Thus, sin is essentially rebellion against the claims of the King. Consequently, all humanity stands condemned and guilty as lawbreakers who have violated the will of the King. Yet, the King has decided to make things right through the coming of a Redeemer into the world. One day (in the new creation), all sin and rebellion will be eradicated, ushering in the fullness of God's kingdom.

Third, God's saving reign is advanced primarily through the biblical covenants. "It is *through* the progression of the covenants that God chooses to reverse the disastrous effects of sin and usher in his saving reign to this world."[89] The Old Testament covenants failed to usher in the kingdom due to Israel's persistent sin. It is only the arrival of the Son of God that inaugurates the long-awaited kingdom.

Fourth, even in the midst of faithlessness and even apostasy, the Old Testament prophets declare the promises and hopes of restoration to Israel and the world. But the saving reign of God will arrive only with the coming of the Redeemer or Messiah, since he will inaugurate a new covenant that will fulfill all previous covenants.

In the New Testament, Jesus inaugurates God's promised kingdom. Similar to the Old Testament, the kingdom of God "refers primarily to God's *kingly* and *sovereign rule*, and it is especially tied to God's *saving reign* that will come in the Messiah, which the New Testament announces has now begun in Christ's coming, life, death,

---

88. Gentry and Wellum, *Kingdom through Covenant,* 648–54.

89. Ibid., 653 (emphasis original).

and resurrection."[90] Consequently, until the consummation when God's rule will be coextensive with the new creation, it does *not* refer to a geographic location.

Did Jesus Bring the Kingdom?

Progressive covenantalism affirms that Jesus brought the kingdom, but not fully. That is, as the promised Son of David, King Jesus ushered in (at least in part) the kingdom God. In his earthly ministry, Jesus reversed the effects of sin and death when he healed the sick and raised the dead. According to the New Testament, the long-awaited kingdom has come and is witnessed by Jesus' life and his death. As Wellum writes, "Thus, through Jesus' obedient life and cross work, he has *inaugurated* the kingdom of God over which he now rules and reigns—it is *already* here."[91] Furthermore, his kingdom's presence is demonstrated by Jesus' coronation as the King as he reigns on his throne at his Father's side. And as King, he commands all people everywhere to repent, confess him as Lord and King, and enter into his kingdom.[92]

At the same time, although the kingdom has come, it has not come fully. That is, because sin and death persist, there is still a *not yet* aspect of the kingdom. Indeed, it is not until the second coming of Christ that the kingdom will be consummated. This "already/not yet" tension is known as "inaugurated eschatology." The "last days" that the Old Testament anticipated and predicted have already arrived with the coming of Jesus, yet they still await their full consummation. The coming of the Spirit at Pentecost is further evidence of the kingdom's presence. Because of his victory over sin and death, Jesus has poured out his promised Spirit. Yet, the gift of the Spirit is only a deposit or guarantee of the full inheritance awaiting believers at

---

90. Ibid., 718 (emphasis original).

91. Gentry and Wellum, *Kingdom through Covenant*, 1st ed., 596 (emphasis original).

92. The following coincide with the arrival of the new covenant: "the arrival of God's saving reign, the pouring out of the Spirit, a new temple, the full forgiveness of sin, the judgment and defeat of God's enemies, resurrection life, eschatological rest, a restored Israel, a transformed people composed of believing Jews and Gentiles, and a new creation" (Gentry and Wellum, *Kingdom through Covenant*, 735).

the consummation. Thus, even though the "last days" have already arrived, the kingdom will not fully arrive until Jesus' second advent.

In sum, Jesus is the fulfillment of all the Old Testament predictions, hopes, and expectations.[93] As such, with his coming there was an epochal shift in redemptive history. The present phase in redemptive history represents a new age and a new covenant, with many concepts being transposed or transformed. By his death, resurrection, and ascension, Jesus has ushered in the kingdom of God which will only be fully consummated at his second coming.

How Is the Kingdom Consummated?

Simply stated, the kingdom will be consummated at the return of Christ. He will right all wrongs by punishing those who oppose him and his people. Once he has subdued all his enemies (including the last enemy, death), he will hand over the kingdom to his Father (1 Cor 15:24–28). Then, God will be all in all and every created being will submit to his will.

Progressive covenantalists have divergent views when it comes to the millennium. Many align themselves with historic premillennialism, though dispensational premillennialism is rejected. Others prefer amillennialism, the view that rejects a *future-only* millennium but instead argues that the binding of Satan took place at the resurrection and the millennium is the period of time between Christ's advents.

Because of these different positions and because of the paucity of specific references to a millennium (only occurring in Rev 20:1–8),[94] progressive covenantalists do not seem to be overly concerned regarding one's millennial position. One consistent view of this position, however, is that if the millennial kingdom follows the return of Christ, the nation of Israel will not be given the land of Palestine in fulfillment

---

93. Wellum states, "In every aspect of Jesus's life, ministry, and cross work, *he fulfills* all the promises, instruction, and typological patterns of the previous covenants and their covenant heads, thus bringing God's eternal plan to its intended end. … [Consequently,] all God's promises find their fulfillment, terminus, and 'summing up' in him (Eph. 1:9–10)" (ibid. [emphasis original]).

94. Reisinger argues, "We must not … allow six verses in Revelation 20 to frame our understanding of the promised eternal kingdom of God" (*New Covenant Theology and Prophecy*, 3–4).

of Old Testament prophecies.[95] Instead, such Old Testament restoration prophecies are fulfilled in Christ and are thus expanded
to include the entire earth. Nowhere is the land promise to Israel
repeated in the New Testament. Oren Martin explains: "Israel's land
promise ultimately reaches its fulfillment when redeemed people from
every nation fill and inhabit the whole earth. What believing Israel
obtains is far greater than the land of Canaan, for they—along with
the nations—will inherit the whole earth in fulfillment of God's gracious and irrevocable promises."[96]

ASSESSMENT

Progressive covenantalism offers a *via media* between dispensationalism and covenant theology. Thus, one of its strengths is that it seeks
to offer a more balanced approach than those views which are sit-
uated on either side. This view seeks to affirm both continuity and
discontinuity, acknowledging that the final revelation is given in Jesus
Christ who fulfills all the previous promises and covenants. A related
weakness of progressive covenantalism is the newness of the theological system. It was officially launched in 2012, though proponents
claim their view goes back into history and that most of what they
say is not new but is simply a minor tweaking of some of the details.[97]
Some leaders of this view see it as building upon many of the insights
of covenant theology but rejecting their imposition of a "covenant
of works" and a "covenant of grace" on the Bible without allowing
Scripture to first define those concepts.

---

95. See, e.g., Gentry and Wellum, *Kingdom through Covenant*, 743–44. Wellum comments,
"It is difficult, then, to argue that various *spiritual* blessings of the new covenant are *now* here *in the
church* but that the material-physical blessings of the new covenant are still *future* and *for national
Israel*" (744 [emphasis original]). According to Reisinger, "not a single New Testament text lit-
eralizes the temple, the priesthood, or the sacrifices" (*New Covenant Theology and Prophecy*, 78).

96. Martin, "The Land Promise," 270–71.

97. New covenant theology began in the late 1970s and early 1980s. Furthermore, in her
book on the history of new covenant theology, Heather Kendall includes several chapters and
an appendix demonstrating that the essence of new covenant theology is not new but can be
traced throughout the church (*One Greater Than Moses*). Her chapter titles include "Glimpses
of New Covenant Theology Developing Before the Reformation" (ch. 2), "Glimpses of New
Covenant Theology Developing After the Reformation" (ch. 3), "Laying the Groundwork: The
Doctrines of Grace (From the Late 1940s)" (ch. 4), and "Further Glimpses of New Covenant
Theology Developing Before the Reformation" (appendix).

A second strength of progressive covenantalism is their use of biblical theology and the priority of interpreting each passage in relation to its place in redemptive history. There is a danger of either flattening out the Bible so that every passage applies equally and in the same way or emphasizing discontinuity to the extent that a particular passage does not apply at all. Progressive covenantalists have sought to treat all the Bible as Scripture that is relevant for the believer—but only in light of redemptive history and fulfillment in Christ. A possible weakness is that they give little attention to debated texts, especially those that deal with the relationship between Israel and the church. For example, in his review of the first edition of *Kingdom through Covenant*, Darrell Bock writes, "It is amazing to see no detailed treatment of Romans 9–11 or how Israel is seen in several texts within Luke-Acts."[98] Although Gentry and Wellum added a few more pages on Romans 9–11 in the second edition, Bock's critique still has merit.

A final strength of progressive covenantalism is its flexibility or openness related to one's millennial position. Currently, there are advocates who embrace historical premillennialism as well as those who prefer amillennialism (and no doubt a few who hold to postmillennialism). Such flexibility is welcomed by many who are persuaded that one's millennial position should not be a litmus test for orthodoxy or evangelical faithfulness.[99]

Although such flexibility is refreshing, it perhaps reveals an inherent weakness in this theological system. That is, because the millennium is not a central feature of their system (cf. dispensationalism), and because there are divergent views represented by its adherents, there is a tendency to downplay or ignore the millennium altogether. For example, in the 900-plus pages of *Kingdom through Covenant*, "Revelation 20" is only listed once (Rev 20:4) and the term "millennium"

---

98. Darrell Bock, "Kingdom through Covenant: A Review by Darrell Bock," The Gospel Coalition, September 11, 2012, https://www.thegospelcoalition.org/reviews/kingdom-through-covenant-a-review-by-darrell-bock/.

99. Interestingly, Reisinger declares, "I am not a premillennialist, an amillennialist, or a postmillennialist. I am a millennial agnostic" (*New Covenant Theology and Prophecy*, 1).

is never listed in its indices. So, although there is a healthy appreciation for eschatology (especially as various themes are fulfilled in Christ), certain elements of eschatology (e.g., the millennium) seem to receive very little attention.

CHAPTER 6
COVENANT THEOLOGY

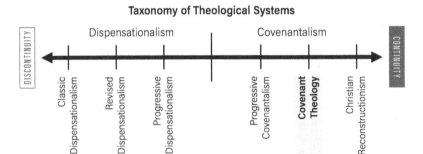

Taxonomy of Theological Systems

ovenant theology (also called federal theology or Reformed theology) represents a theological system that emphasizes the unity and continuity of the Bible. Consequently, it contrasts with dispensationalism with respect to the relationship between the old covenant and the new covenant. For example, not only do covenant theologians speak of the one people of God in both Testaments, they also affirm that the church existed in the Old Testament. One key linchpin for seeing continuity between the covenants revolves around the centrality of the covenant of grace. Because God is working out his unified plan to redeem humanity through this covenant, all historical covenants fall under this larger covenant and thus are expressions of it.

Although they are often accused of espousing "replacement theology" or "supersessionism," most covenant theologians insist that God has not abandoned his promises to Israel or replaced Israel with the church. Instead, they assert that God has fulfilled his promises to national Israel in Jesus, the Messiah. Thus, there is an organic continuity as the church is grafted into the covenant promises given to God's Old Testament people. As its name suggests, covenant theology understands the concept of covenant as the controlling principle for understanding the Bible and redemptive history. This system not only affirms the historical covenants (Noahic, Abrahamic, Mosaic, Davidic, and new) but also three overarching theological covenants (redemption, works/creation, and grace). The three key proponents who will be used to represent this view are (1) Meredith Kline, (2) O. Palmer Robertson, and (3) Michael Horton.

Meredith G. Kline (1922–2007) received his AB from Gordon College of Theology and Missions (later abbreviated to Gordon College), his ThB and ThM from Westminster Theological Seminary in Philadelphia, and his PhD from Dropsie College. His teaching career spanned over fifty years, mainly in four seminaries: Westminster Theological Seminary in Philadelphia (1948–1977), Gordon-Conwell Theological Seminary (1965–1993), Reformed Theological Seminary (1979–1983), and Westminster Theological Seminary, California (1981–2002). He was also an ordained minister in the Orthodox Presbyterian Church.

Some of Kline's major works include *Treaty of the Great King* (which demonstrated how the structure of Deuteronomy and the Ten Commandments closely paralleled suzerain-vassal treaties), *By Oath Consigned* (which treated the covenant symbols of circumcision and baptism as curse sanctions), *The Structure of Biblical Authority* (which sought to demonstrate the covenantal, and thus canonical, nature of all Scripture[1]), *Kingdom Prologue* (which contended that Genesis provided the historical background for the Israelite kingdom through the renewal of the Sinai covenant), and *Images of the Spirit* (which illustrated how the glory of God related to the human royal, priestly, and prophetic functions). Because of his commitment to covenant theology and because of the recent discovery of Hittite diplomatic treaties, much of Kline's writing emphasized how the biblical

---

1. "Because the Bible *is* the old and new covenants and because canon is inherent in covenant of the biblical type, canonicity is inherent in the very form and identity of Scripture as the Old Testament and the New Testament" (Meredith G. Kline, *The Structure of Biblical Authority*, 2nd ed. [Eugene, OR: Wipf & Stock, 1989], 75).

covenants (especially the covenant at Sinai) were patterned after the suzerain-vassal covenants.

O. Palmer Robertson (1937–present) is a graduate of Belhaven College, Westminster Theological Seminary in Philadelphia (BD), and Union Theological Seminary in Richmond (ThM and ThD). Like Kline, he taught at several theological institutions including Westminster, Reformed Theological Seminary, Covenant Theological Seminary, and Knox Seminary. He also taught at Bible colleges in Malawi and Uganda, serving as the principal of the latter institution (African Bible University). Robertson is best known for his book *The Christ of the Covenants* where he argues that a covenant is defined as "a bond in blood, sovereignly administered."

Michael Horton (1964–present) received his BA from Biola University, his MA from Westminster Theological Seminary, California (studying under Kline), and his PhD from Wycliffe Hall, Oxford and Coventry University. He is an ordained minister in the United Reformed Churches in North America and is professor of systematic theology and apologetics at Westminster Theological Seminary, California (since 1998) and is a prolific author. He has written or edited more than twenty-five books including *Covenant and Eschatology* (2002), *Lord and Servant: A Covenant Christology* (2005), *God of Promise: Introducing Covenant Theology* (2006), *Covenant & Salvation: Union with Christ* (2007), *The Christian Faith: A Systematic Theology for Pilgrims on the Way* (2011), and *Pilgrim Theology: Core Doctrine for Christian Disciples* (2013). He is also the founder and host of *White Horse Inn*, a nationally syndicated radio talk-show that discusses Reformational theology and the intersect of American Christianity and culture. Additionally, he is the editor-in-chief of *Modern Reformation* magazine. Just how central is the concept of *covenant* to this theological system? Horton clarifies, "Whenever Reformed theologians attempt to explore and explain the riches of Scripture, they are always thinking *covenantally* about every topic they take up."[2]

---

2. Michael Horton, *Introducing Covenant Theology* (Grand Rapids: Baker, 2006), 14 (emphasis original). Originally published under the title *God of Promise*.

1. WHAT IS THE BASIC HERMENEUTIC?

Is a Literal or Symbolic Hermeneutic Employed?

Covenant theologians reject a literalistic or wooden method of interpreting Scripture. They affirm a literal interpretation in the sense of a grammatico-historical approach that interprets the Bible according to the intention of the author as opposed to an allegorical interpretation. But they also embrace a Christocentric or Christotelic hermeneutic that sees Christ as the fulfillment of all the promises of God.[3] As such, they interpret the Old Testament in light of the New Testament,[4] using the interpretive methods of the inspired New Testament authors.[5]

Many, if not most, covenant theologians are comfortable with the notion of *sensus plenior*,[6] the idea that earlier revelation can later take on an expanded or fuller meaning.[7] The expanded meaning, however, "is organically related to the historical meaning," just as an oak tree is related to an acorn.[8] Beale explains:

---

3. See Peter Enns, "Fuller Meaning, Single Goal: A Christotelic Approach to the New Testament Use of the Old in Its First-Century Interpretive Environment," in *Three Views on the New Testament Use of the Old Testament*, ed. Kenneth Berding and Jonathan Lunde (Grand Rapids: Zondervan, 2008), 167–217. It should be noted that Enns's view is more extreme than others in his camp since he views the biblical authors as employing first-century Jewish exegetical methods that sometimes forced the OT text to find its fulfillment in Christ.

4. So Sidney Greidanus, *Preaching Christ from the Old Testament: A Contemporary Hermeneutical Method* (Grand Rapids: Eerdmans, 1999), 51.

5. Silva writes, "If we refuse to pattern our exegesis after that of the apostles, we are in practice denying the authoritative character of their scriptural interpretation—and to do so is to strike at the very heart of the Christian faith" (Moisés Silva, "The New Testament Use of the Old Testament: Text Form and Authority," in *Scripture and Truth*, ed. D. A. Carson and John D. Woodbridge [Grand Rapids: Zondervan, 1983], 164).

6. Beale, e.g., hesitatingly approves of *sensus plenior*: "we may legitimately speak of a *sensus plenior* of Scripture, although it is probably best not to use this phrase since it is not often understood in this precise manner" (G. K. Beale, "Did Jesus and His Followers Preach the Right Doctrine from the Wrong Texts? An Examination of the Presuppositions of Jesus' and The Apostles' Exegetical Methods," in *The Right Doctrine from the Wrong Texts? Essays on the Use of the Old Testament in the New* [Grand Rapids: Baker Academic, 1994], 392).

7. See, e.g., Dan McCartney and Charles Clayton, *Let the Reader Understand: A Guide to Interpreting and Applying the Bible*, 2nd ed. (Phillipsburg, NJ: P&R, 2002), 164; Graeme Goldsworthy, *According to Plan: The Unfolding Revelation of God in the Bible* (Downers Grove, IL: InterVarsity Press, 1991), 67–68.

8. McCartney and Clayton, *Let the Reader Understand*, 165.

On this view it is quite possible that the Old Testament authors did not exhaustively understand the meaning, implications, and possible applications of all that they wrote. Subsequently, New Testament Scripture interprets the Old Testament Scripture by expanding its meaning, seeing new implications in it and giving it new applications. I believe, however, that it can be demonstrated that this expansion does not contravene the integrity of the earlier texts but rather develops them in a way which is consistent with the Old Testament author's understanding of the way in which God interacts with his people—which is the unifying factor between the Testaments.[9]

Whereas dispensationalists employ a consistently literal hermeneutic when interpreting the Bible, covenant theologians emphasize a Christocentric interpretation that often involves an expanded meaning (*sensus plenior*) beyond what was originally given in the Old Testament. Because the Old Testament is only part of the canon of the Christian Scriptures, it must be interpreted in light of the New Testament. To ignore the way the New Testament writers understand Old Testament prophecies is to employ a non-Christian hermeneutic.

What Is the Proper Role of Typology?

Typology plays a prominent part in the hermeneutical approach of covenant theology.[10] Beale offers a standard definition of typology: "the study of analogical correspondences among revealed truths about

---

9. Beale, "Did Jesus and His Followers Preach the Right Doctrine from the Wrong Texts?," 393. Goldsworthy comments, "The *sensus plenior* of an OT text, or indeed of the whole OT, cannot be found by exegesis of the texts themselves. Exegesis aims at understanding what was intended by the author, the *sensus literalis*. But there is a deeper meaning in the mind of the divine author which emerges in further revelation, usually the NT. This approach embraces typology but also addresses the question of how a text may have more than one meaning. While typology focuses on historical events which foreshadow later events, *sensus plenior* focuses on the use of words" (Graeme Goldsworthy, "The Relationship of the Old Testament and New Testament," in *New Dictionary of Biblical Theology*, ed. T. Desmond Alexander et al. [Downers Grove, IL: InterVarsity Press, 2000], 88).

10. See G. K. Beale, *Handbook on the New Testament Use of the Old Testament* (Grand Rapids:

persons, events, institutions, and other things within the historical framework of God's special revelation, which, from a retrospective view, are of a prophetic nature and are escalated in their meaning."[11] Accordingly, there are five key aspects related to typology: (1) analogical correspondence, (2) historicity, (3) a pointing-forwardness, foreshadowing, or presignification, (4) escalation, and (5) retrospection.[12]

For example, Robertson insists that the land of Israel is typological, anticipating new covenant realities.[13] This is similar to how the sacrificial system prefigured the offering of Jesus' body, how the priesthood anticipated the permanent priesthood of Christ, and how the tabernacle foreshadowed the abiding presence of God's glory in Jesus. Robertson states, "The land of the Bible served in a typological role as a model of the consummate realization of the purposes of God for his redeemed people that encompasses the whole of the cosmos. Because of the inherently limited scope of the land of the Bible, it is not to be regarded as having continuing significance in the realm of redemption other than its function as a teaching model."[14]

Thus, Robertson maintains that the possession of the land under the old covenant was not an end in itself but was a type or shadow that pointed to a greater reality.[15] What are the implications for a typological understanding of the land? Robertson asserts that once the greater reality of the antitype appears, God's people should not desire to return to the old, typological ways under the old covenant. "Progression toward consummation in the new covenant cannot allow for a retrogression to the older, shadowy forms."[16] In fact, Paul declares

Baker Academic, 2012), 13–25; Goldsworthy, *According to Plan*, 67–69; McCartney and Clayton, *Let the Reader Understand*, 162–69.

11. Beale, *Handbook on the New Testament Use of the Old Testament*, 14.

12. See also Hans K. LaRondelle, *The Israel of God in Prophecy: Principles of Prophetic Interpretation* (Berrien Springs, MI: Andrews University Press, 1983), 35–59.

13. O. Palmer Robertson, *The Israel of God: Yesterday, Today, and Tomorrow* (Phillipsburg, NJ: P&R, 2000), 3–31.

14. Ibid., 194.

15. Horton suggests that the land was "typological of the heavenly reality, particularly of the true Israelite who would come down from heaven to keep the covenant faithfully" (*Introducing Covenant Theology*, 103). See also Robert L. Reymond, "The Traditional Covenantal View," in *Perspectives on Israel and the Church: 4 Views*, ed. Chad O. Brand (Nashville: B&H, 2015), 36–37.

16. Robertson, *The Israel of God*, 17.

that Abraham is an heir of "the world" (Rom 4:13). Therefore, the fulfillment of the promise to Abraham is no longer merely a small sliver of the earth in the middle east, but the entirety of the new heavens and the new earth.[17] Old Testament types pointed to a greater New Testament reality brought about by the death and resurrection of Jesus Christ who was the fulfillment of the promises of God to his people.

How Are Old Testament Restoration Prophecies Fulfilled?

Based on their stance of rejecting a literalistic hermeneutic but allowing for typology and symbolism, covenant theologians maintain that Old Testament restoration prophecies given to the nation of Israel are fulfilled in Christ and his church. Their position can be seen when considering the restoration prophecy announced in Amos 9:11–15.[18] In this prophecy, future blessings to Israel are stated in very concrete terms (both physically and geographically). This text mentions Israel's return from exile, the restoration of the Davidic dynasty, the conversion of the nations, the continued fruitfulness of the land, the rebuilding of the desolated cities, and the permanent occupation of Israel in the land. But the question is how do these Old Testament concepts reach fulfillment in Christ? Covenant theologians look to the New Testament authors who provide an inspired commentary as to fulfillment of this prophecy.

In response to whether gentiles need to be circumcised to be saved, James quotes Amos 9: "After this I will return, and I will rebuild the tent of David that has fallen; I will rebuild its ruins, and I will restore it, that the remnant of mankind may seek the Lord, and all the Gentiles who are called by my name, says the Lord, who makes these things known from of old" (Acts 15:16–18). Dispensationalists claim that this verse signifies God's twofold plan: God is now calling out a people for himself that includes gentiles but in the future, he shall fulfill specific

---

17. Ibid., 26.

18. See O. Palmer Robertson, "Hermeneutics of Continuity," in *Continuity and Discontinuity: Perspectives on the Relationship Between the Old and New Testaments*, ed. John S. Feinberg (Wheaton: Crossway, 1988), 89–108; LaRondelle, *The Israel of God in Prophecy*, 147–50; Michael Horton, *The Christian Faith: A Systematic Theology for Pilgrims on the Way* (Grand Rapids: Zondervan, 2011), 946–47.

geopolitical promises to the nation of Israel. Thus, Amos' prophetic vision is still future-oriented since it has not yet been fulfilled. This next phase in God's redemptive plan will take place at the second coming of Christ which is indicated by the phrase "I will return" (Acts 15:16).

Robertson argues, however, that James' citation of Amos 9 has *direct* and *immediate* bearing on the question being debated at the Jerusalem Council. Robertson remarks, "To suggest that James introduced these words to resolve the question at hand, knowing all along that Amos' prophecy actually did not speak directly to the matter before the Council, has the effect of cutting the lifeline of the appeal to the authority of Scripture."[19] Consequently, the addition of the uncircumcised gentiles into the church as God's elect people should be interpreted as directly fulfilling Amos 9. Covenant theologian Anthony Hoekema summarizes: "James is saying that the wonderful thing which is now happening, namely, that Gentiles are now coming into the fellowship of God's people, is a fulfillment of the words of the prophet Amos about the building up again of the fallen tabernacle of David." He continues, "In other words, the fallen tabernacle of David is being built up not in a material way (by means of a restored earthly kingdom) but in a spiritual way (as Gentiles are coming into the kingdom of God)."[20] Thus, the restoration prophecy of Amos 9 is symbolically fulfilled as the gentiles receive salvation and expand the people of God.

2. WHAT IS THE RELATIONSHIP BETWEEN THE COVENANTS?

As witnessed by its very name, the concept of *covenant* is central to covenant theology. This section will (1) define the term "covenant," (2) describe the three overarching covenants, and (3) briefly delineate the historical covenants. Perhaps the most referenced definition

---

19. Robertson, "Hermeneutics of Continuity," 102.

20. Anthony A. Hoekema, "An Amillennial Response," in *The Meaning of the Millennium: Four Views*, ed. Robert G. Clouse (Downers Grove, IL: InterVarsity, 1977), 110.

of covenant comes from Robertson, who states that it is a "bond in blood sovereignly administered."[21] The covenantal signs (e.g., the rainbow, circumcision, and the Sabbath) enforce the binding nature of the covenant. Kline offers a slightly different definition: "a covenant may be defined as a relationship under sanctions. The covenantal commitment is characteristically expressed by an oath sworn in the solemnities of covenant ratification."[22]

Three Overarching Covenants

Most covenant theologians affirm three overarching covenants: (1) the covenant of redemption, (2) the covenant of works (creation), and (3) the covenant of grace. All of God's interactions with humanity take place within various covenants. As Robertson observes, "The extent of divine covenants reaches from the beginning of the world to the end of the age."[23] These covenants (along with the historical covenants) are all related to each other and are ultimately one.[24] Horton summarizes these three covenants as "the covenant of redemption (an eternal pact between the Father, Son, and Holy Spirit), the covenant of creation (made with humanity in Adam), and the covenant of grace (made with believers and their children in Christ)."[25] All other covenants in Scripture are grouped under the umbrella of these three overarching biblical covenants. Horton calls these three covenants "the heart of covenant theology."[26]

Covenant of Redemption.[27] Although not explicitly referenced as a covenant in Scripture, the notion of a covenant of redemption is typically embraced by covenant theologians. This is the covenant

---

21. O. Palmer Robertson, *The Christ of the Covenants* (Phillipsburg, NJ: P&R, 1980), 4.

22. Meredith G. Kline, *By Oath Consigned* (Grand Rapids: Eerdmans, 1968), 16.

23. Robertson, *The Christ of the Covenants*, 25.

24. See, e.g., Robertson, *The Christ of the Covenants*, 28, 44, 52, 53. He states, "the covenants of God relate organically to one another. From Adam to Christ, a unity of covenantal administration characterizes the history of God's dealing with his people" (45).

25. Horton, *Introducing Covenant Theology*, 77–78.

26. Ibid., 77.

27. See Louis Berkhof, *Systematic Theology*, 4th rev. and exp. ed. (Grand Rapids: Eerdmans, 1941), 265–71; R. C. Sproul, *What Is Reformed Theology? Understanding the Basics* (Grand Rapids: Baker, 1997), 107–9; Horton, *Introducing Covenant Theology*, 78–83.

between the three persons of the Trinity made in eternity. As Horton explains, "The Father elects a people in the Son as their mediator to be brought to saving faith through the Spirit."[28] Similarly, R. C. Sproul highlights the Trinitarian nature of this covenant: "the Father sends the Son and the Spirit, the Son accomplishes the mediatorial work of redemption in our behalf, and the Holy Spirit applies the work of Christ to us."[29] This covenant is somewhat unique since all other biblical covenants are made between God and man but this covenant is made between the three persons of the Godhead. Those God elects are chosen from among the mass of fallen humanity based on the grace of God alone. This covenant is grounded on the biblical texts which speak of unconditional election, predestination, and adoption. Furthermore, Christ is spoken of as "the Lamb who was slain from the creation of the world" (Rev 13:8 NIV) and believers were chosen in Christ "before the foundation of the world" (Eph 1:4).

Covenant of Works.[30] The covenant of works (also called the covenant of creation or the pre-redemptive covenant) is the pact that God made with Adam, the federal head of humanity. This pre-fall covenant assumes that Adam is capable of perfect righteousness and thus can fulfill all of God's stipulations. In addition, it promised reward upon obedience and retribution upon disobedience. Thus, God implicitly promises Adam that upon his complete obedience, he will be given the right to eat from the Tree of Life.[31] Horton asserts, "Humankind was created to pass through the probationary period and attain the right to eat from the Tree of Life. Thus, the telos of human existence was not fully present in creation, but was held out as a future reward."[32] In all of this, Adam acts as the representative head of humanity.

---

28. Horton, *Introducing Covenant Theology*, 78.

29. Sproul, *What Is Reformed Theology?*, 109. Berkhof describes this covenant as "the agreement between the Father, giving the Son as Head and Redeemer of the elect, and the Son, voluntarily taking the place of those whom the Father had given Him" (*Systematic Theology*, 271).

30. See Kline, *The Structure of Biblical Authority*, 155; idem, *By Oath Consigned*, 26–35; Robertson, *The Christ of the Covenants*, 54–57; Sproul, *What Is Reformed Theology?*, 109–11; Horton, *Introducing Covenant Theology*, 83–104; idem, *The Christian Faith*, 414–23; idem, *Lord and Servant: A Covenant Christology* (Louisville: Westminster John Knox, 2005), 128–49.

31. Sproul comments: "Life is promised as a reward for obedience, for satisfying the condition of the covenant" (*What Is Reformed Theology?*, 109).

32. Horton, *Introducing Covenant Theology*, 106. He also writes, "God commands such

What is the basis for this covenant? Besides the implicit covenant elements in the arrangement God made with Abraham, many cite Hosea 6:7 which states, "like [*adam*] Adam they transgressed the covenant." Based on this text, Robertson declares, "Hosea 6:7 would appear to apply covenantal terminology to the relation of God to man established by creation."[33] Furthermore, Romans 5:12–21 emphasizes the representational roles of both Adam and Christ. Reformed theologians also look to the Westminster Confession of Faith as support for this covenant: "The first covenant made with man was a covenant of works, wherein life was promised to Adam; and in him to his posterity, upon condition of perfect and personal obedience" (7.2).

Although he readily acknowledges the presence of a covenant between God and Adam in the garden, Robertson is reluctant to use the terminology "covenant of *works*" to describe that relationship. Instead, he prefers the phrase "covenant of *creation*" (which is also preferred by Horton, for different reasons). According to Robertson, the nomenclature "covenant of works" should be avoided because it "suggests that grace was not operative in the covenant of works. As a matter of fact, the totality of God's relationship with man is a matter of grace."[34] Kline (as well as Horton), however, maintains that the problem is just the opposite. The problem with using the phrase "covenant of grace" is that it suggests that law is not part of the covenant. But, according to Kline, "The satisfaction of the divine law underlies every administration of divine promise."[35] For Kline, the one common denominator among all covenants is the principle of works (even if grace surrounds the covenant). In the covenant of grace, the law was kept by the covenant head, Jesus Christ.

---

complete obedience, and he promises, upon that condition, the *right* (not the *gift*) to eat from the Tree of Life. While creation itself is a gift, the entrance into God's Sabbath rest was held out as the promise for loyal obedience in the period of testing" (89 [emphasis original]).

33. Robertson, *The Christ of the Covenants*, 24.

34. Robertson, *The Christ of the Covenants*, 56. In addition, Robertson maintains that the phrase "covenant of grace" suggests that works have no place in the covenant. But, in reality, Christ's works were essential for the salvation of his people.

35. Kline, *By Oath Consigned*, 33.

Covenant of Grace.[36] The third overarching covenant is the "covenant of grace," the covenant that God made with Adam immediately after his failure in the garden under the covenant of works. God's relationship with man did not terminate after the fall. Instead, God bound himself to redeem a people for himself as was first announced in Genesis 3:15 (the *protoeuangelion*). The goal of this new covenant is for man to realize the blessings originally promised under the covenant of creation. It represents God's commitment to redeem his now fallen creation.[37] This covenant is related to the previous covenants in that it is based on God's commitment to redeem a people for himself (covenant of redemption) and will ultimately be fulfilled by the faithful law-keeping of the second Adam (covenant of works).[38] As Robertson explains, "Covenant theology understands the whole of history after man's fall into sin as unifying under the provisions of the covenant of [grace]. Beginning with the first promise to Adam-in-sin and continuing throughout history to the consummation of the ages, God orders all things in view of his singular purpose of redeeming a people to himself."[39]

Again, this theological covenant is specifically mentioned in the Westminster Confession of Faith:

> Man, by his fall, having made himself incapable of life by that covenant, the Lord was pleased to make a second, commonly called the covenant of grace; wherein He freely offers unto sinners life and salvation by Jesus Christ; requiring of them faith in Him, that they may be saved, and promising to give unto all those that are

---

36. See Berkhof, *Systematic Theology*, 272–83; Robertson, *The Christ of the Covenants*, 54–57, 87; Sproul, *What Is Reformed Theology?*, 111–14; Horton, *Introducing Covenant Theology*, 104–7. Robertson also calls this the "covenant of redemption," since he does not affirm the inter-Trinitarian covenant that was earlier given that title.

37. See Robertson, *The Christ of the Covenants*, 91, 93.

38. Sproul, *What Is Reformed Theology?*, 113.

39. Robertson, *The Christ of the Covenants*, 206. Berkhof defines it as "that gracious agreement between the offended God and the offending but elect sinner, in which God promises salvation through faith in Christ, and the sinner accepts this believingly, promising a life of faith and obedience" (*Systematic Theology*, 277).

ordained unto eternal life His Holy Spirit, to make them willing, and able to believe. (7.3)

Accordingly, this covenant has both conditional and unconditional elements. It is *unconditional* in the sense that God himself fulfills the conditions of the covenant for all the elect, and it is *conditional* since Jesus met all the conditions originally given in the covenant of works through his active and passive obedience.

Following traditional Reformed theology, Horton insists that the covenant of grace is not limited to the elect (believers with genuine faith). Instead, this covenant also includes believing *and* unbelieving children of the elect. He writes, "There are real partners in this covenant (God with believers and their children) and real conditions (repentance and faith), but as it is grounded in the eternal covenant of redemption and the Mediator's fulfillment of the covenant of works, even the meeting of these conditions is graciously given and not simply required."[40] Because this covenant is made with believers and their children, not everyone in this covenant is elect, just as not everyone of the nation of Israel was a true believer.[41]

Chart 6.2 represents a summary of the three overarching covenants in covenant theology.[42]

	Covenant of Redemption	Covenant of Works	Covenant of Grace
Parties	The Father, the Son, and the Holy Spirit	God and human beings	God and sinful human beings
Initiator	God the Father	God	God
Time	In eternity past	At creation	After the fall
Condition		Perfect obedience	Faith in Christ (who satisfied the condition of the covenant of works)
Reward		Life	Spiritual life
Penalty		Immediate death (physical and spiritual)	Spiritual death

---

40. Horton, *Introducing Covenant Theology*, 105.

41. Ibid., 182.

42. Based on Sproul, *What Is Reformed Theology?*, 112.

Are the Covenants Conditional or Unconditional?

As was seen in the previous section, covenant theology affirms three overarching (theological) covenants. The following historical covenants are viewed as manifestations of the covenant of grace.[43]

- *Adam:* the covenant of commencement
- *Noah:* the covenant of preservation
- *Abraham:* the covenant of promise
- *Moses:* the covenant of law
- *David:* the covenant of the kingdom
- *Christ:* the covenant of consummation

Typically, a distinction is made between the unconditional nature of the Abrahamic covenant and the conditional nature of the Mosaic covenant. Before this question is answered in more detail, however, the nature of the Mosaic covenant will be highlighted.

Kline has argued extensively that the Mosaic covenant is patterned after ancient Near Eastern suzerain-vassal treaties, especially those of the Hittite Empire (1450–1180 BC). Affirming Kline's work, Horton writes, "The great king was the father adopting the captives he had liberated from oppression. Consequently, he was not simply to be obeyed externally, but loved; not only feared, but revered; not only known as the legal lord of the realm, but acknowledged openly as the rightful sovereign."[44] For example, Kline demonstrates how Deuteronomy is a covenant renewal document whose structure parallels the suzerain-vassal treaties.[45] Below is the covenant form and its parallels in the book of Deuteronomy.[46]

---

43. Robertson, *The Christ of the Covenants*, 61.

44. Horton, *Introducing Covenant Theology*, 25.

45. Meredith G. Kline, *Treaty of the Great King* (Eugene, OR: Wipf & Stock, 1963, reprint 2012), 27–44. This same material is found in idem, *The Structure of Biblical Authority*, 131–53. Kline is building on the work of George E. Mendenhall, *Law and Covenant in Israel and the Ancient Near East* (Pittsburgh: Biblical Colloquium, 1955).

46. Kline, *Treaty of the Great King*, 28 (for a more in-depth analysis, see 50–149); Robertson, *The Christ of the Covenants*, 169; Horton, *Introducing Covenant Theology*, 25–27, 31–32; idem, *The Christian Faith*, 151–55; idem, *Covenant and Salvation: Union with Christ* (Louisville: Westminster John Knox, 2007), 13.

- *Preamble:* covenant mediator (Deut 1:1–5)
- *Historical Prologue:* covenant history, e.g., liberation from Egypt (Deut 1:6–4:49)
- *Stipulations:* covenant life (Deut 5–26)
- *Sanctions:* blessings and curses (Deut 27–30)
- *Covenant Continuity:* invocation of witnesses for deposition and public reading (Deut 31–34)

Suzerainty treaties (like the Mosaic/Sinai covenant) represent conditional covenants ("Do this and you shall live"), whereas royal grant covenants (like the Noahic, Abrahamic, Davidic, and new covenants) represent unconditional covenants.[47] Horton avers that with the latter covenants, "Yahweh (the suzerain) freely and mercifully obligates himself to fulfill a promise despite the opposition he encounters even from the beneficiaries of the oath. We may call these 'royal grants,' 'promissory oaths,' 'unconditional dispositions,' or any number of terms drawn from ancient legal custom, but they are distinguished sharply from suzerainty pacts in which a greater party (suzerain) obligates a lesser party (vassal) to serve faithfully and in which blessings or curses are held out as recompense."[48]

In contrast, the Mosaic covenant was a conditional covenant based strictly on law. "There is no mercy in the Sinaitic covenant itself. It is strictly an oath of allegiance by the people to personally perform everything commanded in the book of the law, with long life in the land promised as the blessing and exile and death as the curse."[49] This statement does not deny the fact that God's grace was experienced in the Mosaic covenant. Rather it means that the Sinai covenant "represents a law covenant rather than a promise covenant—in other words, that it is a republication in some sense of the original covenant with Adam."[50] That is, although God is gracious in making the covenant at Sinai with Israel, the covenant itself "is not gracious."[51]

---

47. See Horton, *Introducing Covenant Theology*, 33, 48, 56, 68, 74, 90.
48. Ibid., 74.
49. Ibid., 50.
50. Ibid., 97 (see also 130).
51. Ibid., 54. Robertson disagrees with Horton (and Kline) on this point.

With the Abrahamic covenant, however, God alone walks between the severed halves of the sacrificed animal indicating that God will assume all the responsibility for bringing the promises in the covenant to fruition. Robertson explains: "Abraham does not pass between the divided pieces representing the covenantal curse of self-malediction. The Lord of the covenant does not require that his servant take to himself the self-maledictory oath. Only God himself passes between the pieces."[52] He continues, "By this action, God promises. The Lord assumes to himself the full responsibility for seeing that every promise of the covenant shall be realized. It is not that Abraham has no obligations in the covenant relation. ... [But] this covenant shall be fulfilled because God assumes to himself full responsibility in seeing to its realization."[53]

Robertson does not simply divide the covenants into conditional and unconditional as does Horton. Instead, he notes that each of God's covenants has a conditional aspect. Although it is true that God will make certain that the conditions will be met, it is still conditional nonetheless. The certainty of God's faithfulness in fulfilling the covenant, however, does not relieve the individual from his covenant obligations. Similarly, the Davidic covenant had a conditional element that was fulfilled by Jesus Christ.[54] Finally, the new covenant is not a renewal of the covenant made at Sinai but a renewal of the covenant made with Abraham and is "the consummate fulfillment of the earlier covenants."[55]

---

52. Robertson, *The Christ of the Covenants*, 145.

53. Ibid., 145–46. Similarly, Horton comments, "God swears unilaterally to personally perform all of the conditions and suffer all of the curses for its violation" (*Introducing Covenant Theology*, 41–42).

54. Robertson, *The Christ of the Covenants*, 247–48.

55. Ibid., 41. The old covenant in Scripture is the Mosaic covenant made at Sinai, which was conditional and temporary, whereas the new covenant is a renewal of the Abrahamic covenant, which was unconditional and promissory. This distinction is not the same as the covenant of works and the covenant of grace. The covenant of works specifically involved Adam in his pre-fallen state as the representative of mankind and the covenant of grace is the covenant God made with Adam in his post-fallen state. This latter covenant is the foundation of all other unconditional covenants (Abrahamic, Davidic, and new).

How Were Old Testament Saints Saved?

Covenant theologians consistently teach that Old Testament saints were saved by grace and not by works. This view is consistent with their emphasis on the continuity between the Old Testament and New Testament and affirmation of the overarching covenant of grace. According to Horton, "Salvation has always come through a covenant of grace (founded on an eternal and unilateral covenant of redemption), rather than on a contract or one's personal fulfillment of the law."[56] Thus, the new covenant is not completely new but is a renewal of the covenant of grace that has been in operation since the fall of Adam. "The covenant of grace, as it is revealed in the New Testament, is essentially the same as that which governed the relation of Old Testament believers to God."[57]

In addition, the means of salvation has always been as a result of union with Christ through personal faith in the promised Messiah. Reymond asserts that "Old Testament saints were saved precisely the same way that New Testament saints are being saved, namely, through conscious faith in the (anticipated) sacrificial work of the promised Messiah on their behalf as that work was foresignified by Old Testament promises, prophecies, sacrifices, circumcision, the paschal lamb, and other types and ordinances delivered to the Jewish people."[58] Regardless of the covenant, the ground of salvation has always been the same. Robertson also remarks, "Throughout the Mosaic period of law-covenant, God considered as righteous everyone who believed in him."[59] Abraham is a model for all believers since "he believed the LORD, and he counted it to him as righteousness" (Gen 15:6). In the Old Testament, the faith of believers looked

---

56. Horton, *Introducing Covenant Theology*, 36 (see also 50).

57. Berkhof, *Systematic Theology*, 299–300.

58. Reymond, "The Traditional Covenantal View," 17. Later he adds, "The elect of God [in both the Old Testament and New Testament] were saved, are saved, and will be saved only by grace through faith in either the anticipated (OT) or accomplished (NT) work of the Messiah" (27). Likewise, Horton comments, "No less than new covenant believers, those under the old covenant were united to Christ by faith in the promise that was heard" (*Introducing Covenant Theology*, 74).

59. Robertson, *The Christ of the Covenants*, 174. Likewise, Sproul asserts, "the way of salvation in the Old Testament is substantially the same as in the New Testament. Redemption is always through grace by faith" (*What Is Reformed Theology?*, 114).

forward. In the New Testament, faith is directed backward to Christ's redemptive work. Thus, "Israelites under the old covenant and believers under the new are justified by grace alone through faith alone because of Christ alone."[60]

How Is the Old Testament Law to Be Applied Today?

In covenant theology, not all the Old Testament law is applicable to the New Testament believer. The Old Testament law is often divided into three types: moral, civil (judicial), and ceremonial.[61] Reformed theologians assert that only moral laws apply (continuity) but civil and ceremonial laws do not (discontinuity) because of their temporary status tied to the Mosaic covenant or because they are fulfilled in Christ, pointing to a future fulfillment of New Testament realties. Horton clarifies: "Civil laws ... are obviously in force only so long as the theocracy itself exists. Ceremonial laws ... are similarly 'canonical' only as long as the theocracy stands. ... [But] the moral law, summarized in the Ten Commandments, is inscribed on our consciences by virtue of our being created in God's image."[62] Furthermore, when Jesus summarized the two tables of the Ten Commandments as loving God and loving one's neighbor, he demonstrated continuity between the covenants. Thus, God's expectation of obedience to his moral law has not changed from the Old Testament to the New Testament. "So while the civil and ceremonial laws pertain exclusively to the theocracy and are no longer binding, the moral law is still in force."[63] The tripartite division of the law is consistent with the Westminster Confession of Faith:

> Besides [the Ten Commandments], commonly called
> *moral*, God was pleased to give to the people of Israel, as
> a church under age, *ceremonial laws,* containing several

---

60. Horton, *Introducing Covenant Theology*, 101. He also declares, "No Reformed writer I am aware of has argued that Old Testament believers were saved by works" although corporate obedience was necessary for them to remain in the land (103; see also 75, 101).

61. Ibid., 177–80.

62. Ibid., 177–78.

63. Ibid., 180.

typical ordinances, partly of worship, prefiguring Christ, His graces, actions, sufferings, and benefits; and partly, holding forth divers instructions of moral duties. All which ceremonial laws are now abrogated, under the New Testament. To them also, as a body politic, He gave sundry *judicial laws*, which expired together with the State of that people; not obliging under any now, further than the general equity thereof may require. The *moral law* does forever bind all, as well justified persons as others, to the obedience thereof; and that, not only in regard of the matter contained in it, but also in respect of the authority of God the Creator, who gave it. Neither does Christ, in the Gospel, any way dissolve, but much strengthen this obligation. (19.3–5, emphasis added)

The Reformed position of the law also affirms the three uses of the law in the new covenant:[64]

- *The civil use* (curb): The law restrains criminal behavior (Rom 13:1–3).
- *The pedagogical use* (mirror): The law shows us our sin and drives us to Christ (Rom 7:7–13).
- *The normative use* (ruler): The law provides norms for the Christian life, not as a means of salvation but for those already saved since the threat of the law's curse has been removed (Rom 7:21–24).[65]

---

64. See ibid., 180–82.

65. The Westminster Confession of Faith specially addresses the third use of the law: "Although true believers be not under the law, as a covenant of works, to be thereby justified, or condemned; yet it is of great use to them, as well as to others; in that, as a rule of life informing them of the will of God, and their duty, it directs and binds them to walk accordingly; discovering also the sinful pollutions of their nature, hearts and lives; so as, examining themselves thereby, they may come to further conviction of, humiliation for, and hatred against sin, together with a clearer sight of the need they have of Christ, and the perfection of His obedience. It is likewise of use to the regenerate, to restrain their corruptions, in that it forbids sin: and the threatenings of it serve to show what even their sins deserve; and what afflictions, in this life, they may expect for them, although freed from the curse thereof threatened in the law. The promises of it, in like manner, show them God's approbation of obedience, and what blessings they may expect upon the performance thereof: although not as due to them by the law as a covenant of works.

Kline affirms both continuity and discontinuity of Old Testament law in the life of the believer. In one sense he agrees that the Old Testament is normative for the Christian since it is scriptural revelation given by God.[66] And yet, "the Old Testament's community life-norms for Israel are replaced in the New Testament by a new polity for the church."[67] For Kline, the old covenant had its unique authoritative canon and because the church is under the new covenant, the binding documents have changed. As he explains, "the Old Testament, though possessing the general authority of all the Scriptures, does not possess for the church the more specific authority of canonicity. Under the new covenant the Old Testament is not the current canon."[68] Horton asserts that in his Sermon on the Mount, Jesus "assumes the seat of Moses and announces a regime change."[69] The old covenant was not wrong but was full of types and shadows that pointed to Christ. "Jesus does not set aside the law but fulfills it."[70] Thus, the theocratic polity of the Old Testament is "no longer binding for the people of God."[71] Instead, the teachings of Jesus, such as found in the Sermon on the Mount, are now binding.

And yet, covenant theologians approach the New Testament with the assumption of continuity unless they have specific evidence to the contrary. As Horton comments, "Covenant Theology begins with continuity rather than discontinuity, not because of any a priori bias, but because Scripture itself moves from promise to fulfillment, not from one distinct program to another and then back again."[72] He later adds

---

So as, a man's doing good, and refraining from evil, because the law encourages to the one and deters from the other, is no evidence of his being under the law: and not under grace" (19.6).

66. "As Scriptural revelation the Old Testament provides norms for faith. Indeed, all that the Old Testament teaches concerning God and the history of his relationship to his creation is normative for Christian faith" (Kline, *The Structure of Biblical Authority*, 101).

67. Ibid., 102. He later states that "not all that is contained in Old Testament laws concerning Israelite institutions was intended to be normative in all periods of Israel's history" (103).

68. Ibid., 102. He similarly writes, "The form of government appointment in the old covenant is not the community policy for the church of the new covenant, its ritual legislation is not a directory for the church's cultic practice, nor can the program of conquest it prescribes be equated with the evangelistic mission of the church in this world" (99).

69. Horton, *The Christian Faith*, 538.

70. Ibid., 153.

71. Ibid., 539.

72. Horton, *Introducing Covenant Theology*, 20.

that covenant theology "helps us to see the basic *continuity between the old and new covenants* in terms of a single covenant of grace running throughout."[73]

So, for example, Robertson assumes that the Sabbath requirement is still applicable for the church since the command is nowhere specifically revoked in the New Testament. For him, the "presumptive evidence favors the continuing significance of the essence if not the form of the Mosaic law-covenant into the present day."[74] Furthermore, the Sabbath command remains binding on Christians because it is part of God's moral law established in the Ten Commandments. Indeed, "the 'ten-words' derive their binding power from the fact that they reflect the nature of God himself."[75] But Robertson does affirm some discontinuity. With the arrival of the new covenant, the Sabbath command has been transformed. For instance, the Christian "does not first labor six days, looking hopefully toward rest. Instead, he begins the week by rejoicing in the rest already accomplished by the cosmic event of Christ's resurrection. Then he enters joyfully into his six days of labor, confident of success through the victory which Christ already has won."[76]

3. WHAT IS THE RELATIONSHIP BETWEEN ISRAEL AND THE CHURCH?

Does the Church Replace or Fulfill Israel, or Are the Two Distinct?

Because of their preference for continuity over discontinuity, it is natural for covenant theologians to see an organic relationship between Israel and the church. The New Testament church grows out of the Old Testament church.[77] The promises given to the church are a direct fulfillment of the promises given to Abraham. As such, there is only

---

73. Ibid., 20–21 (emphasis original).

74. Robertson, *The Christ of the Covenants*, 183.

75. Ibid., 74.

76. Ibid., 73.

77. Horton, *The Christian Faith*, 739.

one people of God who are all saved by grace through the atoning work of the Messiah. Thus, the New Testament church, made up of both Jews and gentiles, represents the true Israel of God. Based on texts such as 1 Peter 2:9–10, Horton declares, "it becomes clearer that we are dealing not with two peoples but with one (cf. Eph 2:11–22), and not with a displacement of Israel but with its enlargement."[78]

Horton and other covenant theologians are quick to clarify that their position should not be labeled as "replacement theology." The church is not Israel's replacement but its fruition.[79] Horton clarifies: "the church does not replace Israel; it fulfills the promise God made to Abraham that in him and his seed all the nations would be blessed."[80] The nation of Israel thus functions as a type of God's people which is eschatologically fulfilled in Jesus and the church. Robertson argues that Israel is "a typological representation of the elect people of God. ... If the new covenant people of God are the actualized realization of typological form, and the new covenant now is in effect, those constituting the people of God in the present circumstances must be recognized as the 'Israel of God.' As a unified people, the participants of the new covenant today are 'Israel.'"[81]

How Are Romans 11:26 and Galatians 6:16 Interpreted?

Similar to progressive covenantalism, there is no consistent interpretation of Romans 11:26 offered by covenant theologians. The identity of "Israel" in Paul's phrase, "And in this way all Israel will be saved," is understood to refer to (1) the church, (2) the elect among ethnic Israel throughout history, or (3) a future mass conversion of ethnic Israel. For instance, Horton is an advocate of the last view. He states, "After bringing in the full number of elect Gentiles, God will pour out his Spirit on the Jewish people en masse."[82] He also proposes that the latter part of Romans 11 "seems to argue that although this era is dominated by the widespread ingrafting of Gentiles and only a small

---

78. Ibid., 719.

79. Horton, *Introducing Covenant Theology*, 131–32.

80. Horton, *The Christian Faith*, 730.

81. Robertson, *The Christ of the Covenants*, 288–89.

82. Horton, *Introducing Covenant Theology*, 132.

remnant of Jews, there will be a widespread reingrafting of Jews at the end of the age."[83]

But many covenant theologians do not affirm a future mass conversion position. Robertson, for example, rejects the notion that Romans 11 teaches that at the end of history as we know it, all (or a vast majority of) ethnic Jews will be converted.[84] He argues that in the context of Romans 11, Paul's concern is not so much about the future as the present significance of Israel in God's plan (Rom 11:1, 5, 13–14, 30–31). This emphasis does not mean that Paul's discussion completely omits references to the future. It does, however, caution the exegete from reading into the text a bias that assumes a future mass conversion. In verse 11 Paul asks, "So I ask, did they stumble in order that they might fall?" Robertson notes that people often read this question as "Has God rejected ethnic Israel with respect to his special plan for their future?"[85] But such a reading prejudices one to see a distinctive future for ethnic Israel. Instead, the question asks, "Has God rejected ethnic Israel *altogether* as they might relate to his purposes of redemption?"[86] The issue at stake is whether God has completely rejected them because of their sin. Of course, Paul responds by answering, "By no means!"

Furthermore, the analogy of the olive tree is often misread by some. Paul does not claim that Israel as a nation will be grafted back into the tree representing God's blessings to Abraham. Instead, Paul affirms that those individual Jews who believe in Christ will be grafted back in. Thus, this pattern is the same as believing gentiles who are grafted in after they exercise faith in Christ. Robertson concludes, "Nothing in this figure of ingrafting communicates the idea of a distinctive and corporate inclusion of the Jews at some future date."[87] So, when Paul writes, "in this way all Israel will be saved" (v. 26), he either is referring to the elect remnant of Jewish believers throughout

---

83. Horton, *The Christian Faith*, 949.

84. Robertson, *The Israel of God*, 167–92. See also LaRondelle, *The Israel of God in Prophecy*, 124–34.

85. Robertson, *The Israel of God*, 172.

86. Ibid. (emphasis original).

87. Ibid., 176.

history (Robertson's earlier view)[88] or he is referring to the church—Jewish and gentile believers who have been grafted into the same tree (Robertson's later view).[89] But regardless of which view someone takes, "Nothing in [Romans 11] says anything about the restoration of an earthly Davidic kingdom, or of a return to the land of the Bible, or of the restoration of a national state of Israel, or of a church of Jewish Christians separated from Gentile Christians."[90]

In Galatians 6:16 Paul states, "Peace and mercy to all who follow this rule—to the Israel of God" (NIV). The question is whether Paul's reference to "the Israel of God" relates to Jewish believers only (the dispensationalist view) or to Jewish and gentile believers, that is, the church (the covenant theology view). In the original Greek, the last phrase begins with *kai* (usually translated "and," "even," or "also") which here is interpreted epexegetically. If that is correct, then *kai* functions as an explanatory term, represented in the NIV with an em dash ("—") which functions similarly to "even" or "that is." Such a reading then designates all those to whom Paul is writing (i.e., the church) as the "Israel of God."

This interpretation is consistently held by covenant theologians.[91] Robertson argues that his interpretation best fits the context of the epistle where Paul has been arguing that gentiles are part of God's people without practicing the rite of circumcision. Robertson contends, "Certainly he would include Gentile believers among those he intends to bless, particularly since his point has been to eliminate any distinction between Jews and Gentiles who have faith in Jesus."[92] Citing Galatians 6:16 as support, Horton declares, "The church, in its unity of Jew and Gentile in Christ, is understood as the fulfillment of

---

88. See O. Palmer Robertson, "Is There a Distinctive Future for Ethnic Israel in Romans 11?" in *Perspectives on Evangelical Theology: Papers from the Thirtieth Annual Meeting of the Evangelical Theological Society*, ed. Kenneth Kantzer and Stanley Gundry (Grand Rapids: Baker, 1979), 209–27. See also Robert L. Reymond, *A New Systematic Theology of the Christian Faith*, 2nd ed. (Nashville: Thomas Nelson, 2002), 1024–30.

89. Robertson claims that "a strong case can be made in support of either of these interpretations" (*The Israel of God*, 186).

90. Ibid., 191.

91. See, e.g., Robertson, *The Israel of God*, 39–46, 115; LaRondelle, *The Israel of God in Prophecy*, 108–11.

92. Robertson, *The Israel of God*, 42.

Israel's existence."[93] Thus, the church (both Jew and gentile) in Christ is the true Israel of God.[94]

4. WHAT IS THE KINGDOM OF GOD?

The kingdom of God is the reign and rule of God over his creation. The kingdom, while already here in part, will only finally arrive when Christ returns and all rebellion against the King finally comes to an end. According to Hoekema, "The kingdom of God, therefore, is to be understood as the reign of God dynamically active in human history through Jesus Christ, the purpose of which is the redemption of his people from sin and from demonic powers, and the final establishment of the new heavens and the new earth."[95]

Did Jesus Bring the Kingdom?

It is the consensus among covenant theologians that during his earthly ministry, Jesus ushered in the kingdom of God. This kingdom, however, did not come in its fullness and so believers still await the final consummation. Horton maintains that "the kingdom of Christ is present now but not yet in its consummated form. ... The kingdom is coming, but has also come."[96] Thus, although "the promised messianic kingdom of Jesus Christ has come,"[97] the fullness of the same kingdom in its final, perfected form will not be manifest until Christ's second coming. Consequently, "this present age will come to a climactic conclusion with the arrival of the final phase of the kingdom of the Messiah."[98]

Covenant theology disagrees with dispensationalism regarding Jesus' response to the disciples' question in Acts 1:6 ("Will you at

---

93. Horton, *The Christian Faith*, 795 (see also 719, 730).

94. See also Reymond, "The Traditional Covenantal View," 41.

95. Anthony A. Hoekema, *The Bible and the Future* (Grand Rapids: Eerdmans, 1979), 45.

96. Horton, *The Christian Faith*, 544.

97. Robertson, *The Israel of God*, 195.

98. Ibid., 196.

this time restore the kingdom to Israel?").[99] The problem with the disciples' question must not be limited to the *timing* of the coming kingdom. They also missed the *nature* of the kingdom. Even though the disciples were probably thinking of the kingdom in nationalistic terms with a government centered in Jerusalem, theirs was "a misapprehension of the nature of the kingdom Jesus had in mind."[100] The presence of the kingdom is directly related to Jesus' following statement about the coming of the Holy Spirit. That is, "the power of the kingdom of God would come down on the apostles in the form of the promised Holy Spirit, thereby manifesting the current reality of the kingdom."[101] Robertson further suggests that Jesus' response that the Holy Spirit would come "not many days from now" (Acts 1:5) may even be a partial answer to the disciples' question concerning the timing of the coming kingdom.

Regarding the domain of the kingdom, Robertson notes that Jesus' answer does address the disciples' question. They ask about the restoration of the kingdom to Israel and Jesus declares that the kingdom growth will begin in Israel but will eventually expand to the end of the earth. Consequently, Jesus' "statement should not be regarded as peripheral to the question asked by the disciples. Instead, it is germane to the whole issue of the restoration of the kingdom to Israel. The domain of the kingdom, the realm of the Messiah's rule, would indeed begin at Jerusalem. ... [But] the domain of this kingdom cannot be contained within the Israel of the old covenant."[102]

How Is the Kingdom Consummated?

Most covenant theologians would be classified as amillennialists. Horton clarifies that "amillennialism" is a misnomer since this position affirms a millennial period but just not a purely *future* period. In other words, the millennium is the period between Christ's advents

---

99. See ibid., 129–37.

100. Reymond, "The Traditional Covenantal View," 58.

101. Robertson, *The Israel of God*, 132.

102. Ibid., 133. He later summarizes: "The kingdom of God would be restored to Israel in the rule of the Messiah, which would be realized by the working of the Holy Spirit through the disciples of Christ as they extended their witness to the ends of the earth" (134).

(the current period of gospel proclamation).[103] Thus, he prefers the title "semirealized millennialism."[104] The key text for the millennium, Revelation 20, is consistently interpreted non-chronologically and symbolically.[105] Often the most controversial aspect of their position is the current binding of Satan. Those who disagree with amillennialism insist that the imagery of Satan being chained, locked up, and sealed in the abyss indicates that he has no power or influence during the millennium.[106]

Amillennialists assert, however, that the binding of Satan in Revelation 20 corresponds to the binding of the "strong man" referenced by Jesus (Matt 12:28–29; Luke 10:18). When was Satan bound? According to Horton, "Christ has triumphed over Satan at the cross, and in his resurrection and ascension led captivity captive."[107] Additionally, when Revelation 20 refers to Satan being bound and thrown into the bottomless pit, this is an example of telescoping. That is, it includes both the period of him being bound (already) and the final consummation of his judgment (not yet). This is consistent with other passages found in the New Testament. For example, although Hebrews 2:14 states that by his death Christ *destroyed* the devil, it is not until the end of history that he will be cast into the lake of fire. And although Satan still "prowls around like a roaring lion, seeking someone to devour" (1 Pet 5:8) and still persecutes the church, he is unable to change the outcome of the redemption of God's people (Rev 12). He is called "the god of this world" who "has blinded the minds of the unbelievers, to keep them from seeing the light of the gospel of the glory of Christ" (2 Cor 4:4). Yet, because he is bound his efforts are ultimately thwarted so that the light of Christ shines

---

103. Thus, the coming of the kingdom during Jesus' ministry is also the beginning of the millennium. Consequently, the kingdom and the millennium are essentially two sides of the same coin.

104. Horton, *The Christian Faith*, 935.

105. Regarding the question as to whether Revelation 20 should be taken literally, Horton argues, "What we reject is a literalistic interpretation of the thousand years, since the book of Revelation employs numbers symbolically" (*Introducing Covenant Theology*, 120).

106. Robertson notes that those who make this argument also have the problem regarding the many people who will continue to rebel against Christ during that time (*The Israel of God*, 162n50).

107. Horton, *The Christian Faith*, 940.

"in our hearts to give the light of the knowledge of the glory of God in the face of Jesus Christ" (2 Cor 4:6). And even if it is true that "the whole world lies in the power of the evil one" (1 John 5:19), we also know that Scripture teaches "that the kingdom has been inaugurated and is progressing through the gospel, and that all authority now belongs to Christ in heaven and on earth" and "that the imprisonment of the world is precisely *the condition that Christ's kingdom of grace is overturning.*"[108]

Furthermore, Revelation specifically states that the binding of Satan keeps him from "deceiving the nations" (Rev 20:3). Robertson suggests that this is a good description of the present age where the gospel is being spread to all the peoples of the world. He adds, "In previous ages, the message of redemption was essentially confined to the borders of a single nation of the world. But now all nations are the privileged possessors of God's saving grace."[109] Thus, Satan is restrained so that the good news of salvation in Christ can spread to all the nations of the world.

The amillennial position is also considered the simplest eschatological position. Immediately preceding the second coming is a period of intense tribulation, and then the second coming is followed by the last judgment. "With his second coming will arrive the resurrection of all the dead and the last judgment as one single and sweeping event."[110]

ASSESSMENT

The first strength of covenant theology relates to its hermeneutical approach to Scripture. While affirming a literal approach to Scripture, it rejects a literalistic (overly or woodenly literal) hermeneutic that often is found in dispensationalism. It further sees typology as an important interpretive tool while at the same time avoiding an allegorical approach to the Bible that was popular pre-Reformation. Beale comments, "Most scholars today agree that typology is not allegory because it is based on the actual historical events of the Old Testament

---

108. Ibid., 942 (emphasis original).
109. Robertson, *The Israel of God*, 161.
110. Horton, *The Christian Faith*, 940.

passage being dealt with and because it essentially consists of a real, historical correspondence between the Old Testament and the New Testament event."[111]

Negatively, covenant theology has been accused of inconsistently applying Old Testament typology, especially as it relates to the Abrahamic covenant. For example, whereas covenant theologians insist that the land is a type (and thus fulfilled in Christ and the new heavens and new earth), they reject the notion that the seed of Abraham is also a type (and thus fulfilled in Christ and those united to him by faith). Because the sign of the covenant (circumcision) was given to the children of Israel in the Old Testament, it is argued that the sign of the covenant (baptism) should likewise be given to the children of believers. The principle of continuity assumes that the children of believers should be baptized and welcomed as members in God's church just as the children of Israel were circumcised and welcomed as part of God's covenant community. Stephen Wellum explains that, in one sense, the hermeneutical approach of covenant theology is similar to dispensationalism: "Dispensational thought makes [this argument] in regard to the land promise, while covenant theology makes it in regard to the genealogical principle, both of which are tied to the Abrahamic covenant!"[112] Likewise, Reisinger notes,

> Both the Dispensationalist and the Covenant Theologian want to bring the promise of Abraham and his seed into the present age in a *physical* sense via the lineage of their physical children. They both insist that the promise made to Abraham and his seed is an unconditional covenant and is therefore still in effect for physical seeds. The Dispensationalist naturalizes the seed to mean physical Israel, and the [covenant

---

111. Beale, "Did Jesus and His Followers Preach the Right Doctrine from the Wrong Texts?" 395.

112. Peter J. Gentry and Stephen J. Wellum, *Kingdom through Covenant: A Biblical-Theological Understanding of the Covenants*, 2nd ed. (Wheaton: Crossway, 2018), 100.

theologian] naturalizes the seed to mean the physical children of believers.[113]

A second strength of covenant theology is its focus on the unity and continuity of God's purposes in the Bible. If the sovereign God of the universe purposes to redeem a people for himself through the Messiah and inspires the biblical authors to chronicle the unfolding of this plan, then it naturally leads to the expectation that the Bible will be a unified document. The covenants of redemption, creation (works), and grace provide a coherence to the Bible and to God's plan to redeem humanity.

But not all covenant theologians agree with these three overarching covenants. For example, not all affirm the covenant of redemption—specifically whether it is appropriate to call the inter-Trinitarian agreement a "covenant." Robertson states, "To speak concretely of an intertrinitarian 'covenant' with terms and conditions between Father and Son mutually endorsed before the foundation of the world is to extend the bounds of scriptural evidence beyond propriety."[114] It should be noted that Robertson is the exception and Horton is convinced that it stems from "an overly restrictive definition of covenant" which then leads to the claim "the covenant of redemption is speculative rather than biblical."[115]

A final strength of covenant theology is its rejection of "replacement theology" or "supersessionism," as was noted in the views of Robertson and Horton. For example, Horton writes, "Israel is not replaced by the church, but is the church *in nuce*, just as the church is the anticipation of the kingdom of God."[116] Historically, replacement theology has been associated with racism, including anti-Semitism. Theologically, the concept of fulfillment seems to better represent the relationship between Israel and the church.

---

113. John G. Reisinger, *Abraham's Four Seeds: A Biblical Examination of the Presuppositions of Covenant Theology and Dispensationalism* (Frederick, MD: New Covenant Media, 1998), 94.

114. Robertson, *Christ of the Covenants*, 54.

115. Horton, *Introducing Covenant Theology*, 82.

116. Horton, *The Christian Faith*, 731.

Unfortunately, not all covenant theologians agree here. For example, commenting on the parable of the vineyard, Reymond states, "*Here is a biblical 'replacement theology,'* and it is Jesus himself who enunciated it." The special standing of Israel would be judged "and the special standing that it had enjoyed during the old dispensation would be transferred to the already existing and growing *international* church of Jesus Christ."[117] Ridderbos does not use the term "replacement theology" but does use the word "replace." He writes, "On the one hand, in a positive sense it presupposes that the church springs from, is born out of Israel; on the other hand, the church takes the place of Israel as the historical people of God."[118] Similarly LaRondelle comments that Christ's pronouncement of judgment given in Matthew 21:43 means that "Israel would no longer be the people of God and would be *replaced* by a people that would accept the Messiah and His message of the kingdom of God." He later adds that the church "would replace the Christ-rejecting nation."[119]

---

117. Reymond, "The Traditional Covenantal View," 49 (emphasis original).

118. Herman Ridderbos, *Paul: An Outline of His Theology* (Grand Rapids: Eerdmans, 1975), 333–34.

119. LaRondelle, *The Israel of God in Prophecy*, 101 (emphasis original).

CHAPTER 7
CHRISTIAN RECONSTRUCTIONISM

Taxonomy of Theological Systems

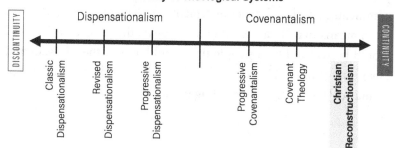

C hristian reconstructionism represents the position of extreme (though not absolute) continuity between the Old Testament and New Testament. It can be defined as a "version of Reformed, postmillennial theology that emphasizes the concepts of theonomy and dominion."[1] Reconstructionists believe that both church *and* state are under God's rule and thus should both be governed by God's laws. The concepts of the sacred and secular represent a false dichotomy introduced by unbiblical thought. Instead, society should be *reconstructed* based on Christian principles found in the Bible. Michael Gabbert offers the following summary:

> Christian reconstructionism is a complex movement
> of neo-Puritan scholars and evangelical Calvinist

---

1. Alan Cairns, ed., *Dictionary of Theological Terms* (Greenville, SC: Ambassador-Emerald International, 1998), 296.

theology. Drawing history and the Scriptures together, Reconstructionists attempt to combine a dominion-oriented, postmillennial understanding of theonomy with various historical examples of anti-Erastian church-state structures. The goal of the movement is to integrate every aspect of American life into a consistent world view based upon the abiding validity of the Old Testament law in exhaustive detail.[2]

The main tenets of Christian reconstructionism can be summarized according to the following five points:[3]

1. *Calvinism:* Christian reconstructionists hold to the historic, orthodox faith affirmed by the major Reformed confessions.[4] They also assert that because God is sovereign over all things, the Christian faith should apply to all of life (including education, art, technology, politics, etc.). Regeneration (salvation by grace through faith) is man's only hope since only those who reflect the image of Christ can effect real change in society.[5]

2. *Theonomy:* Reconstructionists believe that society should be ruled by biblical law, including the Old Testament civil law. They maintain that the Bible provides the basis for all ethics and should therefore be the enduring standard for all government, including

2. Michael D. Gabbert, "An Historical Overview of Christian Reconstructionism," *CTR* 6.2 (1993): 281.

3. These tenets come from Andrew Sandlin, often cited in the *Chalcedon Report.* See also Gary DeMar, *The Debate over Christian Reconstruction* (Fort Worth, TX: Dominion Press, 1988), 63–71; Gary North and Gary DeMar, *Christian Reconstruction: What It Is, What It Isn't* (Tyler, TX: Institute for Christian Economics, 1991), 81–82; Cairns, ed., *Dictionary of Theological Terms,* 296–97.

4. Sandlin avers, "All reconstructionists are Calvinists" (Andrew Sandlin, "The Genius of the Thought of Rousas John Rushdoony," in *A Comprehensive Faith: An International* Festschrift *for Rousas John Rushdoony,* ed. Andrew Sandlin [San Jose, CA: Friends of Chalcedon, 1996], 7).

5. DeMar writes, "Society cannot change unless people change, and the only way people can change is through the regenerating work of the Holy Spirit" (*The Debate over Christian Reconstruction,* 63).

the church, the family, *and* the public sector. This view is necessarily based on the authority, sufficiency, and unity of Scripture.

3. *Presuppositional Apologetics:* The Bible's truthfulness is self-attesting and is not subject to human proofs since it is the highest authority and is therefore the very foundation of all proofs. Because of the noetic effect of sin on humanity, the problem with unbelievers is not lack of evidence but lack of repentance and submission to God's word. Reconstructionism is thus founded on the presuppositional apologetics of Cornelius Van Til.[6]

4. *Postmillennialism:* Christ's second coming will occur *after* the millennium (which is John's image for the kingdom of Christ which was established in the first century). Through the power of the Holy Spirit and the word of God, the church will continue to advance Christ's kingdom until most of society has become Christianized. This process will be incremental and difficult, with many ups and downs in history, but the outcome is certain. Christ's kingdom will triumph in the end.

5. *Dominion Theology:*[7] From the beginning, God gave man the mandate to subdue and take dominion over the earth (Gen 1:28). Thus, the goal of the gospel and the Great Commission is to fulfill the task originally given to Adam. This includes the Christianization of all areas of life—the individual, family, church, and government—through the application of divinely revealed scriptural precepts and principles.

---

6. Van Til has been called the grandfather of the reconstructionist project (though he never condoned or affiliated with Christian reconstructionism). See Greg L. Bahnsen, *Van Til's Apologetic: Readings and Analysis* (Phillipsburg, NJ: P&R, 1998).

7. Christian reconstructionism can be viewed as a subset of dominion theology. Other groups adhere to a type of dominion theology (e.g., Roman Catholics, integralism; Charismatics/Pentecostals, Kingdom Now theology; and New Apostolics, Reformation).

The three proponents who perhaps best represent the thought of Christian reconstructionism are (1) Rousas Rushdoony, (2) Greg Bahnsen, and (3) Gary North.[8]

Rousas J. Rushdoony (1916–2001) is known as the founder or father of modern Christian reconstructionism.[9] He was born in New York City to Armenian immigrants who had recently fled to America to escape genocide. His family soon moved to California where he would eventually receive a BA in English (1938) and an MA in education from the University of California in Berkeley (1940). In 1944 he graduated from the Pacific School of Religion and was ordained in the Presbyterian Church (USA) later that year. After serving as a missionary to the Shoshone and Paiute tribes for more than eight years, he then pastored in Santa Cruz, California. In 1965 he founded the Chalcedon Foundation and its monthly newsletter, *Chalcedon Report* (which became a magazine in 1987). In 1970 he resigned as a minister in the Orthodox Presbyterian Church in order to focus his attention on writing and speaking.

Rushdoony based his philosophy and theology on the work of Cornelius Van Til.[10] Van Til's presuppositional approach recognizes the noetic effect of sin and therefore holds that human thinking is fallen or depraved, which even affects a person's ability to reason, leading one either consciously or subconsciously to suppress the truth in righteousness. Consequently, there are no neutral facts—all

---

8. Adam English notes, "Rushdoony, Bahnsen, and North together formed the original triumvirate of the Reconstructionists" (Adam C. English, "Christian Reconstructionism after Y2K: Gary North, the New Millennium, and Religious Freedom," in *New Religious Movements and Religious Liberty in America*, ed. Derek H. Davis and Barry Hankins [Waco, TX: Baylor University Press, 2002], 168). Similarly, Gabbert declares that "the real leadership of the movement rests with three men who provide the inspiration and intellectual framework for the crusade." He then goes on to list R. J. Rushdoony, G. Bahnsen, and G. North ("An Historical Overview of Christian Reconstructionism," 283). Finally, Neuhaus calls these three "the chief architects of the movement" (Richard John Neuhaus, "Why Wait for the Kingdom? The Theonomist Temptation," *First Things* 3 [May 1990]: 13).

9. See Mark Rousas Rushdoony, "A Biographical Sketch of My Father," in *A Comprehensive Faith*, 21–29.

10. Sandlin writes that Rushdoony's Calvinism was "interpreted through the grid of the epistemology and apologetics of Cornelius Van Til" which then propelled his "Reformed convictions to their most consistent and logical conclusions" ("The Genius of the Thought of Rousas John Rushdoony," 7). See Rousas John Rushdoony, *By What Standard? An Analysis of the Philosophy of Cornelius Van Til* (Vallecito, CA: Ross House, 1995).

propositions are either biased toward God's law or toward secular humanism. Additionally, non-Christian knowledge is corrupt, and where it is valid, it is borrowed from a Christian theistic worldview. Rushdoony sought to apply Van Til's philosophical approach to all spheres of life. Some of his works include *By What Standard?* (1958), *The One and the Many: Studies in the Philosophy of Order and Ultimacy* (1971), several works related to education and homeschooling, history, and, most importantly, law and politics (*The Institutes of Biblical Law* [3 vols.; 1973, 1982, 1999], *Law and Liberty* [1984], and *Christianity and the State* [1986]), and biblical studies (*Systematic Theology* [2 vols.; 1994] and *Romans and Galatians* [1997]). His *Institutes of Biblical Law* (modeled after Calvin's *Institutes of the Christian Religion*) is a massive three-volume work that is Rushdoony's most significant contribution.

Greg Bahnsen (1948–1995) is known for being a philosopher, theologian, apologist, and ethicist. He graduated *magna cum laude* from Westmont College with a BA in philosophy (1970), from Westminster Theological Seminary (Philadelphia) with an MDiv and ThM (1973), and from the University of Southern California with a PhD (1978). He was raised in the Orthodox Presbyterian Church and later became an ordained minister of that denomination. While still in high school, he began reading Van Til and in college started writing for Rushdoony's Chalcedon Foundation. He is best known for his advocacy of presuppositional apologetics, theonomy, and postmillennialism. Because of his strong defense of Christian reconstructionism, he was dismissed from Reformed Theological Seminary (Jackson, MS).

He had a fruitful writing and speaking career as a full-time scholar in residence for the Southern California Center for Christian Studies until his untimely death in 1995 at the age of forty-seven. Some of Bahnsen's key works include *Theonomy in Christian Ethics* (1977, 1984), *By This Standard: The Authority of God's Law Today* (1985), *House Divided: The Break-Up of Dispensational Theology* (1989), *No Other Standard: Theonomy and Its Critics* (1991), as well as chapters in *God and Politics: Four Views* (1989), *Five Views on Law and Gospel* (1996), and *Van Til's Apologetic: Readings and Analysis* (1998).

Gary North (1942–present) is a well-known reconstructionist who has authored or coauthored over fifty books on theology, economics, and history. He received a PhD in history from the University of California, Riverside in 1972. North later married Rushdoony's daughter, though was estranged from Rushdoony for about twenty years due to a theological disagreement. Among his many endeavors, North served as research assistant for congressman Ron Paul (1976). North is also involved in promoting homeschool curriculum since he believes that it is important to educate the next generation with the truth. He is also the founder of the Institute for Christian Economics (ICE) and Dominion Press in Tyler, Texas. Some of his more relevant books to the current study are *Dominion Covenant: Genesis* (1982), *The Sinai Strategy: Economics and the Ten Commandments* (1986), *Millennialism and Social Theory* (1990), *Tools of Dominion: The Case Law of Exodus* (1990), *Christian Reconstruction: What It Is, What It Isn't* (1991, coauthored with Gary DeMar), *Theonomy: An Informed Response* (1991), and *Westminster's Confession: The Abandonment of Van Til's Legacy* (1991).

1. WHAT IS THE BASIC HERMENEUTIC?

Is a Literal or Symbolic Hermeneutic Employed?

In one sense the hermeneutical approach of Christian reconstructionists is similar to that of traditional covenant theologians. They often employ a redemptive-historical method that allows for both a literal and symbolic hermeneutic, depending on the particular genre and context. They reject the literalistic interpretation of dispensationalism and embrace the use of figurative language and symbolism in prophecy and apocalyptic literature, especially the book of Revelation. Chilton explains that essentially Revelation is a book of signs and that such "symbols are not to be understood in a literal manner."[11] For example, the thousand-year binding of Satan does not refer to a literal thousand years but designates "a vast, undefined period of time."[12]

---

11. David Chilton, *Paradise Restored: A Biblical Theology of Dominion* (Tyler, TX: Dominion Press, 1985), 151.

12. Ibid., 199.

Christian reconstructionists hold to strong continuity between the Old Testament and New Testament. Because of progressive revelation, however, the New Testament has the final say as to how we should understand the Old Testament. For example, Bahnsen asserts, "If the Scriptures are seen as a progressive revelation, then the New Testament must be used to understand, not undermine, the Older Testament."[13] Elsewhere he adds that "we must be committed to the rule that *the New Testament should interpret the Old Testament for us.*"[14]

And yet, Christian reconstructionists apply a rather literal hermeneutic when it comes to the Old Testament law. The Ten Commandments and the other Old Testament commands (minus those considered ceremonial law) are to be strictly applied today.[15] Because the law represents the eternal and binding character of God, both individuals and institutions should submit to biblical law. Rushdoony argues the laws should be interpreted and followed literally since "God requires that He be worshiped according to His own word."[16] The law is literal, and the consequences for breaking the law are literal and physical as well.[17] In sum, reconstructionists employ somewhat of a mixed hermeneutic—one that allows for symbolism but maintains that (most) Old Testament laws must be followed literally.

Christian reconstructionists consistently assume continuity between the Testaments unless the New Testament says otherwise.[18] Bahnsen argues, "We should presume that Old Testament

---

13. Greg L. Bahnsen, *Theonomy in Christian Ethics*, 3rd ed. (Nacogdoches, TX: Covenant Media Press, 2002), 306.

14. Greg L. Bahnsen, *By This Standard* (Tyler, TX: Institute for Christian Economics, 1985), 4 (emphasis original).

15. Gabbert suggests that the sociological background of Rushdoony's insistence on keeping the Old Testament law springs from an exhaustive literalness that characterizes Armenian biblical exegesis. For example, in Armenia even in the modern era, Old Testament animal sacrifices were performed with a Christian significance ("An Historical Overview of Christian Reconstructionism," 284). See Rousas John Rushdoony, *The Institutes of Biblical Law*, 3 vols. (Phillipsburg, NJ: P&R, 1973, 1982, 1999), 1:782–83.

16. Rushdoony, *Institutes of Biblical Law*, 1:22.

17. Ibid., 1:65.

18. Greg L. Bahnsen, "The Theonomic Reformed Approach to Law and Gospel," in *Five Views on Law and Gospel*, ed. Stanley N. Gundry (Grand Rapids: Zondervan, 1999), 113.

standing laws continue to be morally binding in the New Testament, unless they are rescinded or modified by further revelation."[19] He clarifies his hermeneutical presuppositions: "To approach the New Testament with the premise that only that which is *repeated* from the Old Testament is still binding is faulty procedure; everything God has said should be that by which man lives (Matt. 4:4), not simply those things which God has spoken *twice* (and at the right places)."[20] North has a similar approach: "we must affirm that *unless* the New Testament explicitly announces that the *former application* of a *still morally binding* law has been changed by God, we should still honor it in its Old Testament details."[21]

What Is the Proper Role of Typology?

Although typology may not play a prominent role, it nevertheless plays a crucial role. Rushdoony defines typology as "God's predestined and developing pattern in history."[22] Furthermore, "all the factors are real and historical; they represent necessary stages in the unfolding of God's revelation and His plan in history."[23] Because of the overarching themes present in Scripture, the biblical text reveals reoccurring people and events as types that tie the texts together. Types are not just symbols but have historical referents. One of the most important examples of typology in Scripture is the connection between Israel and Jesus Christ. Rushdoony cites the typology of sonship in Hosea 11:1 and Galatians 4:4–7 to show the connection between Old Israel (an adopted son), Jesus (the natural son), and new Israel (an adopted son in Christ). Thus, the citation of Hosea 11:1 in Matthew 2:15 teaches us that "Christ, as the Greater Moses, shall lead His people out of bondage into world conquest, so that, as heirs of

---

19. Ibid., 142; also found in *Theonomy*, xxvi.

20. Bahnsen, *Theonomy*, 184 (emphasis original). He also states, "We presume our obligation to obey any Old Testament commandment unless the New Testament indicates otherwise. We must assume continuity with the Old Testament" (*By This Standard*, 3; see also 7).

21. Gary North, *75 Bible Questions Your Instructors Pray You WON'T Ask: How to Spot Humanism in the Classroom or Pulpit*, 2nd ed. (Tyler, TX: Institute for Christian Economics, 1988), 88 (emphasis original).

22. Rushdoony, *Institutes of Biblical Law*, 2:597.

23. Ibid.

all things in Christ, they shall reign with Him. The birth of our Lord is thus a joyful word of victory; it declares the ordained continuity of grace and law, and of God's Israel by adoption."[24]

Typology is especially crucial in making a distinction between laws that must be kept today and laws that are no longer applicable. In other words, how is it that some laws are directly applicable to believers and some are not? Those Old Testament *ceremonial* laws that typologically pointed to Christ's perfect life and atoning death are fulfilled in him. Thus, certain Old Testament requirements fore-shadowed realities that are replaced by the New Testament antitype. The Old Testament ceremonial laws of sacrifice served as shadows of Christ's perfect sacrifice. Additionally, the land of Canaan foreshad-owed the kingdom of God. Bahnsen states, "What God was doing with the nation of Israel was but a type looking ahead to the inter-national church of Christ."[25] Consequently, laws regulating circum-stances related to the land of Canaan such as family plots, location of cities of refuge, and the law of the levirate have been put aside and are now inapplicable since they have served their God-ordained, temporal purpose.[26]

How Are Old Testament Restoration Prophecies Fulfilled?

Amos 9:11–15 describes the future (from Amos' perspective) res-toration of Israel, promising prosperity, blessing, and physical res-toration of the land. Although very little is said about this passage by Christian reconstructionists, in general they employ a symbolic interpretation of prophecy and, because of their preterist leanings, see many prophecies of Christ's kingdom as already fulfilled in the first century AD. Furthermore, they do not argue for a restoration of the literal geopolitical, nation-state of Israel, as true Israel is now spiritual Israel, which includes both ethnic Jews as well as gentiles.

---

24. Ibid., 2:600.

25. Bahnsen, "The Theonomic Reformed Approach to Law and Gospel," 105; see also idem, *By This Standard*, 6.

26. Bahnsen, *By This Standard*, 6. See Greg L. Bahnsen, "M. G. Kline on Theonomic Politics: An Evaluation of His Reply," *Journal of Christian Reconstruction* 6.2 (Winter 1979–80): 195–211, for Bahnsen's response to Kline.

Bahnsen insists that the New Testament redefines the people of God and transforms the significance of the promised land.[27] Yet, there is a sense in which such prophecies will be fulfilled both symbolically and literally: symbolically because the church is the new Israel and literally because the fulfillment will occur on the earth where God's people rule the nations. Thus, such prophecies often point to "the visible prosperity of Christ's established kingdom on earth."[28]

2. WHAT IS THE RELATIONSHIP BETWEEN THE COVENANTS?

Covenant is a central concept of Christian reconstruction, as its proponents see God's primary interaction with humankind occurring through covenants. Rushdoony notes that all covenants are acts of grace and that all covenants also include a law relationship.[29] Thus, both law and grace are essential components of the covenant. God gives his covenant as an act of grace, but his word is law and law-keeping demands holiness. Rushdoony claims, "*Grace* and *law* are covenantal. God's covenant is a covenant of grace because for Him to enter into a covenant or treaty with man is an act of grace from the superior to the inferior. At the same time, a covenant is a treaty of law whereby in this case the greater tells the lesser how to live under His care and protection."[30] The covenants are never abolished, and thus God's covenant relationship (including his expectations) with his people continues on as an act of grace and law.

Although Rushdoony embraces the covenant of grace,[31] he rejects the covenant of works affirmed by traditional covenant theologians.

---

27. Bahnsen, *Theonomy*, xxvi.

28. Gary North, "Common Grace, Eschatology, and Biblical Law," *The Journal of Christian Reconstruction* 3.2 (Winter 1976–77): 63.

29. Rousas John Rushdoony, *Systematic Theology*, 2 vols. (Vallecito, CA: Ross House, 1994), 1:374.

30. Rushdoony, *Institutes of Biblical Law*, 3:3 (emphasis original); see also idem, *Systematic Theology*, 1:376–77.

31. Rushdoony states, "The covenant which exists between God and His people has been rightly called the *covenant of grace*" (*Institutes of Biblical Law*, 1:695 [emphasis original]).

He offers four reasons as to why the nomenclature of "covenant of works" should be rejected.[32] First, all covenants between God and humanity are initiated and executed by God and are thus acts of grace. Works that the law requires are always a response of gratitude to grace previously received. Second, any covenant based on works undermines God's sovereignty and predestination. Third, even in his state of innocence, man does not have "any capacity to render anything to God in the way of works."[33] Fourth, there is nothing man can do to change his relationship with God since only God can alter that relationship. Any covenant that does not stress God's grace "is deadly wrong" and can lead to "serious error."[34]

North maintains that the primary covenant in the Bible is the dominion covenant found in Genesis 1:26–28.[35] This covenant was made with Adam, confirmed with Noah, and has never been repealed. "In this sense, there is only one covenant. It will never end. It will extend into eternity, for it defines both man and the creation."[36] North proposes five main components of a covenant:[37]

1. An announcement that God is *transcendent*: God is different from and superior to man and yet he is also present with his creation (*immanence*).
2. The establishment of a *hierarchy* to enforce God's authority on earth.
3. A set of *ethical rules* or laws man must follow in exercising his dominion over the earth.
4. A list of *judgments* that will be imposed by God, who blesses man for obedience and curses man for disobedience.

---

32. See Rushdoony, *Systematic Theology*, 1:376–79. Cf. also Brian Abshire, "The Covenant of Grace and Law: Rushdoony and the Doctrine of the Covenant," in *A Comprehensive Faith*, 47.

33. Rushdoony, *Systematic Theology*, 1:377.

34. Ibid., 1:376, 377.

35. Notice how North avoids the terminology of the "covenant of works."

36. Gary North, *God's Covenants* (Dallas, GA: Point Five Press, 2014), 47.

37. North and DeMar, *Christian Reconstruction*, 57.

5. A program of *inheritance*: a lawful transition that moral men need in order to extend their dominion over creation.

All of these features are present in all of the covenants that God made with his people throughout the Bible. The new covenant does not replace the dominion covenant. Thus, there is a single covenant with four manifestations: pre-Adamic, pre-fall, post-fall, and post-resurrection.[38]

Consequently, all the covenants in the Bible serve as reiterations of the same covenant that God made in the garden with Adam and Eve. All people are under the dominion covenant of Genesis 1:28.[39] God charged the first human beings to rule over the earth and to submit to the Lord's sovereign domain, and that charge continues to this day. Each covenant pictured in the Old Testament refers to the same promise of God and demonstrates God's everlasting word to his people. Even the new covenant is a reissuing of the broken original covenant.[40]

Although critics of Christian reconstruction sometimes overlook references to discontinuity, Bahnsen readily acknowledges discontinuity between the Old Testament and New Testament. Some discontinuities are redemptive-historical in nature due to the coming of Christ whereas others may be cultural in nature due to changes of time, place, or lifestyle.[41]

Are the Covenants Conditional or Unconditional?

Christian reconstructionists do not distinguish between conditional and unconditional covenants since they affirm all covenants are a recapitulation of the same promise. They also do not differentiate

---

38. North, *God's Covenants*, 48.

39. Ibid., 56.

40. See Bahnsen, "The Theonomic Reformed Approach to Law and Gospel," 96; Abshire, "The Covenant of Grace and Law," 48. Rushdoony comments, "Scripture gives us one Lord, one covenant, one plan of salvation, and one law. The members of that one covenant live and die; the covenant is renewed and continues. The old Israel gives way to the new, but the covenant continues. It is an everlasting covenant" (*Institutes of Biblical Law*, 2:317).

41. Bahnsen, "The Theonomic Reformed Approach to Law and Gospel," 100.

between certain components of the covenant or even use the language of conditionality. The covenants are universal and apply to all men.[42] North claims that in addition to forming covenants with men, God also establishes covenants with the institutions of family, church, and state, and all parties are expected to comply with the covenant stipulations.[43] Breaking the covenant "places the violators thereof directly under the ban of God, who, by His providential government, brings judgment upon them."[44] God's law is eternal, and he is sovereign over the whole earth, even if people and institutions do not obey him. Thus, if individuals or society do not comply with God's law, then judgment is coming, just as God judged and condemned the nations in the Old Testament for failing to observe his commands.[45] It could be stated, then, that the covenants are unconditional in the sense that God will impose his will and he will rule the world, but they are conditional in the sense that non-compliance to the law results in judgment.

How Were Old Testament Saints Saved?

Christian reconstructionists are convinced that in every age and under every covenant, people are saved by grace through faith in Christ. This position is expected based on their view of the continuity between the covenants. Indeed, as was mentioned earlier, they essentially affirm one biblical covenant that is periodically renewed. Bahnsen clarifies, "The old covenant administration of law (or the Mosaic administration itself) did not offer a way of salvation or teach a message of justification that differs from the one found in the gospel of the new covenant."[46] He continues, "The old covenant … was a covenant of *grace* that offered salvation on the basis of grace through faith, just as does the Good News found in the New Testament."[47] The main difference was that the old covenant anticipated the prophesied Messiah whereas the new covenant proclaims the accomplishments.

---

42. Rushdoony, *Institutes of Biblical Law*, 1:655.
43. North and DeMar, *Christian Reconstruction*, 56.
44. Rushdoony, *Institutes of Biblical Law*, 2:476.
45. Ibid., 1:694; North and DeMar, *Christian Reconstruction*, 57.
46. Bahnsen, "The Theonomic Reformed Approach to Law and Gospel," 96.
47. Ibid., 97 (emphasis original).

Bahnsen argues, "The Old Covenant was *not* a covenant of works which proposed salvation by works of the law. It was rather a covenant of *grace* which offered salvation on the basis of grace through faith, just as does the good news found in the New Testament. The law-covenant *looked ahead* to the coming of the Savior, administering God's covenants by means of promises, prophecies, ritual ordinances, types, and foreshadows that anticipated the Savior and His redeeming work."[48] This position is also affirmed by DeMar who writes that "the Bible teaches that the church since Adam has always been under grace and not law! The New Testament did not set forth any new way to be saved."[49] Salvation was always by grace through faith in the Savior, whether in the Old Testament or New Testament. The law points to God but does not justify the believer. Instead, believers abide by God's law as a response to grace. Law-keeping enables the believer to grow closer to the Lord and please him as an act of obedient worship.[50]

How Is the Old Testament Law to Be Applied Today?

Because the topic of law is the most distinctive element of Christian reconstruction, this section will necessarily receive more attention.[51] First, because there are no neutral facts in their system, Christian reconstructionists reject *natural law* since it ultimately undermines the possibility of a truly Christian society. Rushdoony comments, "Neither positive law nor natural law can reflect more than the sin and apostasy of man: *revealed law* is the need and privilege of Christian

---

48. Greg L. Bahnsen, *No Other Standard: Theonomy and Its Critics* (Tyler, TX: Institute for Christian Economics, 1991), 76–77 (emphasis original). Elsewhere he states that "the New Testament condemns any legalistic (i.e., Judaizing) use of God's law to establish one's personal justification or sanctification before him" (Bahnsen, "The Theonomic Reformed Approach to Law and Gospel," 113; see also idem, *Theonomy*, 136–37; idem, *By This Standard*, 144).

49. North and DeMar, *Christian Reconstruction*, 100 (see also 36).

50. Rushdoony takes this a step further when he writes, "Man's *justification* is by the *grace* of God in Jesus Christ; man's *sanctification* is by means of the *law* of God" (*Institutes of Biblical Law*, 1:4 [emphasis original]).

51. DeMar defines theonomy as "The continuing validity and applicability of the whole law of God, including, but not limited to, the Mosaic case laws is the standard by which individuals, families, churches, and civil governments should conduct their affairs" (North and DeMar, *Christian Reconstruction*, 81).

184

society. It is the *only* means whereby man can fulfil his creation mandate of exercising dominion under God."[52]

Second, they reject the *tripartite division of* Old Testament law. Although most Reformed Christians maintain that the civil and ceremonial laws of the Old Testament are no longer applicable to believers, Christian reconstructionists claim that believers are still obligated to keep both the moral *and* civil laws. Thus, such divisions of the law are not helpful since it was the moral obligation of God's people to keep the civil (or judicial) statutes. According to Rushdoony,

> It is a serious error to say that the *civil law* was also abolished, but the *moral law* retained. What is the distinction between them? At most points, they cannot be distinguished. Murder, theft, and false witness are clearly civil offenses as well as moral offenses. In almost every civil order, adultery and dishonoring parents have also been civil crimes. Do these people mean, by declaring the end of civil law, that the Old Testament theocracy is no more? But the kingship of God and of His Christ is emphatically asserted by the New Testament and especially by the book of Revelation. The state is no less called to be under Christ than is the church. It is clearly *only* the sacrificial and ceremonial law which is ended because it is replaced by Christ and His work.[53]

Thus, Rushdoony endorses extreme continuity between the Old Testament and New Testament, especially in relation to the role of the law. In fact, unless there is (explicit) evidence to the contrary, we should assume the eternal validity of the law in the life of the believer. He states:

> The law is done away with only as an indictment against us; it stands as the righteousness of God which

---

52. Rushdoony, *Institutes of Biblical Law*, 1:10 (emphasis original).

53. Ibid., 1:304–5 (emphasis original).

we must uphold. Every aspect of the Old Testament law still stands, except those aspects of the ceremonial and priestly law specifically fulfilled by the coming of Christ, and those laws specifically re-interpreted in the New Testament.[54]

Third, *all law*, not just the Ten Commandments, *is eternally binding* and thus applicable to all people at all times and in all places. In the beginning of his *Institutes of Biblical Law*, Rushdoony specifies his position on the law:

> It is a modern heresy that holds that the law of God has no meaning nor any binding force for man today. It is an aspect of the influence of humanistic and evolutionary thought on the church, and it posits an evolving, developing god. This "dispensational" god expressed himself in an earlier age, then later expressed himself by grace alone. ... But this is not the God of the Scripture, whose grace and law remain the same in every age, because He, as the sovereign and absolute lord, changes not, nor does He need to change.[55]

The "law" mentioned throughout the Bible does not refer merely to the Mosaic legal codes but is rather God's divine word.[56] There is one God and one law throughout time. Therefore, the law of Christ and the law of Moses are synonymous.[57] God's law reflects his unchangeable character and is absolutely binding for all people in all time because God is the one true God.[58]

Most Old Testament law (including civil or judicial law) provides "case law," or specific examples of how to apply the Ten Commandments.

---

54. Rousas John Rushdoony, *The Roots of Reconstruction* (Vallecito, CA: Ross House Books, 1991), 553.

55. Rushdoony, *Institutes of Biblical Law*, 1:2.

56. Ibid., 1:6.

57. Ibid., 1:17; North and DeMar, *Christian Reconstruction*, 107.

58. Bahnsen, *No Other Standard*, 12.

"Without case law, God's law would soon be reduced to an extremely limited area of meaning."[59] In essence, then, there are really only ceremonial and moral laws, with so-called "civil" laws simply providing specific examples ("case laws") of how the moral law should be applied. The contextual case laws reveal the moral character of God applied to a particular situation and provide direction for bringing society under the reign of God.

Bahnsen also claims that the "demands of God's law are *universal* in their character and application" and are "not confined in validity to Old Testament Israel."[60] His thesis is that "the Christian is obligated to keep the whole law of God as a pattern of sanctification and that his law is to be enforced by the civil magistrate where and how the stipulations of God so designate."[61] Thus, the ethical standards of the new covenant are the same as the old covenant. Because moral standards do not change, what is sinful in the Old Testament is likewise sinful in the New Testament.[62] This continuity between the Testaments is confirmed by his stance that there is essentially only one covenant (the covenant of grace). Consequently, there is only one code of ethics that governs God's covenant-keeping people.[63]

Matthew 5:17–20 provides a crucial text for Christian reconstructionism.[64] In this text, it is argued, Jesus is in no way setting aside Old Testament law but declaring that he came to fulfill the law by enforcing it. Our relationship to the ceremonial law has changed because such laws were fulfilled by Christ and his sacrificial death.[65] Jesus came not to remove the law of God but "to confirm and restore the

---

59. Rushdoony, *Institutes of Biblical Law*, 1:12.

60. Bahnsen, "The Theonomic Reformed Approach to Law and Gospel," 112 (emphasis original). He defines theonomy as the "verbalized law of God which is imposed from outside man and revealed authoritatively in the words of Scripture" (*Theonomy*, 35).

61. Bahnsen, *Theonomy*, 36.

62. Bahnsen, *By This Standard*, 37.

63. Ibid., 42.

64. Waltke calls Matthew 5:17 "the Golden Text of theonomy" (Bruce K. Waltke, "Theonomy in Relation to Dispensational and Covenant Theologies," in *Theonomy: A Reformed Critique*, ed. William S. Barker and W. Robert Godfrey [Grand Rapids: Zondervan, 1990], 80).

65. Bahnsen states, "The ceremonial observations were stop-gap and anticipatory; Christ and the New Covenant are the *fulfilled reality*. Therefore, all Christians have had the ceremonial laws observed for them finally and completely *in Christ*" (*Theonomy*, 205 [emphasis original]).

full measure, intent, and purpose of the Older Testamental law."[66] He did not come to invalidate God's law since God's word abides forever (1 Pet 1:25–25). Consequently, "*every* single stroke of the law must be seen by the Christian as applicable to *this* very age between the advents of Christ."[67] Christ's perfect obedience to the law does not cancel the demands of the law for believers, though it does remove the condemning aspect of the law. Furthermore, the Holy Spirit provides the power needed for believers to obey and comply with God's glorious law. Thus, the Sermon on the Mount, for example, is binding on Christians today since it should be viewed as "a proclamation of the absolute will of God."[68]

The law of Moses is applicable not only to the individual, but also to human government. It is the proper function of civil officials to obey what the Bible says regarding crime and punishment.[69] The civil laws of the Old Testament model perfect social justice for all times and all cultures, even the punishment of law-breakers.[70] All nations have a responsibility to follow the law of God as revealed by Moses to the nation of Israel.[71] Because both the law and the consequences for law-breaking are still binding, some Christian reconstructionists support the sanctions of Old Testament law such as public executions and stonings. In fact, rejecting the prescriptions set forth in the Bible would be an act of heresy reminiscent of Marcionism.[72]

---

66. Ibid., 67.

67. Ibid., 84 (emphasis original).

68. Ibid., 44.

69. Bahnsen, "The Theonomic Reformed Approach to Law and Gospel," 128.

70. Bahnsen, *Theonomy*, xxvii.

71. Based on the redefinition of the people of God in the New Testament, certain aspects of the Old Testament are no longer applicable such as (1) loyalty to Israel as a nation, (2) the tribal division of the land and cities of refuge, and (3) Jewish dietary laws (Bahnsen, "The Theonomic Reformed Approach to Law and Gospel," 105).

72. Gary North, "Editor's Conclusion," in *Theonomy: An Informed Response*, ed. Gary North (Tyler, TX: Institute for Christian Economics 1991), 316–19.

3. WHAT IS THE RELATIONSHIP BETWEEN ISRAEL AND THE CHURCH?

Does the Church Replace or Fulfill Israel, or Are the Two Distinct?

According to Christian reconstructionism, the church is best described as *replacing* Israel. Because there is continuity between the Testaments, there is only one people of God. In the Old Testament the people of God was Israel, and in the New Testament it is the church, the new Israel. The nation of Israel had a special covenant relationship with God but because Israel rejected the Lord, God formed a covenant with a new nation, the church. Thus, the kingdom was taken from the Jews and given to the church.[73] Therefore, the church replaces Israel as the people of God and now receives the promises once given to Israel (1 Pet 2:9–10). As Bahnsen explains, "The kingdom that was once focused on the nation of Israel has been taken away from the Jews ... and given to an international body, the church of Jesus Christ."[74]

Rushdoony contends that Jesus replaced the twelve patriarchs of Israel with the twelve apostles and the council of the elders with his seventy disciples and tasked them to keep his covenant by bringing the world under his command.[75] Judgment to Israel came in AD 70 with the destruction of Jerusalem and the temple. Indeed, most Christian reconstructionists are preterists who interpret the first part of the Olivet Discourse (Matt 24:3–34) and most of the book of Revelation (except Rev 20:7–15) as being already fulfilled, specifically when God judged Israel in the first century.[76] It is important to note,

---

73. Chilton, *Paradise Restored*, 78–79.

74. Bahnsen, "The Theonomic Reformed Approach to Law and Gospel," 104–5. Bahnsen and Gentry claim that "Israel as a nation has once for all been set aside as the specially favored nation of God" (Greg L. Bahnsen and Kenneth L. Gentry Jr., *House Divided: The Break-Up of Dispensational Theology* [Tyler, TX: Institute for Christian Economics, 1989], 173).

75. Rushdoony, *Systematic Theology*, 1:382.

76. Chilton, *Paradise Restored*, 85–113. See also David Chilton, *The Days of Vengeance: An Exposition of the Book of Revelation* (Fort Worth: Dominion Press, 1987), 15–17; Kenneth L. Gentry Jr. *The Olivet Discourse Made Easy* (Draper, VA: ApologeticsGroup Media, 2010), ch. 8; idem, "A Preterist View of Revelation," in *Four Views on the Book of Revelation*, ed. C. Marvin Pate (Grand Rapids: Zondervan, 1998), 37–92; Greg L. Bahnsen, *Victory in Jesus: The Bright*

however, that the strong divide between Israel and the church is not unsurpassable. God has one covenant people, which now consists of the church. If an ethnic Jew is saved, he or she will become part of the church.[77] Israel once held a favored position, but because they rejected God, God widened his elected people to the entire world, of which ethnic Jews may be a part.

How Are Romans 11:26 and Galatians 6:16 Interpreted?

In Romans 11:25–26 Paul writes that "a partial hardening has come upon Israel, until the fullness of the Gentiles has come in. And in this way all Israel will be saved." Reconstructionists consistently affirm that Romans 11 teaches that "Jews will someday be converted to Christ, and that this will spark a massive revival, which will produce abundant blessing for the entire world."[78] Bahnsen and Gentry note that this passage indicates that there will be "mass conversions" of Jews.[79] This position fits within their larger framework of postmillennialism and dominion theology. It should be noted that "Israel" in Romans 11:26 is usually taken to mean ethnic Jews. North maintains that Romans 11 teaches "the fulness of converted physical Israel grafted back into the people of God."[80] Likewise, Bahnsen and Gentry assert, "It is true that racial Jews in great mass will be saved later in the development of the kingdom in history."[81] Thus, it is specifically "physical Israel" or "racial Jews" that will be converted. In contrast, Rushdoony, following Calvin, uses Galatians 6:16 to interpret this passage, claiming, "Since the church is 'the Israel of God' (Gal. 6:16), 'all Israel' refers to the 'fulness of the Gentiles' and of the Jews."[82] For him, "all Israel" refers to spiritual Israel consisting of both Jews and gentiles.

Chilton explains the interrelationship between the salvation of Israel and the gentiles. He writes, "The people of Israel, as a whole,

---

Hope of Postmillennialism (Texarkana, AR: Covenant Media Press, 1999), ch. 1.

77. Ibid., 126, 130.
78. North and DeMar, *Christian Reconstruction*, 133.
79. Bahnsen and Gentry, *House Divided*, 217.
80. North, "Common Grace, Eschatology, and Biblical Law," 63.
81. Bahnsen and Gentry, *House Divided*, 166.
82. Rousas John Rushdoony, *Romans and Galatians* (Vallecito, CA: Ross House, 1997), 222.

will turn back to the faith of their fathers and will acknowledge Jesus Christ as Lord and Savior."[83] This restoration will then result in an even greater revival among the gentiles. Below is a summary of Chilton's position:[84]

1. The entire gentile world will be converted to faith in Jesus Christ.
2. Genetic Israel will be converted to faith in Jesus Christ.
3. Not every individual gentile or Jew will be converted.
4. The conversion of both Jews and gentiles will take place through the normal means of evangelism in this age.
5. The motive for the conversion of Israel will be jealousy.
6. Converted Jews, in every age, belong to the church of Jesus Christ; they are not a distinct group.
7. Israel will not be restored as the kingdom.
8. The conversion of Israel will result in an era of great blessings for the entire world.

At the closing of his epistle to the churches of Galatia, Paul adds the following benediction: "And as for all who walk by this rule, peace and mercy be upon them, and upon the Israel of God" (Gal 6:16). Christian reconstructionists consistently claim that in this closing statement, Paul identifies his entire audience (both Jews *and* gentiles) as the "Israel of God." Thus, it is argued, in the passage Paul clearly redefines Israel as the church.

Rushdoony claims that because Israel rejected their own Messiah, God judged them by taking away their special status and applying it to the church. He comments, "For Paul, the old Israel had been cut off from the root, Jesus Christ, and the new Israel grafted in. ... Israel rejected the Messiah and was set aside, and the church became the new Israel of God (Gal. 6:16)."[85] North makes a similar argument: "Repeatedly, Israel had disobeyed God. With the crucifixion of Christ,

---

83. Chilton, *Paradise Restored*, 126.

84. Ibid., 129–31.

85. Rushdoony, *Romans and Galatians*, 409 and *Institutes of Biblical Law*, 3:154 (see also 2:429, 431; 3:176).

God finally severed His covenantal relation with the nation of Israel" and made a new covenant with the church, the new Israel of God.[86] Finally, Chilton argues, "From the beginning, God has always had His one covenant people. The New Testament church is simply the continuation of the true 'Israel of God' (Gal. 6:16), after the false Israel had been cut off."[87] The Israel of God refers to God's covenant people, which is now spiritual, not ethnic or political.

4. WHAT IS THE KINGDOM OF GOD?

Because Christian reconstructionists emphasize God as the true authority and sovereign king over the world, the kingdom of God holds a central position in their hermeneutic. North's definition of the kingdom of God is quite broad: it is "the *civilization* of God."[88] That is, it is the entire creation (in both heaven *and* earth) which belongs under God's dominion. It is therefore the goal of Christian reconstruction to help society submit to God and his laws and fulfill the creation mandate given in Genesis 1:28.

In its current state, the world has turned away from God and has set itself up as a false god. The hope of the kingdom of God is that Jesus Christ will save and rule the world. Christian reconstructionists affirm a postmillennial eschatology. Currently, people participate in the kingdom of God by embracing the gospel and living according to God's commands in the Bible. But as the gospel spreads further bringing the majority of people in the world to salvation, Christians will look more deeply at the implications of their faith for all of life and will seek to promote the kingdom on earth by urging the application of God's revealed law.[89]

---

86. North, *God's Covenants*, 34.

87. Chilton, *Paradise Restored*, 126. See also Bahnsen, *Theonomy*, 188; idem, "The Theonomic Reformed Approach to Law and Gospel," 105.

88. North and DeMar, *Christian Reconstruction*, 30 (emphasis original).

89. Rushdoony, *Institutes of Biblical Law*, 3:176; Gary North, "Editor's Introduction to Part III," in *Theonomy: An Informed Response*, 203; North and DeMar, *Christian Reconstruction*, 99.

Did Jesus Bring the Kingdom?

Although one of the major goals of Christian reconstructionism is to spread the kingdom of God through both individual and institutional evangelism, Christians should not be viewed as the ones bringing the kingdom because it is already here (see, e.g., Matt 3:2; 10:7; 12:28).[90] Furthermore, Jesus did not so much bring the kingdom as extend the kingdom. God has always been the sovereign king over his creation but through Christ the visible reign and rule of God is extended. As opposed to the dispensational teaching that Jesus will one day rule from a physical throne in Jerusalem, reconstructionists affirm he is already ruling. Jesus' kingdom is spiritual and physical in scope. Because Jesus is the sovereign king over all creation (including all society), not only the family and the church but every sphere of life—including the state, the school, the arts and science, economics, etc.—should be brought into conformity to his word and under his lordship. No area of life is exempt from his dominion.[91] The purpose of man and society goes back to Genesis 1:27–30 and the dominion mandate to subdue and fill the earth.[92] As an institution, the state falls under the jurisdiction of God's rule and thus belongs to the kingdom of God.[93] Those nations that attempt to build a society

---

90. North and DeMar, *Christian Reconstruction*, 97.

91. Rushdoony states: "The gospel is for all of life: the good news is precisely that the whole of life is restored and fulfilled through Jesus Christ, that, in the counsel of God, the kingdom is destined to triumph in every sphere of life. This gospel cannot be proclaimed and the dominion of the kingdom extended except on Christian presuppositions. The answer to the question, how wide a gospel do we have, is simply this: as wide as life and creation, as wide as time and eternity" (*By What Standard?*, 176). Bahnsen notes that "theonomists are committed to the transformation or reconstruction of every area of life, including the institutions and affairs of the socio-political realm, in accordance with the holy principles of God's revealed Word (theonomy)" ("The Theonomic Reformed Approach to Law and Gospel," 118).

92. Rushdoony, *Institutes of Biblical Law*, 1:163.

93. Rushdoony comments, "Not only is every church a religious institution, but every state or societal order is a religious establishment. Every state is a law order, and every law order represents an enacted morality, with procedures for the enforcement of that morality. Every morality represents a form of theological order, i.e., is an aspect and expression of a religion. The church thus is not the only religious institution; the state also is a religious institution. More often than the church, the state has been the central religious institution of most civilizations through the centuries" (Rousas John Rushdoony, *Christianity and the State* [Vallecito, CA: Ross House, 1986], 7).

and legal system on a foundation other than God's perfect law are destined for failure.

Jesus' kingdom is here, but it is not in its final state. Following a postmillennial view of eschatology, Bahnsen claims that Christ is presently reigning over his creation and will continue to do so until he subdues every enemy under his feet. Christ is progressively plundering Satan's house and is rescuing the nations from his deception.[94] Thus, we cannot separate God's kingdom from this world. To do so is to surrender the world to Satan.[95] The kingdom will emerge progressively through history and spread across the whole earth (cf. Dan 2:44; Luke 13:18–21).[96] When Christ does return, he will enforce his law across the entire world and cast out those who do not submit to his authority and dominion.

How Is the Kingdom Consummated?

When the disciples asked Jesus in Acts 1:6 about the restoration of the kingdom to Israel, they did not understand the nature of the kingdom of God.[97] Jesus related the kingdom directly to witness and discipleship. The disciples were to go and make disciples of all nations through the power of the Holy Spirit, which will spread the kingdom of God on earth (Matt 28:18–20; Acts 1:8). The goal of Christian reconstruction (and of the church) is to roll forward Christ's earthly kingdom by "rolling back Satan's earthly kingdom."[98]

Because of their view of humanity, reconstructionists do not believe that progress toward the millennium will be the result of humanity's actions. Christians cannot institute the kingdom on their own through social good or through political power. Rather, the transformation toward the reign of peace will come about through the divine work of the Holy Spirit on both individuals and institutions.

---

94. Bahnsen, "The Theonomic Reformed Approach to Law and Gospel," 120.

95. North and DeMar, *Christian Reconstruction*, 29.

96. Chilton, *Paradise Restored*, 68, 73–74.

97. Bahnsen and Gentry claim, "Absolutely nothing in either the question or the answer demands the notion that *national* Israel would be restored to a *political*, earthly kingdom" (Bahnsen and Gentry, *House Divided*, 171). Additionally, the disciples could have been in error as they often were.

98. North and DeMar, *Christian Reconstruction*, 29.

It is not conquest by force but "conquest by conversion."[99] The key is not legal reform but lifechanging regeneration brought about by the Spirit of God.[100] Rushdoony explains: "It is *not* the purpose of the state and its law to change or reform men: this is a spiritual matter and a task for religion. Man can only be changed by the grace of God through the ministry of His word. Man cannot be changed by statist legislation; he cannot be legislated into a new character."[101] The law can restrain people but cannot change or save them. "God's kingdom advances by means of the Great Commission."[102]

Christians should transform society from the bottom up and bring all spheres of society under the lordship of Jesus. Comprehensive evangelism involves engaging in politics to save the state and imposing biblical sanctions to save society.[103] Christians serve the kingdom by spreading God's law outside of the walls of the church. Rushdoony argues, "The Bible is God's word for man in his family life, in church, state, school, business, the arts and sciences, law, economics, politics, and all things else. We cannot claim to affirm God's sovereignty, or believe in the lordship of Jesus Christ, if we limit God's word to the church."[104] The kingdom comes in its fullness through reconstructing society to form a Christian civilization under the rule of Jesus Christ, the true authority and sovereign king.

As stated earlier, to be a Christian reconstructionist is to be postmillennial. DeMar provides the following definition:

---

99. Gary North, *Millennialism and Social Theory* (Tyler, TX: Institute for Christian Economics, 1990), 273. See also idem, "Common Grace, Eschatology, and Biblical Law," 68; idem, *Westminster's Confession: The Abandonment of Van Til's Legacy* (Tyler, TX: Institute for Christian Economics, 1991), 337–38; North and DeMar, *Christian Reconstruction*, 40, 63.

100. See Bahnsen, "The Theonomic Reformed Approach to Law and Gospel," 140; North and DeMar, *Christian Reconstruction*, 51, 126.

101. Rousas John Rushdoony, *Law and Liberty* (Vallecito, CA: Ross House, 1984), 3 (emphasis original). Rushdoony declares, "The key to remedying the situation is *not* revolution, nor any kind of resistance that works to subvert law and order. The New Testament abounds in warnings against disobedience and in summons to peace. The key is regeneration, propagation of the gospel, and the conversion of men and nations to God's law-word" (*Institutes of Biblical Law*, 1:113 [emphasis original]). He later adds, "Clearly, there is no hope for man except in regeneration" (1:449).

102. Bahnsen, *By This Standard*, 9.

103. North and DeMar, *Christian Reconstruction*, 34.

104. Rushdoony, *Romans and Galatians*, 1.

Postmillennialism is the belief that, before Christ returns, by the power of the Spirit, the kingdom of Jesus Christ will grow to enjoy a period of prosperity and growth throughout the world through the Church's faithfulness in fulfilling the Great Commission. ... [Additionally,] the converted nations will seek to order their common social and political life according to the Word of God in Scripture.[105]

North offers the following summary: Christ returns at the end of the millennium (i.e., the spiritual kingdom of Christ spanning the church age), but only after unprecedented advancement of the gospel to all nations. It is a time of peace, righteousness, and prosperity as God's visible kingdom expands through the influence of the church. The return of Christ will coincide with the resurrection and judgment at the end of the church age. Thus, for North, "the millennium or kingdom of Christ is a present reality spanning the interadventual [sic] age."[106] At the end of the period of millennium righteousness and prosperity, Satan will be released and "will bring apostasy from these blessed conditions."[107] Chilton summarizes his position: "On the Last Day, at the end of the world, Jesus Christ will return to resurrect all men for the Judgment, both the righteous and the wicked. Those Christians who are still living at the Second Coming will be raptured to join the Lord and the resurrected saints in the Glory-Cloud, where they will be transformed, fully restored into the image of God."[108]

ASSESSMENT

The first strength of Christian reconstructionism is their effort to employ a hermeneutic that produces a consistent biblical, theological, and ethical system. By focusing on continuity between the Testaments (and between all covenants), reconstructionists affirm the universal

105. North and DeMar, *Christian Reconstruction*, 127.

106. North, "Common Grace, Eschatology, and Biblical Law," 63.

107. Ibid.

108. Chilton, *Paradise Restored*, 148.

applicability of Old Testament law to all cultures and contexts. As such, they attempt to provide a coherent and unified presentation of the word of God and demonstrate its relevance in a modern context. Christian reconstructionists also take a clear stand against secular humanism, which has permeated Western society so that many Christians hold humanistic ideas without recognizing them, compromising some of the core doctrines of Christianity. Thus, it provides a clear avenue to honor God and spread his kingdom on earth.

But here is where a major critique has been noted by those skeptical of this view. In their quest for continuity, reconstructionists seem to neglect important distinctions between the covenants. Interestingly, many traditional covenant theologians, who are known for their affirmation of the continuity between the covenants, criticize Christian reconstructionists for failing to see sufficient discontinuity. For example, Kline insists that the problem with Christian reconstructionism "is a failure to do justice to the discontinuity between the old and new covenants."[109] Similarly, Knudsen states that "we may not assume that every law in the Old Testament age without exception continues to apply until it has been revoked. The sharp distinction between the old and the new ages will not allow us to assume this."[110]

Because of their focus on continuity, reconstructionists are often accused of ignoring the progress of redemptive history, especially as it relates to the distinction between Israel and modern America (or any nation). Longman writes, "Before applying a case law from the Old Testament today, therefore, we must consider not only cultural adaptations but also discontinuities that result because of the difference in redemptive status between Israel and any modern society." He continues, "Theonomy tends to grossly overemphasize continuity to the point of being virtually blind to discontinuity."[111] Kline identifies their failure to see the typological aspect of the Old Testament theocracy. Commenting on this error specifically in Bahnsen's *Theonomy*,

---

109. Meredith G. Kline, "Comments on an Old-New Error," *WTJ* 41 (1978): 173.

110. Robert D. Knudsen, "May We Use the Term 'Theonomy' for Our Application of Biblical Law?" in *Theonomy: A Reformed Critique*, 36.

111. Longman, "God's Law and Mosaic Punishments Today," in *Theonomy: A Reformed Critique*, 48, 49.

Kline declares, "Dispensationalism says the theocratic kingdom of Israel is to be resumed in the future beyond the alleged new covenant parenthesis" whereas "Bahnsen says the kingdom structure of Old Testament Israel is pretty much the same thing as the state in all ages or as the Chistocracy of the millennium (especially in its later stage)."[112] Thus, because he is constrained by a certain type of literalism, Bahnsen fails to recognize that the prophetic idiom used by Old Testament authors was conditioned and limited to a particular context. Instead, the proper correlation is not between Israel and America but between Israel and the church. As Clowney states, "To suppose that the body of Christ finds institutional expression in both the church and the state as religious and political spheres is to substitute a sociological conception of the church for the teaching of the New Testament. Christ does not give the keys to the kingdom to Caesar, nor the sword to Peter before the *parousia*. The church is the new nation (I Pet. 2:9)."[113]

The second strength of Christian reconstructionism is that it has a high view of the law. After all, the law was graciously given to Israel based on God's covenantal love and their status as his chosen people. The psalmist took great delight in God's law (Ps 119:47). Paul affirmed that the law was "holy and righteous and good" (Rom 7:12) and that he delighted in the law of God in his inner being (Rom 7:22). James exhorts his readers to keep "the royal law" and claims that breaking one part of the law makes one guilty of breaking all of it (Jas 2:8–10). Peter urges his audience to live holy lives based on an Old Testament injunction (1 Pet 1:15–16, citing Lev 11:44–45). John indicates that those who truly love God will keep his commands (1 John 2:3–6; 5:3).

A correlated weakness, however, is that there is an inconsistent application of the law. Although the Old Testament case law (i.e., civil law) is given the utmost importance, one is often left wondering how such laws should be applied for Christians today. For example, in noting the differences among Christian reconstructionists, Bahnsen

---

112. Kline, "Comments on an Old-New Error," 182n7. Bahnsen disputes this claim in *By This Standard*, 4–7.

113. Edmund P. Clowney, "The Politics of the Kingdom," *WTJ* 41 (1978–79): 306.

admits that "many (like myself) do not affirm R. J. Rushdoony's view of the dietary laws, Gary North's view of home mortgages, James Jordon's stance on automatic infant communion (without sessional examination), or David Chilton's attitudes toward bribery and 'ripping off' the unbeliever."[114] If people today must keep the Old Testament law, and if those who refuse to obey the law are considered antinomian or unregenerate, then such diversity of opinions regarding the application of the law is not comforting.[115]

Furthermore, Bahnsen insists that all the law of God (minus the ceremonial law) is applicable today. But wisely recognizing that certain Old Testament laws are culturally conditioned, he maintains that the application of some laws cannot be carried out as stated. So, when Deuteronomy 22:8 states that railings should be put on roofs to protect people from falling and getting hurt or killed, Bahnsen suggests that a proper application of the law in our context is installing a fence around a swimming pool.[116] He identifies the principle of the law, which is also the same principle found in the sixth commandment ("you shall not murder"), and then applies it to a modern context. If that is the case, then is it really the law we are required to follow or merely the principles upon which the laws are founded?

In addition, there is not agreement among reconstructionists as to what sins are deserving of capital punishment. Bahnsen lists murder, adultery, homosexuality, sodomy and bestiality, incest, incorrigibility in children, Sabbath-breaking, kidnapping, apostasy, idolatry, witchcraft, and blasphemy.[117] He states, "Knowing that God's standard of righteousness (which includes temporal, social relations) is

---

114. Bahnsen, *Theonomy*, xxix.

115. Bahnsen recognizes this objection when he writes, "I certainly do *not* believe that theonomists have all the answers. Indeed, in a number of cases I believe the answers they offer are positively wrong! Theonomy was never *intended* to be 'rich enough to *determine* the answer to all questions of exegesis and application'—much less an apostate effort to gain a system of ultimate continuity for understanding reality! (Frame, pp. 97, 98). With Frame, I agree the exegetical work on specific texts remains to be done. It seems that theonomists, though, are more often the one doing it (even with occasional errors), not so much their critics" (*No Other Standard*, 28n19 [emphasis original]). See also Rushdoony, *Institutes of Biblical Law*, 1:2–3.

116. Bahnsen, *Theonomy*, xxiv, 517–18; idem, *By This Standard*, 138; idem, "The Theonomic Reformed Approach to Law and Gospel," 102.

117. Bahnsen, *Theonomy*, 431.

as immutable as the character of God Himself, we should conclude that crimes which warrant capital punishment in the Older Testament continue to *deserve* the death penalty today."[118] For Rushdoony, however, the death penalty is not applicable for breaking the Sabbath. He explains: "The modern state is not in covenant with God but is an enemy of God. Sabbath-breaking has no specific penalty of death, just as there is no death penalty for adultery (Hosea 4:14), because the nations are not in covenant with God and are therefore under sentence of death."[119] Such ambiguity concerning the application of the law is troubling if it is our duty to keep such commands. Thus, reacting to this problem, Moo comments, "the subjectivity that is ostentatiously ushered out the front door is therefore smuggled in through the side door again."[120]

The third strength of Christian reconstructionism is their optimism tied to their belief in the certain expansion of the kingdom of God. They are convinced that, based on passages such as the Great Commission in Matthew 28:19–20, the gospel message will not only increasingly transform hearts but also cultures. North maintains that postmillennialism is distinct from other eschatological views because of "its essential *optimism* for the kingdom in the *present age*."[121] Christian reconstructionists unashamedly affirm the success of the Great Commission in the church age. Thus, what distinguishes postmillennialism from both premillennialism and amillennialism is "the optimistic confidence that the world nations will become disciples of Christ, that the church will grow to fill the earth, and that Christianity will become the dominant principle rather than the exception to the rule."[122]

But this optimism often seems to slide into a type of triumphalism and even cockiness. Sandlin writes in a volume dedicated to

---

118. Ibid., 427–28 (emphasis original).

119. Rushdoony, *Institutes of Biblical Law*, 2:685 (see also 2:28). North supports capital punishment by public stoning (see Gary North, *Tools of Dominion: The Case Law of Exodus* [Tyler, TX: Institute for Christian Economics, 1990], 44–45). He even states, "The privatization of execution is immoral" (45).

120. Douglas Moo, "Response to Greg L. Bahnsen," in *Five Views on Law and Gospel*, 166.

121. North, "Common Grace, Eschatology, and Biblical Law," 66 (emphasis original).

122. Ibid., 68.

Rushdoony: "[Christian reconstructionism] thereby constitutes the purest form of Christianity, a comprehensive Faith and worldview capable of meeting and defeating the forces of secularism and other rival religions." He continues, "Our Faith cannot but triumph. We can meet all rival faiths, point by point, issue by issue, law by law, practice by practice, and, by the grace of God, defeat each. We demand of all rival faiths unconditional surrender *in every dimension of existence* to the King of kings and Lord of lords."[123] North, by far the most polemic reconstructionist, was so convinced that his position was correct that he maintained that the theological battle is already over and that they were now in the "mopping up" phase.[124] Based on these types of comments (which were made frequently by North), Gabbert declares that reconstructionists suffer from "an oppressive arrogance."[125] But any momentum that reconstructionists had in the 1980s and early 1990s is clearly gone.[126]

Finally, one wonders if the type of evangelism that Christian reconstructionists propose to expand the kingdom is not somewhat distorted. Bahnsen speaks of fulfilling the Great Commission as "exhorting others to obey the law of God."[127] Even more troubling is North, who states, "A basic aspect of evangelism is calling upon God to bring His negative sanctions against His enemies in history." He then adds, "Having churches pray the imprecatory psalms (e.g., Psalm 83) is an important and neglected aspect of evangelism."[128] This type of evangelism seems to be very distant from what one finds in the New Testament.

---

123. Andrew Sandlin, "Afterword: Why We Will Win," in *A Comprehensive Faith*, 241, 242 (emphasis original).

124. North and DeMar, *Christian Reconstruction*, 176.

125. Gabbert, "An Historical Overview of Christian Reconstructionism," 296.

126. Worthen calls Christian reconstructionism "an obscure religious movement" and maintains that the movement "is largely dead," having imploded sometime in the mid-1990s (Molly Worthen, "The Chalcedon Problem: Rousas John Rushdoony and the Origins of Christian Reconstructionism," *Church History* 77.2 [June 2008]: 399, 435).

127. Bahnsen, *Theonomy*, 461.

128. North and DeMar, *Christian Reconstruction*, 76 (emphasis original).

CONCLUSION
SUMMARY OF THE SIX
THEOLOGICAL SYSTEMS

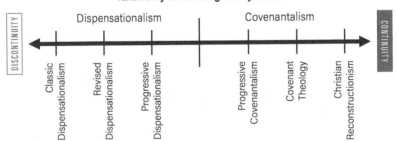

Taxonomy of Theological Systems

The purpose of this study was primarily descriptive in nature. That is, I have described the basic doctrines of six major theological systems by way of answering four key questions related to each system's (1) basic hermeneutic, (2) view of the covenants, (3) view of Israel and the church, and (4) view of the kingdom of God. I started from those views that represent more discontinuity (dispensationalism) and worked toward those views that represent more continuity (covenantalism).

It should be noted that these theological systems are not the only major hermeneutical or theological systems that can be studied. For example, some approach Scripture with the hermeneutical grid of Luther's law-gospel distinction as the primary tool for correctly interpreting the message of the Bible. Although such a system does not correspond precisely to the six views covered in this book, it is still helpful to relate these systems to Luther's approach. In other words, although a Lutheran hermeneutic may be asking different questions than the four major questions presented throughout each chapter, it is helpful to ask where a Lutheran might fall on the theological spectrum and how the questions asked in this book relate to the questions Lutherans are asking.

Luther's view often centers on the use of the law in the new covenant. For Luther, the law and the gospel were contrary ideas in the sense that they have contrary functions. Although the law reflects God's holy character, it can never save since it was not designed for that purpose. On the contrary, the law was given to reveal sin and drive a person to Christ (the gospel). Because he often focused on the negative function of the law, and because most of the law is found in the Old Testament, Luther and modern Lutherans often highlight the Old Testament's negative function, concentrating on Luther's second use of the law (the pedagogical function of revealing sin). Here is one place where covenant theologians differ from Lutherans. Because they affirm a greater amount of continuity between the Testaments, covenant theologians are often quick to acknowledge the positive functions of the law.

And yet, Lutherans should not be viewed as dispensationalists. The Lutheran understanding of law and gospel cannot be nicely divided between the Old Testament and New Testament so that the Old Testament represents law and the New Testament represents gospel. Rather, for Luther, law and gospel are found in both Testaments. When it comes to the issue of law and gospel, therefore, Lutherans probably have most affinity with progressive covenantalism or new covenant theology. Indeed, Douglas Moo, who contributed a chapter to *Fives View on Law and Gospel*, describes his view as a "Modified Lutheran View."[1] Moo associates himself with new covenant theology since he endorsed Wells and Zaspel's book. In the foreword, Moo declares that their analysis of the biblical texts "is impressive and persuasive."[2] He later adds that their perspective

---

1. Douglas J. Moo, "The Law of Christ as the Fulfillment of the Law of Moses: A Modified Lutheran View," in *Five Views on the Law and Gospel*, ed. Stanley N. Gundry (Grand Rapids: Zondervan, 1999), 319–76.

2. Douglas J. Moo, foreword to *New Covenant Theology: Description, Definition, Defense* by Tom Wells and Fred Zaspel (Frederick, MD: New Covenant Media, 2002), xiii.

of the discontinuity and continuity between the Old Testament and New Testament "is close to the right one."[3] Thus, although Lutherans have unique controlling issues that drive their theological system, their system at times overlaps with the issues of continuity and discontinuity covered in his book. In the remainder of this chapter, I will briefly summarize the six theological systems.

CLASSIC DISPENSATIONALISM

Classic dispensationalism interprets the Bible literally, allowing for symbolism or typology (and even allegory) if a text relates to the church and not Israel. Consequently, Old Testament restoration texts given to the nation of Israel demand a literal fulfillment. New Testament texts that quote Old Testament prophecies as being fulfilled must be understood as partial fulfillments or applications. Final fulfillment will occur during the millennium and will relate to ethnic Jews.

Rather than focus on biblical covenants, classic dispensationalists emphasize seven dispensations (innocence, conscience, human government, promise, law, grace, and kingdom). Each dispensation includes a period of time in which man is tested as to whether he will obey God's revelation. The major covenants in the Bible (Abrahamic, Davidic, new) are considered eternal and unconditional since God will fulfill them and man cannot break them. The new covenant belongs primarily to Israel, though the church participates in its benefits (Darby), partially fulfills it (Scofield), or has a separate and distinct new covenant (Chafer). Although some statements made by classic dispensationalists seems to suggest that salvation was by works under the Mosaic covenant, defenders of this view claim that such statements are misrepresented. Because the church age is a distinct dispensation, both Old Testament law and much of Jesus' teaching, such as the Sermon on the Mount, do not directly apply to Christians today.

The major doctrine of dispensationalism is that Israel and the church are distinct peoples and thus have distinct futures. There is a sharp duality between Israel as *earthly* and the church as *heavenly*.

---

3. Ibid., xiv.

Romans 11:26 teaches that God will fulfill his promises to ethnic Israel and remove their blindness when the nation as a whole is saved. In Galatians 6:16 Paul does not address the entire church (Jews and gentiles) as "the Israel of God" but only ethnic Jews within the congregation.

The "kingdom of heaven" refers to God's earthly rule over the Jews whereas the "kingdom of God" refers to his authoritative rule over the church. In his earthly ministry, Jesus did not usher in the promised kingdom. He offered the earthly, messianic kingdom to Israel but, because they rejected it, that kingdom was postponed (until the millennium). Therefore, the current "church age" is an unpredicted parenthesis in God's plan. After the church is raptured from earth, God will once again focus his attention on the nation of Israel, fulfilling Old Testament restoration prophecies. Christ will reign on the throne of David for a literal 1,000 years at the end of which time Satan will be released and then ultimately will be defeated by Christ.

REVISED DISPENSATIONALISM

Revised dispensationalists are firmly committed to a literal hermeneutic, meaning that they attempt to take every word according to its normal usage or at face value. Furthermore, they claim to apply this method *consistently* to every text. Although they allow for typology, they maintain that the New Testament authors almost always use the Old Testament in the historical-grammatical sense. On those rare occasions when typology is used, the New Testament antitype does not necessarily make void the Old Testament type. The Old Testament is also given priority over the New Testament so that the message of the Old Testament cannot be altered by the New Testament but must mean what it meant to the original (Jewish) audience. When the New Testament claims fulfillment of an Old Testament passage, this often indicates a partial fulfillment. For example, when the restoration prophecy of Amos 9:11–15 is quoted in Acts 15, it is interpreted not as being fulfilled in the church with the inclusion of the gentiles, but as still awaiting its full and final fulfillment which will take place when Christ returns.

According to revised dispensationalists, each dispensation involves a test, a failure, and a judgment. The Abrahamic, Davidic, and new covenants are all eternal unconditional covenants that God will fulfill. Although there are sometimes conditional elements within these unconditional covenants that require obedience (e.g., Abraham was told, "Go!"), the final fulfillment of these covenants is certain because it is ultimately based on God's faithfulness. Revised dispensationalists fervently deny that the Old Testament teaches salvation by works but maintain that salvation in every dispensation is based on Christ's death by means of faith in God. The conscious *content* of the faith of Old Testament saints was not necessarily in Jesus Christ or a coming Messiah but differed according to the revelation given at the time. Old Testament law does not apply to Christians today because it belongs to a previous dispensation. Because the Sermon on the Mount represents all law and no gospel, it does not relate directly to the church (though some principles can be gleaned) but rather to Jews during Jesus' ministry and will again apply to them during the tribulation and millennium.

The essence of dispensationalism is maintaining a clear distinction between Israel and the church. The two are separate and distinct entities and should never be confused. Israel is an ethnic people who are promised physical blessings, whereas the church is the body of Christ whose members are indwelt with the Holy Spirit. Additionally, the church age is a parenthesis in God's plan and the church itself did not come into existence until Pentecost. In Romans 11:26, Paul teaches that at the second advent of Christ, ethnic Jews *en masse* will be saved and the Jewish nation restored. Galatians 6:16 ("the Israel of God") is addressed only to Jewish Christians.

The "kingdom of God" and the "kingdom of heaven" are not necessarily viewed as distinct realities. Jesus offered the kingdom to Israel but because they rejected his offer, the kingdom was postponed. Jesus is currently reigning from his Father's throne but not from the Davidic throne. After the seven-year tribulation, the church will be raptured to heaven and Christ will return and establish his kingdom on earth. During the millennium, Jesus will physically reign in Jerusalem. At the end of the thousand years, Satan will be released and will lead a rebellion only to be defeated and thrown into the lake of fire. After this is the resurrection and the judgment followed by the eternal state.

PROGRESSIVE DISPENSATIONALISM

Although progressive dispensationalists embrace a literal hermeneutic, they also claim that such an approach is inadequate since the historical-grammatic method also needs a literary-theological component. This "complementary" hermeneutic allows the meaning of a text to develop or expand, though the text retains its original meaning (unless explicitly stated by the New Testament). Because of this expanded hermeneutic, typology is more readily affirmed. Restoration prophecies regarding Israel can also relate to the church, but such fulfillment is not the ultimate fulfillment since the original text concerned Israel.

Instead of seven dispensations found in traditional dispensationalism, progressive dispensationalists have only four: (1) Patriarchal, (2) Mosaic, (3) Ecclesial, and (4) Zionic. The Abrahamic, Davidic, and new covenants are unconditional grant covenants that emphasize the grace of God (though they do not exclude demands of the recipients). In contrast, the Mosaic covenant was based on the suzerain-vassal treaty that required obedience (i.e., a conditional covenant). But since the Mosaic covenant was dependent on the Abrahamic covenant, salvation under the Mosaic law (as in every era) was through faith in God (though not necessarily faith in Christ). Christians today are not obligated to keep the Old Testament law, though the moral components of the Mosaic law are still authoritative for new covenant believers.

Consistent with all dispensationalists, progressive dispensationalists view the church as beginning at Pentecost. And yet, they view both Israel and the church as the one people of God. They affirm both continuity (one people) and discontinuity (distinct futures). Whereas the church receives spiritual blessings, Israel will receive physical blessings as a national, political entity. This unique future for Israel is confirmed by Romans 11:26, which indicates that God will remove ethnic Israel's temporal hardening, resulting in the salvation of the nation as a whole. At the end of Galatians, Paul once again affirms the unique status of Jews as he pronounces a benediction on the "Israel of God" (Gal 6:16).

God's plan in history is one unified plan. Consequently, the church age is not a parenthesis because each dispensation progressively reveals the kingdom of God. Furthermore, there is no distinction between the "kingdom of God" and the "kingdom of heaven." In his earthly ministry, Jesus ushered in the kingdom—at least in part (inaugurated but not consummated)—and is currently seated in heaven having inaugurated the eschatological kingdom. Israel's physical restoration is confirmed by the disciples' question in Acts 1:6, which demonstrates they were on the right track. The restoration of Israel will occur after the church is raptured, then Christ will rule over Israel for a thousand years. At the end of this reign of peace, Satan will be released to lead a rebellion against Christ, only to be defeated. After the great judgment, Christ's people will experience the new heavens and the new earth.

PROGRESSIVE COVENANTALISM

Progressive covenantalists interpret the Bible literally or according to the intention of the author as conveyed through various literary forms (*sensus literalis*). When the literal sense includes symbols and types as part of the feature of divine revelation, then they seek to interpret Scripture accordingly, allowing for a spiritual or typological interpretation (and even *sensus plenior*), especially when affirmed by the New Testament authors. Because the Bible contains progressive revelation, the New Testament brings Christological clarity to Old Testament passages. It does so by expanding the implications of Old Testament authors without contravening the original meaning. Biblical texts, therefore, should be interpreted according to textual, epochal, and canonical horizons, giving hermeneutical priority to the New Testament since it is the culmination of God's revelation. Many Old Testament persons, events, and institutions are typologically fulfilled in Christ, which is crucial for understanding the storyline of the Bible and the relationship between the Testaments. This is also true of Old Testament restoration prophecies which are fulfilled in Christ, the true Israelite.

Progressive covenantalism affirms six biblical covenants (Adamic, Noahic, Abrahamic, Mosaic, Davidic, and the new covenant). The

Bible develops according to these biblical covenants which reveal God's one eternal plan. Affirming both discontinuity and continuity, this view sees God's purpose as it progresses through the covenants which are all fulfilled in Christ. Every covenant possesses both unconditional elements (which are guaranteed by God's power and grace) and conditional elements (which demand obedience). This is true even of the new covenant since Christ perfectly fulfills the demands of the covenant. Saints in both the Old Testament and New Testament have always and only been saved by grace through faith, though their personal experience may have differed based on the revelation and covenant under which they lived. This view affirms that all Scripture is authoritative and thus provides the norm for Christian ethics. At the same time, progressive covenantalists reject the tripartite division of the law as the means of determining what is morally binding on believers since the Old Testament law should be viewed as a covenantal package and since the law-covenant was temporary. Instead, Christians must appeal to the entirety of Scripture viewed through the new covenant, especially in light of its fulfillment in Christ. Thus, the Sabbath command still applies to Christians today, but because we are under the new covenant, it does not apply directly to us but must be filtered through Christ who is the fulfillment of the law.

Both Israel and the church represent the one people of God, though they are not wholly the same. Thus, the church neither replaces nor is equated with Israel. Instead, the church is a typological fulfillment of Israel which is therefore only related to Israel *indirectly*. Jesus is the direct fulfillment of Israel and therefore the church only has access to the promises given to Israel through its union with Christ. There is no unified interpretation of Romans 11:26, though all proponents of progressive covenantalism reject the notion that the restoration of Israel includes physical qualities such as the land and temple. In Galatians 6:16, Paul address the Galatian believers (including gentiles) as "the Israel of God," demonstrating a connection between Israel and the church.

As the promised Son of David, Jesus inaugurated the kingdom during his first coming. His death, resurrection, and ascension to his father's throne signify that he has been coronated as the reigning

King. But the kingdom will only be fully consummated at his second coming when he subdues all his enemies (including death) and hands the kingdom over to his Father. Various views of the millennium (especially historical premillennialism and amillennialism) are held.

COVENANT THEOLOGY

Covenant theologians affirm a literal hermeneutic in that they embrace the grammatico-historical method that seeks the intention of the author (as opposed to an allegorical interpretation), but they also reject a literalistic or overly literal hermeneutic. Instead, they embrace a Christ-centered hermeneutic that views Christ as the fulfillment of all God's promises and, at times, are comfortable with the notion of *sensus plenior*. Any expanded or fuller meaning, however, must be organically related to the historical meaning. Because the New Testament represents God's final and fullest revelation, the Old Testament must be interpreted in light of the New Testament, which often includes a typological fulfillment of messianic prophecy. For example, the promised land under the old covenant pointed toward the greater reality of the new heavens and the new earth. Thus, Old Testament restoration prophecies also find their fulfillment in Christ and his church. Overall, they assume continuity between the Testaments unless the New Testament specifically states otherwise.

The concept of covenants is central to covenant theology, which affirms both theological covenants (redemption, works/creation, and grace) and historical covenants (associated with Adam, Noah, Abraham, Moses, David, and Christ). The theological covenants are the overarching covenants and, together with the historical covenants, are all ultimately one. The covenant of redemption is an inter-Trinitarian covenant made in eternity to redeem humanity. The covenant of works (creation) is a pre-fall covenant given to Adam, the federal head of humanity. The covenant of grace is a post-fall covenant made with Adam where God promises to redeem a people for himself through a coming Messiah (made with the elect and their children). Most covenant theologians view the Abrahamic covenant as unconditional and the Mosaic covenant (following suzerain-vassal treaties) as conditional. Yet, under all post-fall covenants, humanity is saved by grace through faith in the Messiah and not by works. Old Testament law can be divided into three types: civil, ceremonial, and moral. Because both civil and ceremonial laws are fulfilled in Christ, believers are obligated to keep only the Old Testament moral law as summarized in the Ten Commandments (including keeping the Sabbath). God's law has three uses: civil (it restrains criminal behavior), pedagogical (it shows us our sin and drives us to Christ), and normative (it provides guidelines for the Christian life).

Stressing continuity, covenant theologians see an organic relationship between Israel and the church as the one people of God. The church does not replace Israel but fulfills promises given to Abraham. In Romans 11:26 "Israel" refers to either (1) the church, (2) the elect among ethnic Israel throughout history, or (3) a future mass conversion of ethnic Jews. The most natural reading of Galatians 6:16 is that Paul is addressing the entire church (Jews *and* gentiles) as "the Israel of God."

The kingdom of God is the rule and reign of God over his creation. His kingdom came in a fresh way with the arrival of King Jesus but it did not come in its fullness, and so believers still await the final consummation. When the disciples question Jesus in Acts 1:6 ("Will you at this time restore the kingdom to Israel?"), they not only missed the *timing* of the kingdom but they also missed the *nature* of the kingdom. Jesus' answer is found in the arrival of the Spirit and his commission to be witnesses to the end of the earth. Finally, most covenant theologians are amillennialists, affirming that the church is currently in the millennium and that Satan was bound at the resurrection and ascension of Jesus. Immediately following the second coming is the last judgment and the eternal state.

CHRISTIAN RECONSTRUCTIONISM

The main tenets of reconstructionism are (1) Calvinism, (2) theonomy, (3) presuppositional apologetics, (4) postmillennialism, and (5) dominion theology. Christian reconstructionists employ a redemptive-historical hermeneutic that allows for both a literal and symbolic interpretation (especially for apocalyptic literature and the book of Revelation). They affirm a strong continuity between the

Old Testament and New Testament and employ a literal hermeneutic when applying Old Testament law. Typology is crucial in deciding which Old Testament laws are still applicable today. Old Testament *ceremonial* laws that are typologically fulfilled in Christ are set aside, being replaced by the New Testament antitype. Thus, Old Testament sacrificial laws and the land of Canaan point to greater gospel-realities. For example, Old Testament restoration prophecies no longer apply to ethnic Israel since the New Testament redefines the people of God as the church.

All covenants are acts of grace that also include a law relationship. Reconstructionists (such as Rushdoony) affirm the covenant of grace but reject the covenant of works (since all covenants involve grace). For North, the primary covenant in the Bible is labeled the "Dominion Covenant." There is one unifying covenant with various manifestations (pre-Adamic, pre-fall, post-fall, and post-resurrection). They do not distinguish between conditional and unconditional covenants since all covenants are recapitulations of the same promise. Yet, biblical covenants have both unconditional elements (God imposing his will) and conditional elements (non-compliance results in judgment). In every age and under every covenant, however, people are saved by grace through faith in Christ. The law points to God but cannot save. In contrast, natural law must be rejected since it undermines a Christian society. A unique element of Christian reconstructionism is theonomy, which is the belief that all Old Testament law, not just the Decalogue, is binding on believers today. Thus, they affirm that even Old Testament civil law should be enforced since God's law reflects his unchanging character. Jesus affirmed the eternal validity of God's law in Matthew 5:17–20.

Because the nation of Israel rejected the Lord, their special status as God's people has been revoked and given to the church. Thus, the church has replaced Israel. Israel's judgment came in AD 70 when Jerusalem and the temple were destroyed. Most reconstructionists are preterists who interpret many New Testament prophetic texts (e.g., Matt 24; Mark 13; and Revelation) as being fulfilled in the first century. Jews, however, are not completely forsaken since they can be grafted back into the people of God if they trust in Jesus as Messiah. Indeed,

Romans 11:26 teaches that the vast majority of Jews will someday be converted to Christ, which will cause a widespread global revival resulting in worldwide blessing—a teaching consistent with postmillennialism. In Galatians 6:16, Paul identifies both Jews and gentiles as "the Israel of God," thereby redefining the church as the new Israel.

The kingdom of God is already present and will progressively expand until it ushers in a time of unparalleled peace, righteousness, and prosperity. This transformation will only take place as individuals and communities submit to God's law. Such a change cannot be brought about by man but must be the work of the Holy Spirit. Social change is not enough. Regeneration is needed for real change to occur. Thus, the kingdom will progress slowly but surely over the earth until Christ returns again. At his coming those who do not submit to his authority will be cast out, but believers will be transformed and restored to God's image.

BIBLIOGRAPHY

Abshire, Brian. "The Covenant of Grace and Law: Rushdoony and the Doctrine of the Covenant." Pages 45–52 in *A Comprehensive Faith: An International* Festschrift *for Rousas John Rushdoony*. Edited by Andrew Sandlin. San Jose, CA: Friends of Chalcedon, 1996.

Aldrich, Roy L. "An Apologetic for Dispensationalism." *Bibliotheca Sacra* 112 (1955): 46–54.

Allis, Oswald. *Prophecy and the Church*. Grand Rapids: Baker, 1947.

Bahnsen, Greg L. *By This Standard*. Tyler, TX: Institute for Christian Economics, 1985.

———. "M. G. Kline on Theonomic Politics: An Evaluation of His Reply." *Journal of Christian Reconstruction* 6.2 (Winter 1979–80): 195–211.

———. *No Other Standard: Theonomy and Its Critics*. Tyler, TX: Institute for Christian Economics, 1991.

———. "The Theonomic Reformed Approach to Law and Gospel." Pages 93–143 in *Five Views on Law and Gospel*. Edited by Stanley N. Gundry. Grand Rapids: Zondervan, 1999.

———. *Theonomy in Christian Ethics*. 3rd ed. Nacogdoches, TX: Covenant Media Press, 2002.

———. *Van Til's Apologetic: Readings and Analysis*. Phillipsburg, NJ: P&R, 1998.

———. *Victory in Jesus: The Bright Hope of Postmillennialism*. Texarkana, AR: Covenant Media Press, 1999.

Bahnsen, Greg L., and Kenneth L. Gentry Jr. *House Divided: The Break-Up of Dispensational Theology*. Tyler, TX: Institute for Christian Economics, 1989.

Baker, David L. "Typology and the Christian Use of the Old Testament." Pages 313–30 in *The Right Doctrine from the Wrong Texts? Essays on the Use of the Old Testament in the New Testament*. Edited by G. K. Beale. Grand Rapids: Baker, 1994.

Barker, Kenneth L. "False Dichotomies between the Testaments." *Journal of the Evangelical Theological Society* 25.1 (1982): 3–16.

———. "The Scope and Center of Old and New Testament Theology and

Hope." Pages 293–328 in *Dispensationalism, Israel and the Church: The Search for Definition.* Edited by Craig A. Blaising and Darrell L. Bock. Grand Rapids: Zondervan, 1992.

Bass, Clarence B. *Backgrounds to Dispensationalism: Its Historical Genesis and Ecclesiastical Implications.* Grand Rapids: Eerdmans, 1960.

Bateman, Herbert W., IV, ed. *Three Central Issues in Contemporary Dispensationalism: A Comparison of Traditional and Progressive Views.* Grand Rapids: Kregel, 1999.

Beacham, Roy E. "Progressive Dispensationalism: An Overview and Personal Analysis." *Detroit Baptist Seminary Journal* 9 (2004): 5–32.

Beale, G. K. "Did Jesus and His Followers Preach the Right Doctrine from the Wrong Texts? An Examination of the Presuppositions of Jesus' and The Apostles' Exegetical Methods." Pages 387–404 in *The Right Doctrine from the Wrong Texts? Essays on the Use of the Old Testament in the New.* Edited by G. K. Beale. Grand Rapids: Baker Academic, 1994.

———. *Handbook on the New Testament Use of the Old Testament.* Grand Rapids: Baker Academic, 2012.

———, ed. *The Right Doctrine from the Wrong Texts? Essays on the Use of the Old Testament in the New Testament.* Grand Rapids: Baker Academic, 1994.

Berding, Kenneth, and Jonathan Lunde, eds. *Three Views on the New Testament Use of the Old Testament.* Grand Rapids: Zondervan, 2008.

Berkhof, Louis. *Systematic Theology.* 4th rev. and expanded ed. Grand Rapids: Eerdmans, 1941.

Bigalke, Ron J., Jr., and Thomas D. Ice. "History of Dispensationalism." Pages xvii–xlii in *Progressive Dispensationalism: An Analysis of the Movement and Defense of Traditional Dispensationalism.* Edited by Ron J. Bigalke Jr. Lanham, MD: University Press of America, 2005.

Blaising, Craig A. "Biblical Hermeneutics: How Are We to Interpret the Relation between the Tanak and the New Testament on This Question?" Pages 79–105 in *The New Christian Zionism: Fresh Perspectives on Israel and the Land.* Edited by Gerald R. McDermott. Downers Grove, IL: IVP Academic, 2016.

———. "A Critique of Gentry and Wellum's, *Kingdom Through Covenant*: A Hermeneutical Response." *The Master's Seminary Journal* 26.1 (2015): 111–27.

———. "Development of Dispensationalism by Contemporary Dispensationalists." *Bibliotheca Sacra* 145 (1988): 254–80.

———. "Dispensation, Dispensationalism." Pages 343–45 in *Evangelical Dictionary of Theology*. 2nd ed. Edited by Walter A. Elwell. Grand Rapids: Baker Academic, 2001.

———. "Dispensationalism: The Search for Definition." Pages 13–34 in *Dispensationalism, Israel and the Church: The Search for Definition*. Edited by Craig A. Blaising and Darrell L. Bock. Grand Rapids: Zondervan, 1992.

———. "Israel and Hermeneutics." Pages 151–65 in *The People, the Land, and the Future of Israel: Israel and Jewish People in the Plan of God*. Edited by Darrell Bock and Mitch Glaser. Grand Rapids: Kregel, 2014.

———. "Premillennialism." Pages 157–227 in *Three Views on the Millennium and Beyond*. Edited by Darrell Bock. Grand Rapids: Zondervan, 1999.

———. "A Theology of Israel and the Church." Pages 85–100 in *Israel, the Church and the Middle East: A Biblical Response to the Current Conflict*. Edited by Darrell L. Bock and Mitch Glaser. Grand Rapids: Kregel, 2018.

Blaising, Craig A., and Darrell L. Bock. "Dispensationalism, Israel and the Church: Assessment and Dialogue." Pages 377–94 in *Dispensationalism, Israel and the Church: The Search for Definition*. Edited by Craig A. Blaising and Darrell L. Bock. Grand Rapids: Zondervan, 1992.

———, eds. *Dispensationalism, Israel and the Church: The Search for Definition*. Grand Rapids: Zondervan, 1992.

———. *Progressive Dispensationalism*. Grand Rapids: Baker, 1993.

Bock, Darrell L. "Biblical Reconciliation between Jews and Arabs." Pages 165–84 in *Israel, the Church and the Middle East: A Biblical Response to the Current Conflict*. Edited by Darrell L. Bock and Mitch Glaser. Grand Rapids: Kregel, 2018.

———. "Covenants in Progressive Dispensationalism." Pages 169–203, 211–23 in *Three Central Issues in Contemporary Dispensationalism: A Comparison of Traditional and Progressive Views*. Edited by Herbert W. Bateman IV. Grand Rapids: Kregel, 1999.

———. "Current Messianic Activity and OT Davidic Promise: Dispensationalism, Hermeneutics, and NT Fulfillment." *Trinity Journal* 15.1 (1994): 55–87.

———. "Hermeneutics of Progressive Dispensationalism." Pages 85–101, 105–18 in *Three Central Issues in Contemporary Dispensationalism: A Comparison of Traditional and Progressive Views*. Edited by Herbert W. Bateman IV. Grand Rapids: Kregel, 1999.

———. "The Reign of the Lord Christ." Pages 47–55 in *Dispensationalism, Israel and the Church: The Search for Definition*. Edited by Craig A. Blaising and Darrell L. Bock. Grand Rapids: Zondervan, 1992.

———. "Response." Pages 155–63 in *Three Central Issues in Contemporary Dispensationalism: A Comparison of Traditional and Progressive Views*. Edited by Herbert W. Bateman IV. Grand Rapids: Kregel, 1999.

———. "Single Meaning, Multiple Contexts and Referents: The New Testament's Legitimate, Accurate and Multifaceted Use of the Old." Pages 105–51 in *Three Views on the New Testament Use of the Old Testament*. Edited by Kenneth Berding and Jonathan Lunde. Grand Rapids: Zondervan, 2008.

———. "The Son of David and the Saints' Task: The Hermeneutics of Initial Fulfillment." *Bibliotheca Sacra* 150 (1993): 440–57.

Burns, J. Lanier. "The Future of Ethnic Israel." Pages 188–229 in *Dispensationalism, Israel and the Church: The Search for Definition*. Edited by Craig A. Blaising and Darrell L. Bock. Grand Rapids: Zondervan, 1992.

———. "Israel and the Church of a Progressive Dispensationalist." Pages 263–91, 294–303 in *Three Central Issues in Contemporary Dispensationalism: A Comparison of Traditional and Progressive Views*. Edited by Herbert W. Bateman IV. Grand Rapids: Kregel, 1999.

Cairns, Alan, ed. *Dictionary of Theological Terms*. Greenville, SC:

Ambassador-Emerald International, 1998.

Caneday, Ardel B. "Covenantal Life with God from Eden to the Holy City." Pages 101–26 in *Progressive Covenantalism: Charting a Course between Dispensational and Covenant Theologies.* Edited by Stephen J. Wellum and Brent E. Parker. Nashville: B&H, 2016.

Carson, D. A., ed. *From Sabbath to Lord's Day: A Biblical, Historical, and Theological Investigation.* Grand Rapids: Zondervan, 1982.

———. "Matthew." Pages 25–670 in *Expositor's Bible Commentary.* Rev. ed. Edited by Tremper Longman III and David E. Garland. Vol. 9. Grand Rapids: Zondervan, 2010.

Chafer, Lewis Sperry. "Dispensationalism." *Bibliotheca Sacra* 93 (1936): 390–449.

———. "Editorials: Dispensational Distinctions Denounced." *Bibliotheca Sacra* 101 (1944): 257–60.

———. "Editorials: Inventing Heretics Through Misunderstanding." *Bibliotheca Sacra* 102 (1945): 1–5.

———. *Major Bible Themes: 52 Vital Doctrines of the Scripture Simplified and Explained.* Revised by John F. Walvoord. Grand Rapids: Zondervan, 1974.

———. *Systematic Theology.* 8 vols. Dallas: Dallas Seminary Press, 1947–1948.

Chilton, David. *The Days of Vengeance: An Exposition of the Book of Revelation.* Fort Worth: Dominion Press, 1987.

———. *Paradise Restored: A Biblical Theology of Dominion.* Tyler, TX: Dominion Press, 1985.

Clowney, Edmund P. "The Politics of the Kingdom." *Westminster Theological Journal* 41 (1978–1979): 291–310.

Crutchfield, Larry V. "Rudiments of Dispensationalism in the Ante-Nicene Period Part 1 (of 2 parts): Israel and the Church in the Ante-Nicene Fathers." *Bibliotheca Sacra* 144 (1987): 254–76.

———. "Rudiments of Dispensationalism in the Ante-Nicene Period Part 2 (of 2 parts): Ages and Dispensations in the Ante-Nicene Fathers." *Bibliotheca Sacra* 144 (1987): 377–99.

Darby, John Nelson. *The Collected Writings.* Vol. 20. Edited by William Kelly. Oak Park, IL: Bible Truth Publishers, 1962.

DeMar, Gary. *The Debate over Christian Reconstruction*. Fort Worth, TX: Dominion Press, 1988.

DeRouchie, Jason S. "Father of a Multitude of Nations: New Covenant Ecclesiology in Perspective." Pages 7–38 in *Progressive Covenantalism: Charting a Course between Dispensational and Covenant Theologies*. Edited by Stephen J. Wellum and Brent E. Parker. Nashville: B&H, 2016.

Ehlert, Arnold D. *A Bibliographic History of Dispensationalism*. Grand Rapids: Baker, 1965.

English, Adam C. "Christian Reconstructionism after Y2K: Gary North, the New Millennium, and Religious Freedom." Pages 163–79 in *New Religious Movements and Religious Liberty in America*. Edited by Derek H. Davis and Barry Hankins. Waco, TX: Baylor University Press, 2002.

Enns, Peter. "Fuller Meaning, Single Goal: A Christotelic Approach to the New Testament Use of the Old in Its First-Century Interpretive Environment." Pages 167–217 in *Three Views on the New Testament Use of the Old Testament*. Edited by Kenneth Berding and Jonathan Lunde. Grand Rapids: Zondervan, 2008.

Feinberg, John S., ed. *Continuity and Discontinuity: Perspectives on the Relationship Between the Old and New Testaments*. Wheaton: Crossway, 1987.

———. "Systems of Discontinuity." Pages 63–86 in *Continuity and Discontinuity: Perspectives on the Relationship Between the Old and New Testaments*. Edited by John. S. Feinberg. Wheaton: Crossway, 1988.

Fuller, Daniel P. "The Hermeneutics of Dispensationalism." ThD diss., Northern Baptist Theological Seminary, 1957.

Gabbert, Michael D. "An Historical Overview of Christian Reconstructionism." *Criswell Theological Review* 6.2 (1993): 281–301.

Gentry, Kenneth L. Jr. "A Preterist View of Revelation." Pages 37–92 in *Four Views on the Book of Revelation*. Edited by C. Marvin Pate. Grand Rapids: Zondervan, 1998.

———. *The Olivet Discourse Made Easy*. Draper, VA: ApologeticsGroup Media, 2010.

Gentry, Peter J., and Stephen J. Wellum. *God's Kingdom through God's Covenants: A Concise Biblical Theology*. Wheaton: Crossway, 2015.

———. *Kingdom through Covenant: A Biblical-Theological Understanding of the Covenants*. Wheaton: Crossway, 2012.

———. *Kingdom Through Covenant: A Biblical-Theological Understanding of the Covenants*. 2nd ed. Wheaton: Crossway, 2018.

Glenny, W. Edward. "The Israelite Imagery of 1 Peter 2." Pages 156–87 in *Dispensationalism, Israel and the Church: The Search for Definition*. Edited by Craig A. Blaising and Darrell L. Bock. Grand Rapids: Zondervan, 1992.

———. "Typology: A Summary of the Present Evangelical Discussion." *Journal of the Evangelical Theological Society* 40.4 (1997): 627–38.

Goldsworthy, Graeme. *According to Plan: The Unfolding Revelation of God in the Bible*. Downers Grove, IL: InterVarsity Press, 1991.

———. "The Relationship of the Old Testament and New Testament." In *New Dictionary of Biblical Theology*. Edited by. T. Desmond Alexander et al. Downers Grove, IL: InterVarsity Press, 2000.

Greidanus, Sidney. *Preaching Christ from the Old Testament: A Contemporary Hermeneutical Method*. Grand Rapids: Eerdmans, 1999.

Hoekema, Anthony A. "An Amillennial Response." Pages 104–14 in *The Meaning of the Millennium: Four Views*. Edited by Robert G. Clouse. Downers Grove, IL: InterVarsity, 1977.

———. *The Bible and the Future*. Grand Rapids: Eerdmans, 1979.

Horton, Michael. *The Christian Faith: A Systematic Theology for Pilgrims on the Way*. Grand Rapids: Zondervan, 2011.

———. *Covenant and Salvation: Union with Christ*. Louisville: Westminster John Knox, 2007.

———. *Introducing Covenant Theology*. Grand Rapids: Baker, 2006.

———. *Lord and Servant: A Covenant Christology*. Louisville: Westminster John Knox, 2005.

House, H. Wayne. "Traditional Dispensationalism and the Millennium." *Criswell Theological Review* 11.1 (Fall 2013): 3–27.

Johnson, Elliot E. "Covenants in Traditional Dispensationalism." Pages 121–55, 163–68 in *Three Central Issues in Contemporary*

Dispensationalism: A Comparison of Traditional and Progressive Views. Edited by Herbert W. Bateman IV. Grand Rapids: Kregel, 1999.

———. "A Traditional Dispensational Hermeneutic." Pages 63–76, 82–84 in *Three Central Issues in Contemporary Dispensationalism: A Comparison of Traditional and Progressive Views.* Edited by Herbert W. Bateman IV. Grand Rapids: Kregel, 1999.

———. "Response." Pages 203–11 in *Three Central Issues in Contemporary Dispensationalism: A Comparison of Traditional and Progressive Views.* Edited by Herbert W. Bateman IV. Grand Rapids: Kregel, 1999.

Johnson, S. Lewis Jr. "Paul and the 'Israel of God': An Exegetical and Eschatological Case-Study." *The Master's Seminary Journal* 20.1 (2009): 41–55.

———. "Paul and the 'Israel of God': An Exegetical and Eschatological Case-Study." Pages 181–96 in *Essays in Honor of J. Dwight Pentecost.* Edited by Stanley D. Toussaint and Charles H. Dyer. Chicago: Moody, 1986.

Karlberg, Mark W. "Legitimate Discontinuities Between the Testaments." *Journal of the Evangelical Theological Society* 28.1 (1985): 9–20.

Kendall, Heather A. *One Greater Than Moses: A History of New Covenant Theology.* Orange, CA: Quoir, 2016.

Kline, Meredith G. *By Oath Consigned.* Grand Rapids: Eerdmans, 1968.

———. "Comments on an Old-New Error." *Westminster Theological Journal* 41 (1978): 172–89.

———. *The Structure of Biblical Authority.* 2nd ed. Eugene, OR: Wipf & Stock, 1989.

———. *Treaty of the Great King.* Eugene, OR: Wipf & Stock, 1963, reprint 2012.

Knowles, Louis E. "The Interpretation of the Seventy Weeks of Daniel in the Early Fathers." *Westminster Theological Journal* 7.2 (1945): 136–60.

Knudsen, Robert D. "May We Use the Term 'Theonomy' for Our Application of Biblical Law?" Pages 17–37 in *Theonomy: A Reformed Critique.* Edited by William S. Barker and W. Robert

Godfrey. Grand Rapids: Zondervan, 1990.

Kraus, C. Norman. *Dispensationalism in America: Its Rise and Development.* Richmond: John Knox, 1958.

Ladd, George E. "Historic Premillennialism." Pages 17–40 in *The Meaning of the Millennium: Four Views.* Edited by Robert G. Clouse. Downers Grove, IL: InterVarsity, 1977.

———. *A Theology of the New Testament.* Rev. ed. Grand Rapids: Eerdmans, 1993.

LaRondelle, Hans K. *The Israel of God in Prophecy: Principles of Prophetic Interpretation.* Berrien Springs, MI: Andrews University Press, 1983.

Lehrer, Steve. *New Covenant Theology: Questions Answered.* Self-published, 2006.

Lints, Richard. *The Fabric of Theology: A Prolegomenon to Evangelical Theology.* Grand Rapids: Eerdmans, 1993.

Lioy, Dan. "Progressive Covenantalism as an Integrating Motif of Scripture." *Conspectus* 1 (2006): 81–107.

Long, Gary D. *Biblical Law and Ethics: Absolute and Covenantal.* Charleston, SC: Self-published, CreateSpace, 2014.

———. *New Covenant Theology: Time for a More Accurate Way.* Self-published, CreateSpace, 2013.

Longman, Tremper. "God's Law and Mosaic Punishments Today." Pages 41–54 in *Theonomy: A Reformed Critique.* Edited by William S. Barker and W. Robert Godfrey. Grand Rapids: Zondervan, 1990.

Lowery, David K. "Christ, the End of the Law." Pages 230–47 in *Dispensationalism, Israel and the Church: The Search for Definition.* Edited by Craig A. Blaising and Darrell L. Bock. Grand Rapids: Zondervan, 1992.

Lucas, Richard J. "The Dispensational Appeal to Romans 11 and the Nature of Israel's Future Salvation." Pages 235–53 in *Progressive Covenantalism: Charting a Course between Dispensational and Covenant Theologies.* Edited by Stephen J. Wellum and Brent E. Parker. Nashville: B&H, 2016.

Martin, John A. "Christ, the Fulfillment of the Law in the Sermon on the Mount." Pages 248–63 in *Dispensationalism, Israel and the Church:*

The Search for Definition. Edited by Craig A. Blaising and Darrell L. Bock. Grand Rapids: Zondervan, 1992.

Martin, Oren R. "The Land Promise Biblically and Theologically Understood." Pages 255–74 in *Progressive Covenantalism: Charting a Course between Dispensational and Covenant Theologies.* Edited by Stephen J. Wellum and Brent E. Parker. Nashville: B&H, 2016.

McCartney, Dan, and Charles Clayton. *Let the Reader Understand: A Guide to Interpreting and Applying the Bible.* 2nd ed. Phillipsburg, NJ: P&R, 2002.

Meade, John D. "Circumcision of Flesh to Circumcision of Heart: The Typology of the Sign of the Abrahamic Covenant." Pages 127–58 in *Progressive Covenantalism: Charting a Course between Dispensational and Covenant Theologies.* Edited by Stephen J. Wellum and Brent E. Parker. Nashville: B&H, 2016.

Mendenhall, George E. *Law and Covenant in Israel and the Ancient Near East.* Pittsburgh: Biblical Colloquium, 1955.

Meyer, Jason C. "Mosaic Law, Theological Systems, and the Glory of Christ." Pages 69–99 in *Progressive Covenantalism: Charting a Course between Dispensational and Covenant Theologies.* Edited by Stephen J. Wellum and Brent E. Parker. Nashville: B&H, 2016.

Moo, Douglas J. Foreword to *New Covenant Theology: Description, Definition, Defense* by Tom Wells and Fred Zaspel. Frederick, MD: New Covenant Media, 2002.

———. "The Law of Christ as the Fulfillment of the Law of Moses: A Modified Lutheran View." Pages 319–76 in *Five Views on the Law and Gospel.* Edited by Stanley N. Gundry. Grand Rapids: Zondervan, 1999.

———. "Response to Greg L. Bahnsen." Pages 165–73 in *Five Views on the Law and Gospel.* Edited by Stanley N. Gundry. Grand Rapids: Zondervan, 1999.

Neuhaus, Richard John. "Why Wait for the Kingdom? The Theonomist Temptation." *First Things* 3 (May 1990): 13–21.

North, Gary. *75 Bible Questions Your Instructors Pray You WON'T Ask: How to Spot Humanism in the Classroom or Pulpit.* 2nd ed. Tyler, TX: Institute for Christian Economics, 1988.

———. "Common Grace, Eschatology, and Biblical Law." *The Journal of Christian Reconstruction* 3.2 (Winter 1976–77): 13–47.

———. "Editor's Conclusion." Pages 316–19 in *Theonomy: An Informed Response*. Edited by Gary North. Tyler, TX: Institute for Christian Economics 1991.

———. "Editor's Introduction to Part III." Pages 195–206 in *Theonomy: An Informed Response*. Edited by Gary North. Tyler, TX: Institute for Christian Economics 1991.

———. *God's Covenants*. Dallas, GA: Point Five Press, 2014.

———. *Millennialism and Social Theory*. Tyler, TX: Institute for Christian Economics, 1990.

———. *Tools of Dominion: The Case Law of Exodus*. Tyler, TX: Institute for Christian Economics, 1990.

———. *Westminster's Confession: The Abandonment of Van Til's Legacy*. Tyler, TX: Institute for Christian Economics, 1991.

North, Gary, and Gary DeMar. *Christian Reconstruction: What It Is, What It Isn't*. Tyler, TX: Institute for Christian Economics, 1991.

Parker, Brent E. "The Israel-Christ-Church Relationship." Pages 39–68 in *Progressive Covenantalism: Charting a Course between Dispensational and Covenant Theologies*. Edited by Stephen J. Wellum and Brent E. Parker. Nashville: B&H, 2016.

———. "Typology and Allegory: Is There a Distinction? A Brief Examination of Figural Reading." *Southern Baptist Journal of Theology* 21.1 (2017): 57–83.

Pentecost, J. Dwight. "The Purpose of the Sermon on the Mount." *Bibliotheca Sacra* 115 (1958): 128–35.

———. *Things to Come: A Study in Biblical Eschatology*. Grand Rapids: Zondervan, 1964.

———. *Thy Kingdom Come: Tracing God's Kingdom Program and Covenant Promises Throughout History*. Grand Rapids: Kregel, 1995.

Poythress, Vern S. *Understanding Dispensationalism*. 2nd ed. Phillipsburg, NJ: P&R, 1994.

Reisinger, John G. *Abraham's Four Seeds: A Biblical Examination of the Presuppositions of Covenant Theology and Dispensationalism*. Frederick, MD: New Covenant Media, 1998.

———. *New Covenant Theology and Prophecy*. Frederick, MD: New Covenant Media, 2012.

———. *Tablets of Stone and the History of Redemption*. Frederick, MD: New Covenant Media, 2004.

Reymond, Robert L. *A New Systematic Theology of the Christian Faith*. 2nd ed. Nashville: Thomas Nelson, 2002.

———. "The Traditional Covenantal View." Pages 17–68 in *Perspectives on Israel and the Church: 4 Views*. Edited by Chad O. Brand. Nashville: B&H, 2015.

Ridderbos, Herman. *Paul: An Outline of His Theology*. Grand Rapids: Eerdmans, 1975.

Robertson, O. Palmer. *The Christ of the Covenants*. Phillipsburg, NJ: P&R, 1980.

———. "Hermeneutics of Continuity." Pages 89–108 in *Continuity and Discontinuity: Perspectives on the Relationship Between the Old and New Testaments*. Edited by John S. Feinberg. Wheaton: Crossway, 1988.

———. *The Israel of God: Yesterday, Today, and Tomorrow*. Phillipsburg, NJ: P&R, 2000.

———. "Is There a Distinctive Future for Ethnic Israel in Romans 11?" Pages 209–27 in *Perspectives on Evangelical Theology: Papers from the Thirtieth Annual Meeting of the Evangelical Theological Society*. Edited by Kenneth Kantzer and Stanley Gundry. Grand Rapids: Baker, 1979.

Ross, Allen P. "The Biblical Method of Salvation: A Case for Discontinuity." Pages 161–78 in *Continuity and Discontinuity: Perspectives on the Relationship Between the Old and New Testaments*. Edited by John. S. Feinberg. Wheaton: Crossway, 1988.

Rushdoony, Rousas John. *By What Standard? An Analysis of the Philosophy of Cornelius Van Til*. Vallecito, CA: Ross House, 1995.

———. *Christianity and the State*. Vallecito, CA: Ross House, 1986.

———. *The Institutes of Biblical Law*. 3 vols. Phillipsburg, NJ: P&R, 1973, 1982, 1999.

———. *Law and Liberty*. Vallecito, CA: Ross House, 1984.

———. *Romans and Galatians*. Vallecito, CA: Ross House, 1997.

———. *The Roots of Reconstruction*. Vallecito, CA: Ross House, 1991.

———. *Systematic Theology*. 2 vols. Vallecito, CA: Ross House, 1994.

Rushdoony, Mark Rousas. "A Biographical Sketch of My Father." Pages 21–29 in *A Comprehensive Faith: An International* Festschrift *for Rousas John Rushdoony*. Edited by Andrew Sandlin. San Jose, CA: Friends of Chalcedon, 1996.

Ryrie, Charles C. *The Basis of the Premillennial Faith*. Dubuque, IA: ECS Ministries, 2005.

———. *Basic Theology*. Wheaton: Victor, 1982.

———. *Dispensationalism*. Rev. and expanded ed. Chicago: Moody, 2007.

———. "The Necessity of Dispensationalism." *Bibliotheca Sacra* 114 (1957): 243–54.

Sandlin, Andrew. "Afterword: Why We Will Win." Pages 239–42 in *A Comprehensive Faith: An International Festschrift for Rousas John Rushdoony*. Edited by Andrew Sandlin. San Jose, CA: Friends of Chalcedon, 1996.

———. "The Genius of the Thought of Rousas John Rushdoony." Pages 7–20 in *A Comprehensive Faith: An International* Festschrift *for Rousas John Rushdoony*. Edited by Andrew Sandlin. San Jose, CA: Friends of Chalcedon, 1996.

Saucy, Robert L. *The Case for Progressive Dispensationalism: The Interface Between Dispensational and Non-Dispensational Theology*. Grand Rapids: Zondervan, 1993

———. "The Church as the Mystery of God." Pages 127–55 in *Dispensationalism, Israel and the Church: The Search for Definition*. Edited by Craig A. Blaising and Darrell L. Bock. Grand Rapids: Zondervan, 1992.

Sawyer, M. James. "Dispensationalism." Pages 106–12 in *The Blackwell Encyclopedia of Modern Christian Thought*. Edited by Alister E. McGrath. Oxford: Blackwell, 1993.

Schreiner, Thomas R. "Good-bye and Hello: The Sabbath Command for New Covenant Believers." Pages 159–88 in *Progressive Covenantalism: Charting a Course between Dispensational and Covenant Theologies*. Edited by Stephen J. Wellum and Brent E. Parker. Nashville: B&H, 2016.

Scofield, C. I., *Rightly Dividing the Word of Truth*. Rev. ed. Grand Rapids: Meridian, 1989.

———, ed. *The Scofield Reference Bible*. New York: Oxford University Press, 1909, 1917; repr. 1996.

———. *The Scofield Bible Correspondence School*. Vol. 1. Chicago: Moody, 1907.

Scofield, C. I., Frank E. Gaebelein, et al., eds., *New Scofield Study Bible*. New York: Oxford University Press, 1967; repr. 1988 with New American Standard translation.

Silva, Moisés. "The New Testament Use of the Old Testament: Text Form and Authority." Pages 147–65 in *Scripture and Truth*. Edited by D. A. Carson and John D. Woodbridge. Grand Rapids: Zondervan, 1983.

Spencer, Stephen R. "Dispensationalism." Pages 854–55 in *The Encyclopedia of Christianity*. Vol. 1: A–D. Edited by Erwin Fahlbusch et al. Translated by Geoffrey W. Bromiley. Grand Rapids: Eerdmans, 1999.

Sproul, R. C. *What Is Reformed Theology? Understanding the Basics*. Grand Rapids: Baker, 1997.

Thomas, Robert L. "The Hermeneutics of Progressive Dispensationalism." *The Master's Seminary Journal* 6.1 (1995): 79–95.

Toussaint, Stanley D. *Behold the King*. Portland: Multnomah, 1980.

———. "Israel and the Church of a Traditional Dispensationalist." Pages 227–52, 258–62 in *Three Central Issues in Contemporary Dispensationalism: A Comparison of Traditional and Progressive Views*. Edited by Herbert W. Bateman IV. Grand Rapids: Kregel, 1999.

Toussaint, Stanley D., and Jay A. Quine. "No, Not Yet: The Contingency of God's Promised Kingdom." *Bibliotheca Sacra* 164 (2007): 131–47.

Vlach, Michael J. *Has the Church Replaced Israel? A Theological Evaluation*. Nashville: B&H, 2010.

———. "New Covenant Theology Compared with Covenantalism." *The Master's Seminary Journal* 18.1 (2007): 201–19.

Waltke, Bruce K. "Theonomy in Relation to Dispensational and Covenant Theologies." Pages 59–86 in *Theonomy: A Reformed Critique*.

Edited by William S. Barker and W. Robert Godfrey. Grand
Rapids: Zondervan, 1990.

Walvoord, John F. "Israel's Blindness." *Bibliotheca Sacra* 102 (1945):
280–90.

———. *The Millennial Kingdom*. Findlay, OH: Dunham, 1959.

———. "Reflections on Dispensationalism." *Bibliotheca Sacra* 158 (2001):
131–37.

———. "A Review of *Crucial Questions about the Kingdom of God* by George
Eldon Ladd." *Bibliotheca Sacra* 110 (1953): 1–10.

Ware, Bruce. "The New Covenant and the People(s) of God." Pages 68–97
in *Dispensationalism, Israel and the Church: The Search for Definition*.
Edited by Craig A. Blaising and Darrell L. Bock. Grand Rapids:
Zondervan, 1992.

Wells, Tom. *The Priority of Jesus Christ: Why Do Christians Turn to Jesus
First?* Frederick, MD: New Covenant Media, 2005.

Wells, Tom, and Fred Zaspel. *New Covenant Theology: Description,
Definition, Defense*. Frederick, MD: New Covenant Media, 2002.

Wellum, Stephen J. "Introduction." Pages 1–6 in *Progressive Covenantalism:
Charting a Course between Dispensational and Covenant Theologies*.
Edited by Stephen J. Wellum and Brent E. Parker. Nashville: B&H,
2016.

———. "Progressive Covenantalism and the Doing of Ethics." Pages
215–33 in *Progressive Covenantalism: Charting a Course between
Dispensational and Covenant Theologies*. Edited by Stephen J.
Wellum and Brent E. Parker. Nashville: B&H, 2016.

Wellum, Stephen J., and Brent E. Parker, eds. *Progressive Covenantalism:
Charting a Course between Dispensational and Covenant Theologies*.
Nashville: B&H, 2016.

White, A. Blake. *The Law of Christ: A Theological Proposal*. Frederick, MD:
New Covenant Media, 2010.

———. *The Newness of the New Covenant*. Frederick, MD: New Covenant
Media, 2008.

———. *What Is New Covenant Theology? An Introduction*. Frederick, MD:
New Covenant Media, 2012.

Worthen, Molly. "The Chalcedon Problem: Rousas John Rushdoony and the Origins of Christian Reconstructionism." *Church History* 77.2 (June 2008): 399–437.

Zaspel, Fred. *The New Covenant and New Covenant Theology*. Frederick, MD: New Covenant Media, 2008.

Zuck, Roy B. *Basic Bible Interpretation: A Practical Guide to Discovering Biblical Truth*. Wheaton: Victor, 1991.

SCRIPTURE INDEX